AF560230

Sustainable Development Administration

An Analysis of Problems of Economy, Environment and Equity

OTHER BOOKS OF THE AUTHOR

1. Fiscal Policy in the Context of Planning, World Press, Calcutta, 1967.
2. Seminar Papers on Rural Development, ed. Orissa Economics Association, 1984.
3. Capitalism, Socialism and Planning, Oxford and IBH, New Delhi, 4th Edition, 1988.
4. Economics of Public Finance, Macmillan, New Delhi, 3rd Edition, 1992.
5. Agricultural Development, Problems and Prospects, Ashish Publishing House, New Delhi, 1990.
6. Economic Development of Orissa, Edited along with others, 1991.
7. Poverty, Unemployment and Rural Development, Edited, Ashish Publishing House, New Delhi, 1991.
8. Political Economy of Development, Ajanta, New Delhi, 1993.
9. Strategy of Development Planning, Modern Book Depot, Bhubaneswar, 1994.
10. Cooperative Movement in India, Edited, Ashish Publishing House, New Delhi, 1995.
11. Economic Profile of India, Ashish Publishing House, New Delhi, 1997.
12. Contemporary Economic System, Kitab Mahal, Cuttack, 1999.
13. Agro-Industries and Economic Development—A Vision for the 21st Century, Edited along with others, Deep & Deep Publications Pvt. Ltd., New Delhi, 2002.
14. Economic Liberalisation and Regional Disparities in India, Ed. By Baidyanath Misra and Rajkishor Meher, APH Publishing Corporation, New Delhi, 2000.

Sustainable Development Administration

An Analysis of Problems of Economy, Environment and Equity

PROF. BAIDYANATH MISRA

Foreword by

PROF. PRASANTA K. PATTANAIK
Department of Economics
University of California
Riverside, USA

DEEP & DEEP PUBLICATIONS PVT. LTD.
F-159, Rajouri Garden, New Delhi - 110 027

SUSTAINABLE DEVELOPMENT ADMINISTRATION
An Analysis of Problems of Economy, Environment and Equity

ISBN 978-81-8450-415-6

Typeset by RAHUL COMPOSERS
358, Pocket-B, Phase-2, Sector-16B, Dwarka, New Delhi - 110 075

Printed in India at MAYUR ENTERPRISES
WZ Plot No. 3, Gujjar Market, Tihar Village, New Delhi - 110 018

Published by DEEP & DEEP PUBLICATIONS PVT. LTD.
F-159, Rajouri Garden, New Delhi - 110 027 • Phone : 25435369, 25440916
E-mail : ddpubs@gmail.com • ddpubs@yahoo.com
Showroom :
2/13, Ansari Road, Daryaganj, New Delhi - 110 002 • Telefax : 23245122

Dedicated to
my wife and children
whose love and affection have sustained
me so far and enabled me
to pursue intellectual activities

Contents

Foreword

It is a pleasure and honour for me to write a foreword for this volume by Prof. Baidyanath Misra, an eminent economist who has made numerous research contributions and has trained generations of economists in Orissa. This collection of essays is remarkable in many ways. First, it covers a vast range of economic and social issues. India's economic growth, economic development and social ethics, health care, sustainable development, the financing of higher education, and urbanization in India are just a few examples of the diverse problems that Professor Misra takes up in these essays. Second, Professor Misra discusses all these issues in a singularly lucid style. Without losing any analytical rigour, his exposition always remains accessible to non-economists who are willing to do some serious thinking on the problem under consideration. Economics is too important a subject to remain confined to economists, and Professor Misra's essays are a model of how an economist can effectively communicate with the wider public on issues that affect the life of the entire society. Finally, Professor Misra's analysis is suffused with a deep humanism. Underlying many of his essays there is an abiding concern for the huge chunk of the population of India that has remained excluded from the fruits of India's rapid economic growth. This is a volume that both professional social scientists and non-specialists can read with much benefit.

PRASANTA K. PATTANAIK
Professor, Department of Economics
University of California
Riverside, USA

Preface

In the second half of the 20th Century, several changes have taken place in India which have changed the life pattern of the people and drawn the attention of the world. India is now recognised by some outside scholars as an emerging super power. We want to study in this book some such important changes which have drawn the attention of the world. One such change is democratic form of government which has survived more than 60 years. The questions which agitate the minds of people are: How does it function? What is the power structure in democracy? What is its effect on India's nationhood and national culture? And how can it preserve and strengthen India's integrity? These are some of the issues which cannot escape the attention of any conscious citizen.

The second problem which has assumed tremendous importance is economic development. The rate of growth in India has even approached more than 8 per cent per year even when some of the developed countries are struggling to attain 3 or 4 per cent per year after the recession of 2007 and 2008. But the discussions which veer round on issues are: What is the process of change? How does it affect different sections of the community? Who are the gainers and who are the losers? What is its effect on environment and so on. And in the Eleventh Plan there is also an attempt to make the development all embracing so that people of all sections of the community can derive adequate benefit with structural changes in education, health care and social security along with prevention of leakages. What are the measures taken and how will they operate? These are some of the issues for which there is a great deal of debate.

The third question is international relation—how does liberalisation and globalisation affect the people? Whether have they improved the economy or distorted the economy? Whether as a result of this change, is there convergence between North and South or is there integration? How do they influence public sector or private sector? There are diverse views in such cases and discussed at different levels. Some of these issues are examined in the book along with social, political, economic diversity to unravel the puzzle that has far so long confronted scholars and citizens of India as well as foreign scholars. Though the canvas is wide, the central theme of the book is how India can progress towards the realisation of what Huxley has called the fulfilment of a society, based not on power and exploitation, but on scientific knowledge, decent standard of living, humanism and humaneness.

It may be noted here that most of the chapters were written at different periods and some being published in Journals like ISSI Quarterly, University News and Man and Development. I acknowledge with thanks to the editors of above Journals for publishing my papers. I have tried to make some changes in the drafts as per recent events and updated data as far as possible, but allowed some repetitions to continue as they are relevant to the subject under study.

Before I conclude, I must express my deep sense of gratitude to Professor Prasanta Pattanaik, an economist of international repute, who is now working in Department of Economics, University of Carlifornia, Riverside, USA who has kindly written a Foreword in my 'Sustainable Development and Administration'. My thanks are also due to Dr. Nilakantha Panigrahi, a Research Associate of NCDS for providing quite a lot of inputs to me for preparing this book. I also thank my wife and daughter who have spared some time inspite of their busy household work in assisting me to scrutinize the drafts.

And I cannot forget to thank NCDS which is a part of my life and whose assistance I have sought from time to time for my intellectual pursuits.

PROF. BAIDYANATH MISRA

CHAPTER

1

Strengths and Weaknesses in Indian Economy

Horace Walpole, the noted British writer wrote more than 200 years ago, 'the world is a comedy to those that think, a tragedy to those that feel'. When we analyse the statement of Goldman Sachs (2003) that the 21st century is the century of USA, China and India, the same contrast between thinking and feeling is apparent. There are three redeeming features in India for which it is said that India will be more or less a super power in the 21st century, super power in the economic sense.

MORE YOUNG AND LESS DEPENDENCY

One such redeeming feature is that our young population is more and the dependency ratio is less than many other countries of the world. For example, the median age in India in 2000 was less than 24, compared to 38 in Europe, 41 for Japan and 30 for China. The latest study shows that the proportion of young people (0-15) in percentages by 2050 would be 19.7 for India, 16.3 for China, 15.5 for developed world and 21 for the world. When we consider the proportion of working people 16-64 in percentages, by 2050 it would be 59.7 for India, 53.8 for China, 51 for developed world and 58 for the world. On the other hand, the old age dependency ratio (65+) in percentages by 2050 would be 20.6 for India, 29.9 for China, 33.5 for developed world and 21 for world.

Abramovitz in his 'Catching up, forging ahead, and falling behind' points that social capability is a major factor in economic growth. He further points out that social capability gives rise to adaptability and the notion of adaptability suggests that there is an interaction between social capability and technological opportunity. In Solow's new classical model of growth technical progress (which is according to him is an exogenous factor) is the main driving force of long-run growth. Since endogenous growth has a tendency to attract exogenous growth and endogenous growth depends on social capability and adaptability, India has great opportunity in forging ahead due to it's young labour force. All those who have argued that the 21st century is the century of USA, China and India, their main focus is on the capability of Indian people, people who are young, vibrant and prepared to meet any challenge that comes in the way of change.

INDIAN WORKERS ARE INGENIOUS

M.D. Batra writing on 'India's strength and ingenuity' in 'cyber age' indicates how one South Korean businessman compares the working performance of Indian and Chinese workers. According to him, Chinese workers are hard working, but they need clear instructions, a blueprint to follow, to complete the work. Indian workers are probably not as self-disciplined and hard working as the Chinese, but they are resourceful and ingenious. If there is a problem, they won't sit down and wait for someone to come and help them. They would find creative ways to solve the problem. If something is broken or missing, they would improvise a substitute and fix it. He also indicated that Indian workers, those who do not have much education, display the same aptitude for innovativeness.

We can give another example of Indian ingenuity. In 1991, the US state department banned the sale of computers to India that could do more than 900 million operations per second. How did India respond? In no time, the Centre for Development of Advanced Computing developed a powerful series, Param–1000 which at that time was one of the most powerful computers of its kind, capable of diversity of application in fields such as engineering, business, industry, space and nuclear technology. Indian ingenuity served the super computing needs of the Indian scientific community and made possible the development and enhancement of India's nuclear weapons programme. The USA which treated India as a Pariah earlier is now talking of strategic partnership even in case of peaceful transfer of nuclear technology.

INFRASTRUCTURE WOES

The point which worries us is that even though our capability is our people, they cannot work in a vacuum. When a satellite is put to orbit, it requires high velocity to ensure exit from the earth's gravitational force, similarly if our economy is to exit from the gravitational pull of poverty, it requires exit velocity of double digit growth rate over the next two decades. Obviously for attaining such a high level of growth we require improved infrastructure that can help and accelerate the process of growth. It is therefore, said that infrastructure is a *sine qua non* of economic development. Agricultural development needs irrigation, industrial development power, trade depends on transport and communication and such other physical facilities that are prerequisites for development. India's infrastructural woes are so great that even the ablest of the entrepreneurs find difficulty in managing adequate supply of power to increase the productivity of their industries. Industrial states like Maharashtra and Karnataka encounter four to eight hours of power outage in peak months. There is not enough power available but wherever it is available, the supply is not reliable. It is estimated that power theft, transmission and distribution losses and other technical problems drain 40 per cent of power. In irrigation, it is understood that almost 25 per cent of the irrigation facilities that are available is wasted due to lack of proper maintenance, and water harvesting structures which can provide immense benefit for increasing the productivity of agriculture is not given due importance. If India has to succeed in increasing the pace of development and compete with Asian neighbours like Singapore, South Korea, China, Taiwan, it has to upgrade its clogged roads, over-crowded airports, uncertain power and water supply and other important physical infrastructure to effectively utilise the young, active and intelligent labour force to keep the economy in perpetual motion of development.

IMPROVEMENT IN IT SECTOR

Another redeeming feature of India's economy is that there has been tremendous improvement in the IT sector which has been exciting the world's imagination so much so that many outstanding MNCs are competing with each other to hire Indian IT candidates. India has also some fantastic world class companies including INFOSYS Technologies, WIPRO, TATA Consultancy Services, among the software companies for which India has become a world leader. And in the growing field of biotechnology, petrochemicals and pharmaceuticals, India has acquired international reputation. Because of such spectacular improvements, George Evans, the Director of International Equities at the Oppenheimer Funds has shown preference to India for foreign investment than to China.

Simon Wasserman, Chairman of AON Global said at a recent conference on outsourcing, 'India has everything that a multinational needs. It is a young country with creative minds and a huge market with almost 27 cities with more than a million population'. The Confederation of Indian industry in a recent study points out that India would be entering a new threshold of the knowledge economy and could emerge as a global hub for specialised knowledge processing for global corporations.

BUT IT CONFINED TO A FEW

All this makes us proud that India is creating a global buzz, an image that enthrals us. Though we raise a toast to the rising fortunes of IT candidates, let us also begin to realise that a small part of the population has joined the growth process and reap the benefits while the excluded majority watch from the margins, in despair and increasingly sullen. The major problem in India is that even though we have millions and millions of people who are able and willing to work, they have no opportunity to work due to shortage of skill. This is a recipe for not only loss of competitiveness but also social schism and criminality.

We have a rich India where 20 per cent harbours about half of the income of the people of the country and there is a bottom 20 per cent that harbours less than one-tenth of it. One NCAER study shows that we have now three Indias—one that is well on its way to income growth from a good base comprising about 200 million or so people, spread across large and small towns and pockets of rural India as well. We may call it *Arriving India*. The bottom 400 million is a disappointment with less facility for improvement. The remaining 400 million is somewhat in between. The top end is getting richer, the middle is like the middle everything in middle, slow bum, but the average per capita income of this group is growing while there are all kinds of contrast among the bottom—some are getting less poor, some others more poor and some staying at the same level. All this means they are a great liability to the society.

If the civil society wants to help them, they cannot just do it by allocating more funds for education and health or preventing dropouts from schools by providing mid-day meals. Converting a dispersed mass of undernourished and uneducated young fellows into a disciplined army of individuals who learn and apply their knowledge for economic and social change is a political process. What we need is mass politics that will simultaneously make state delivery system work and empower those hitherto marginalised.

LIBERALISATION HAS NOT NEGATED PLANNING

It is heartening to note that inspite of liberalisation and globalisation, the planning process in India has not yet been stalled. The Government has recognised the necessity of planning to improve the economy's productive capacities, involving both physical and human resources to attain the desired economic and social ends (and not just material attainment). Even though during the last decade, there has been some significant change in the growth process, it is admitted that market mechanism alone cannot solve some of the imponderable difficulties that confront the economy. In analysing the 'perspective, objectives and strategy' of the tenth plan, the Planning Commission points out that though more than 60 years that have passed since our independence, the challenges, the imperatives and the capabilities of the nation have undergone profound changes, there are still many hurdles that have to be corrected by planning.

According to the Tenth Plan, the degree of democratization that has been achieved in the political sphere is, however, not matched by its progress on the economic front. There are still too many controls and restrictions on individual initiatives and many of our developmental institutions continue to exhibit paternalistic behaviour which today has become anachronistic. For the country to attain its full economic potential, and for the poorest and weakest to shape their destiny according to their own desires, it requires a comprehensive reappraisal not only of our development strategy, but also of the institutional structures, that guide the development process. The Eleventh Plan aims at achieving these objectives.

SELF-CENTRED POLITICAL AUTHORITY

Though the Planning Commission has pinpointed some of the major constraints in the development process, it has not thrown adequate light on the operational mechanism of the developmental administration that is needed to tackle the difficulties. We can cite only two illustrations to show how there is a big gap between outlay and output for which many of the laudable objectives are not fulfilled. In a democratic form of government, the political party in power generally determines the policy of economic programmes. Even though we have a democratic form of government and frequent elections change the nature of government from time to time, the political authority in India often resorts to populism in order to increase its personal power and privileges and to control economic resources for its own benefit. It does not seem to make any effort to strengthen traditional or institutional resources of authority which result in the weakening of the political organisation. In a heterogeneous social structure and weak economic base, when there are many claimants to secure larger gain from state resources and there is a growing conflict among the contending groups, a self-centred political authority can hardly maintain democratic norm. In order to derive support for personal benefit, the leaders mobilise caste and ethnic groups and demand for reservation in different types of services including representative institutions.

SELF-ASSERTIVE CIVIL SERVICE

On the other hand, the civil service in India with their upper class prejudices could hardly be expected to meet the requirements of social and economic change that development administration entails. Even in some of the developed countries administrative culture became an inhibiting factor in the speedy implementation of welfare programmes. In Great Britain and the USA, the civil service has stalled a number of development programmes ignoring the political authority. Those who have read Peter's Principle (the case of USA) and Yes Minister (the case of Great Britain), they can realise how powerful is the civil service. Indian democratic government is no different from what we see in GB or the USA. On the other hand, it is worse. We can cite just one example how red tape in India takes myriad forms, from expectation of illegal gratification to turf war. Quoting Dr. Jayanta Roy of the Confederation of Indian Industry (CII), the *Financial Times* (London) wrote recently "(A) typical international trade deal from India involved upto 30 separate parties, 257 signatures and 118 copies of the same document. Imports on average sit in Mumbai's port for upto three weeks compared to 24 hours in ports elsewhere in the world". In this digital age, if business transactions are so dilatory, how can India secure cost advantage? One more administrative problem which worries us is close alliance between political authority and senior bureaucracy. It is often seen that senior administrators forge an alliance with politicians not only to brighten their career prospects but also to articulate political views and gain greater share of social resources. It has been commented by many political commentators that there is close collaboration among politicians, bureaucrats and businessmen in India during the planning era to enable politicians to keep their chair, administrators, their power and businessmen, their money through licenses and permits. And this close alliance among three important constituents of India results in colossal black money worth 40 per cent of GDP, amounting to about Rs. 12 lakh crore today.

CONCLUSION

All this implies that even though we have capability to meet the emerging challenges of competition in the 21st century, there are some hurdles which must be carefully and judiciously handled so as to : (a) improve the efficiency of the economy, (b) reduce the harshness of the political system and bureaucratic control, (c) provide wider opportunity to the poor people to get maximum benefit from developmental projects, (d) provide adequate funds for improving both physical and social infrastructure which involves external economies, and (e) make development a people's movement through the help of participatory planning.

We can conclude by stating that, 'the present challenge is not primarily managerial; it is first of all ethical and political, and is aimed at the core of our democratic faith'. In other words, the issue of governance and democratic norm is at the forefront of the development agenda. If we can succeed in achieving these two objectives, we can fulfil the aspirations of our people and meet the challenge of world competition, otherwise it would be the cause of great disappointment and missed development opportunities.

CHAPTER 2

The Role of Natural Resources on Economic Development

IMPORTANCE OF NATURAL RESOURCES

Though there are many countries which have made considerable improvement in their economy without adequate natural resources, the countries which have rich natural resources have greater advantage to register increased pace of development, provided of course there is an incentive on the part of the people to effectively utilise the resources for initiating a process of development. W. Arthur Lewis in his 'The Theory of Economic Growth' has emphasised the role of human behaviour and human institutions for improved use of their resources. As he points out, "Given the country's resources, its rate of growth is determined by human behaviour and human institutions: by such things as energy of mind, the attitude towards material things, willingness to save and invest productively or the freedom and flexibility of institutions".

Another factor which equally important is political leadership particularly in developing countries where traditions play much more important role than creative endeavour. The leadership question comes in because if a community is fortunate to have a good leader, as Lewis says, 'born at a crucial time in its history, who catches the imagination of his people and guides them through a formative experience, he will create traditions and legends and standards which weave themselves into the thinking of his people, and govern their behaviour through many centuries'. This shows that the connection between development of a country and its natural resources is not as vital as is generally imagined. This means the relation between richness of resources and the quality of human response is much more important in determining the process of development than the abundance or scarcity of resources. We have examples of countries which have wrested economic prosperity out of unfavourable natural environment (cases like Japan, South Korea, Taiwan, Singapore and so on). On the other hand, there are instances of countries wasting their rich resources and remaining poor (India is described as a rich country with poor people—so also many parts of Africa).

However, subject to the above observations, we can say that rich natural resources provide great opportunity to accelerate the process of development, particularly in a poor country where agriculture plays a dominant role in meeting the basic requirements of the people. In such cases, natural resources which are important are land, forests, fisheries, animals and so on. These resources provide the necessary wherewithal for maintaining the livelihood of people. In a developed country, some of these resources become less important mainly for two reasons. In the first place, income elasticity of demand for agricultural products is relatively low and therefore, the expenditure incurred on such natural resources, declines reducing their importance. In most of the developed countries the dependence on agriculture is not only less, agriculture also contributes hardly 2 to 3 per cent to total GDP. Further, continuous improvements in technology permit substitution of labour and capital for land and other natural resources. Even in agriculture, because of the application of modern technology, there is a diminution in the land input per unit of output. Roy F. Harrod in his famous growth model, does not give any importance to natural resources. He points out, "I propose to discard the law of diminishing returns from land as a primary determinant in a progressive economy. . . . I discard it only because in our particular context it appears that its influence may be quantitatively unimportant". This is not so in a developing economy.

We may also mention here that natural resources include land, water resources, fisheries, mineral resources, forests, marine resources and so on. Some of these resources like water, and forests are renewable while others like minerals and mineral oils are exhaustible, and can be used only once. Therefore, conservation and economic exploitation of the exhaustible resources and fuller utilisation and proper maintenance of renewable resources are essential in the process of development. We cannot say that we are aware of all the natural resources that are in the bosom of the nature. In order to discover such hidden natural resources, man has to develop necessary techniques to discover them and once such natural resources are discovered, they may change the economic profile of a country. When we talk of natural resources, we only mention the known ones. Advancement of knowledge and improvement of technique may discover some new ones and also their different uses. Take for example the Monazite sand deposits on the beaches on Kerala and Tamilnadu. Even though these resources were known, their uses were not known. Now it is found they are very valuable for producing nuclear energy. Similarly, there may be many unknown natural resources which may be discovered in the course of time along with the knowledge of their uses.

MISUSE OF NATURAL RESOURCES AND THEIR HARMFUL EFFECTS

While natural resources are of great use for the purpose of development, if they are not judiciously used, they may lose their quality and create ecological imbalance. For example, because of increased population and higher demand for food grains, more and more areas have been brought under cultivation by clearing forests along with excessive use of chemical fertiliser, insecticides and pesticides and also of ground water. As a result, India's land area is rapidly turning barren and it is estimated that more than 1 million hectares of crop land and grazing lands are badly affected due to lack of proper maintenance. Some of the estimates of Orissa show that 50 per cent of the cultivable land has now become barren.

In many parts of India, arsenic contamination in ground water has assumed alarming proportions due to intensive digging of tube wells both for drinking and irrigation purposes. Probably such overuse has disturbed the underground geological balance which has resulted in arsenic contamination of water creating skin diseases, conjunctivitis, liver enlargement and diseases of upper and lower limbs. It is also found by a study of Delhi University in Ludhiana District that ground water extraction is 30 per cent higher than replenishment. As a result, water tables are falling at the rate of one metre a year. Orissa is also experiencing the same difficulty even though the ground water exploitation is not as high as in Punjab or Haryana.

Irrigation dams due to lack of proper drainage have created water logging at different parts of the country. It is estimated that the menace of water logging (and consequent salinisation of the soil) has already affected more than 13 mh of good agricultural lands and threatens many more. Due to extensive denudation and soil erosion, the siltation of reservoirs which represent a highly valuable and irreplaceable potential for irrigation, power and flood control is taking place at a much higher rate than was envisaged. It is understood that on an average every hectare loses about 20 tonnes of top soil per year. Again the flood prone area has doubled over the last 10 years from 20 million to 40 million hectares. And millions of people have been displaced and uprooted apart from the fact that the productivity of irrigation dams is not fully utilised and the investment cost for creating irrigation potential is almost galloping from one plan to another.

This shows that canal irrigation instead of becoming a blessing has turned into a curse and allows our renewable resources of water to damage our non-renewable resource of land. What is worse, irrigation and power which are generated from irrigation dams are not fully utilised, the loss of irrigation water is more than 25% due to lack of field channels (it is more than 30% in Orissa) and loss of power due to distribution and transmission loss (it is more than 40 per cent in Orissa). In fact, irrigation and power projects have given birth to powerful engineering interests (which include equipment manufacturers and contractors) backed by decision-makers who have little public interest in view while conceiving of the expenditure intensive projects. As Simon Kuzncts has pointed out the development sequence goes from science to technology and then to engineering.

Forests which provide us with basic needs of life like food and shelter and influence the environment through the supply of clean air by absorbing carbon dioxide and other harmful gases which are by-products are being rapidly destroyed in different parts of the country. In India, of the total officially notified area of 67 m hectares as 'Forest Land', not more than 25 per cent possesses good natural forests (with a crown cover atleast 40 per cent). In Orissa hardly 18 to 19 per cent possesses good natural forests. The loss of forests not only increases pollution and creates acid rains, but also reduces water supply and aggravates floods; forests work like speed breakers to the surface run-off and absorb the water to be released later on in the form of streams. This implies that forest cover in a watershed is the cheapest and best method of water storage in a country where the whole economy revolves around the monsoon. When there is rapid deforestation, there is not only loss on account of surface run-off but reduces ground water table leaving the poor persons' dug well dry.

In addition, the mineral industries along with fossil-fuel-based automobile centred throw away economy have given rise to emission of toxic gases, depletion of the ozone layer, threat of acid rain, pollution of air, water and land surface, etc., in fact, nothing is spared resulting in total pollution. Some of the recent developments in pollution cause great harm to the people. It is true that mineral industries have created abundant opportunities for employment and improvement in the living standards of some people, but at the same time, they have created a serious threat to the environment. Similarly, vehicular smoke is increasing respiratory ailments and many other kinds of serious diseases. And while our air lungs are continually being constricted, the quality of air in our cities worsens every day. Thus todays' environmental challenges arise from unintended consequences of some forms of economic growth.

GUIDING PRINCIPLES OF RESOURCE DEVELOPMENT

The main objective of resource utilisation is to maximise development by utilising such resources in an optimum manner and to see that the benefits accrue not only to the present generation but also to the future generation. As the World Commission on Environment and Development in 'Our Common Future' points out, sustainable development is the development that meets the needs of the present without compromising the ability of the future generation to meet 'their own needs'. For this purpose a number of guiding principles has to be developed. Some of these are mentioned below:

1. Resource Literacy

The first is resource literacy. Probably most of the educated people know that natural resources are not unlimited, but they do not think that misutilisatin of such resources will create health hazards. Some even think that science can invent some substitutes for non-renewable resources and renewable resources can easily be reproduced. All these are not so simple. Many of them do not even imagine that we have already crossed the thresholds of nature and there is a limit beyond which we cannot go. Economic development is necessary, but it should not cross the limits of the carrying capacity of our planet. It is, therefore, imperative to create resource literacy among the people, both educated and non-educated that development should not destroy life support system both for the present and future generation.

2. Control the Growth of Population

Another measure which is necessary to control ecological imbalance is to control the growth of population. The population growth has become a major source of environmental degradation. The huge growth of population increases the demand on scarce resources and the pollution generated by the rising living standards of the relatively affluent. And poverty itself creates further environmental stress. Those who are poor and hungry will often destroy their immediate environment in order to survive. They cut down forests, their livestock over graze grasslands, they over use marginal land and encourage large families as an insurance against high mortality. The consequent destruction of the environment and the pressure exerted by population on natural resources lead to further immiserisation. As pointed out by Paul Kennedy in his 'Preparing for the Twenty-first Century', the poor countries must give more serious attention to controlling population because the poor are not only one of the important agents of ecological degradation, but the poor countries cannot simply cope with the task of providing employment, health care, education, etc. to an ever increasing population. The three key elements in any general effort to reduce the growth of population are education, empowerment of women and enlightened political leadership.

3. Improvement of Healthy Technology

We have already seen that fossil-fuel-based automobile centred, throw away economy leads to reckless exploitation of earth. It assumes that (a) such technology can increase production and guarantee a good quality of life, (b) carrying capacity of the earth is unlimited, and (c) such a society presupposes unlimited resilience in life support systems to keep on absorbing the continued shocks of pollution and co-degradation. But the experiences of development in different parts of the world show that all these assumptions are wrong. Rapid economic development by ruthless exploitation of resources has degraded our physical environment. If poverty in India was the result of under utilisation of natural resources, in post-independence India, poverty and inequality have continued due to the destruction of environment.

This does not mean that economic development should be neglected. Even while defining sustainable development, the Brundland Commission makes this clear: 'Sustainable development seeks to meet the needs and aspirations of the present without compromising the ability to meet those of the future. Far from requiring the cessation of economic growth, it recognises that the problems of poverty and under-development cannot be solved unless we have a new era of growth in which developing countries play a large role and reap large benefits. In the process of development two basic principles have to be followed:

(i) Environment must be protected from avoidable pollution, destruction and exploitation from all resources. Economic development does not mean destruction of nature; it is a part and parcel of nature. In other words, the pattern of development should be in harmony with nature. A cleaner environment would not only result in greater productivity but would also lead to sustainable development.

(ii) The pollutors should be compelled to take measures to prevent pollution. Though such producers derive benefit from their production, the public authority very often incurs heavy expenditure to control such external diseconomies to clear the air before others can use it. It is therefore, imperative that whoever pollutes the air or water, must be held responsible to prevent it or pay for the cost incurred in preventing the pollution.

4. Efficient Use of Natural Resources

The guiding principle in the case of a sustainable society is to satisfy the needs and not greeds of the people, ensure comfort, not luxury and above all bring about equity with social justice. The twin goals of preserving nature are: (a) restoration of the past ecological damage, and (b) insulation of the country from the damage as a consequence of future development. The latter must entail minimum risk to the environment. Each type of development entails some risk. To accomplish both restorative and preventive strategies we have to improve the efficiency of energy use and evolve sources of new energy which do not create pollution, increase the forest area (if necessary the government should have adequate authority to prevent deforestation), reduce wants, increase awareness, provide power and authority to the village units, so that they can take responsibility for protecting the environment. All natural resources have to be conserved and developed by ensuring their efficient, equitable and sustainable use. As we have already pointed out, people have to be educated on the need to preserve and protect our natural habitat and environment.

5. Prevention of Consumerism

Though there are many areas where action can be taken for proper use of natural resources, one and the most important action which is necessary is to prevent consumerism. While eco-friendly and sustainable technologies are important as is population control, we cannot save the planet only through these methods. We have to consider reducing material needs, if anything is to be left for future generation. Often it is assumed that increased consumption will increase production, create more employment and make life happier and easier. But it is forgotten that consumerism increases the rape of the earth and creates more inconvenience than convenience. For example, when cars are multiplied to meet the increased demand for faster commuter travel in our cities, diminishing returns set in with a vengeance. You buy a car to go to work faster, because thousands of others do the same, the cars get in one another's way and traffic slows down to average speeds of below 10 km an hour. Traffic congestion, air pollution and fuel extravagance become the common feature of most of the mega cities.

This shows that unbridled consumerism will undermine even the most concerted efforts to safeguard the planet through eco-friendly technology and family planning. Hence, we can say that judicious use of diminishing resources like fossil fuels, development of alternative energy sources, coupled with population control, improvement of forest area and a less consumerist attitude could actually make it possible for everyone to have a comfortable, though a modest lifestyle and save something for the future generation to live a decent and dignified life.

CHAPTER

3

Emerging Concerns in Development Administration

One of the major concerns that has been agitating the minds of social scientists is the failure of the development strategy in reducing poverty and improving the quality of life of most of the people in the country. The strategy of development which has been formulated in India connotes a movement from poverty to prosperity. It is a cumulative process, which is supposed to make a continuous improvement in the process of change, both physical and human, increasing the gains of real development and providing facilities for percolating such gains to the poorest of the poor.

In fact, India's development pattern is multi-dimensional in character. The objectives of the First Plan clearly stated that this long-term and multi-dimensional process of change would include : (a) a sizeable increase in national income through an increase in the productivity of agriculture and industry so as to improve the living standards of the people, (b) create sufficient employment opportunities so as to absorb in productive work of all those who are able and willing to work, (c) remove poverty and reduce income inequalities, (d) attain self-reliance, and (e) change the traditional economy into a modern one. More or less, all the above objectives have been emphasised in different plans in one form or the other and huge investments have been made in different plans to achieve the goals enunciated in the First Plan. But the baffling problem is that even though, there have been intermittent periods of economic and social growth, the overall development in most of the sectors has been much below the desired level. Even when the policy of distributing resources to the poor and destitutes was accepted at the national level, it could not be properly implemented at the local level due to heavy leakages. Administrative discretion was used to help the privileged and at other times political interference was manipulated to achieve the same results (Mathur).

It is therefore worthwhile to examine the reasons why political and administrative set-up is not geared to meet the challenge of development. Prof. A.H. Hanson in one of his essays analysing Indian Planning said, "The men are able, the organisation is adequate, the procedures are intelligently devised, why then have the plans since 1956, so persistently run into crisis". Prof. V.K.R.V. Rao in analysing the reasons for tardy progress mentions, "What has been wrong with planning so far has not been its conceptual or logical or technical content so much as its implementation, its lack of cohesion with social factors and the impediments imposed by political, social, administrative and cultural forces rather than strictly economic factors".

Another social scientist analysing the reasons for unsatisfactory development points out that the most noticeable impediments are: inadequacy of administrative machinery: inability to develop the collective will to achieve results amidst diverse interest groups and political parties; lack of mass involvement in the process of development; and inappropriateness of policy formulation (Ishwar Dayal). It seems a more satisfactory level of achievement could perhaps be ensured by overcoming all these weaknesses. We therefore propose to analyse the problem of challenges of governance and make some suggestions to overcome the weaknesses. In the 1st section, we analyse the quality of the political elite who are supposed to play a major role in making policy decisions. The second section will be devoted to administrative structure which is the catalytic agent for implementing different programmes. Finally, we try to suggest some measures for institutionalising the system of policy planning and implementing clusters that can involve all the elements in the process of change. Because the economic, social, technological and political areas exert a strong mutual influence and without an integration and interlinkage of different clusters, no single measure, however, effective it is, can solve the extremely sensitive problems of a developing country like India.

QUALITY OF THE POLITICAL ELITE

In a democratic form of government the political party in power generally determines the policy of economic programme. Even though we have a democratic form of government and frequent elections change the nature of government from time to time, the political authority in India does not seem to have sufficient control over economic resources for balanced development. There are several reasons for this. First, the political elite in India often resort to populism in order to increase their personal power and privileges and to control economic resources for their own benefit. There are several examples. One such example of non-too-cheap populism is giving away of telephone connections to 3.2 lakh telecom employees free of registration installation and rental charges which cost about Rs. 1200 crore to the exchequer as reckoned by the Finance Department. Another example is the write off bank loans of farmers to the extent of more than Rs. 60 crore by endangering the credit worthiness of the bankers. They do not seem to make any effort to strengthen traditional or institutional sources of authority which result in the weakening of the political organisation. In a heterogeneous social structure and weak economic base, when there are many claimants to secure larger gain from state resources, there is growing conflict among the contending groups which can be hardly resolved in a democratic process. In order to derive support for securing personal benefit, the leaders mobilise caste and ethnic groups and demand for reservation in different types of services including representative institutions.

Further, India as a democracy is a gift from above, from the elite to masses which enables the elite to acquire more power deteriorating party organisations or institutions which can counter personal interest. These elite groups try to mobilise different socio-economic groups including some passive ones more as power resources for electoral competition rather than satisfying their aspirations. And the political forces are not merely represented by political leaders like ministers or members of the legislative bodies but more importantly by those groups who would like to see a particular policy be made so that they could stand to gain either directly by diverting public resources to themselves or indirectly by getting state patronage to do what would be most advantageous to them (Mathur). These efforts not only increase group conflict but also emasculate fragile institutions. Due to lack of effective institutions which can constrain the powers of a few individuals, there is further increase in centralisation of power which frustrates democratic aspirations of the people. In an environment of eroding institutional system, the political order cannot accommodate disparate interests and promote development. This shows that India's institutional capacity to deal with conflict and initiate solutions to pressing problems is on the decline (Kohli).

Indian political system is characterised by an apparent trichotomy such as, the feudal social order, bourgeois-landlord dominated economy and democratic polity envisaged by the constitution. We pass from an 'institutional democracy' to an 'electoral democracy' which results in 'functioning anarchy'. The political process undermines the role and authority of basic institutions which Rajni Kothari labels as 'institutional decay'. This has converted politics as 'power politics' and politician, the 'power politician' indulging in 'manipulative politics'. Pandit Nehru during his period of stewardship tried to adjust our political structure and political culture to the needs of democratic parliamentary system by his own personal example, but he was a man of his times. Later on, politics became a business, and a lucrative business at that. Instead of a culture-oriented politics, we developed a politics-oriented culture which resulted in wide-spread incidence of public corruption. Corruption at higher level percolated to lower levels. It is said that corruption is rooted in a more pervasive trend towards criminalisation of polity as well as of society. And a society which has a high capacity for corruption has also a higher capacity for violence.

India has a plethora of political parties but the structure of the party system is so authoritarian that no party allows intra-party democracy. They are personality-oriented, not issue or ideology-oriented. The real model is not so much Westminister as Elizabeth I where countries who do not toe the line are either banished from court, exiled from the party or beheaded. Any criticism of the holy cow of leadership is taboo and invites the wrath of the presiding deity. There are those who have to prove that they are more loyal than the king or until it is convenient to dump his or her highness. In the absence of inner party democracy, no party can succeed in establishing a democratic norm of the country. Atrophying the lowest level of the party and depending on sycophancy to maintain oneself in power or climbing to power may improve one's position for some time, but no one can survive in the political game without effective ground level organisation.

Due to lack of effective ground level organisation of political parties, political leadership maintains public contact through government servants blatantly flouting the theory of political neutrality of the permanent services. The nexus between the two, politicians and bureaucrats provides benefit to each one. It enables the bureaucracy to increase intervention and the politicians to assume more discretionary powers to control economic resources in a poor society for personal benefit. A picture emerges of a state that is both centralised and interventionist but that finds it increasingly difficult to accommodate conflicting demands and thus to govern. One unsettling conclusion that follows from this is that India's democracy has itself contributed to over-politicization of the Indian polity (Kohli). The diversity of India's social structure and lack of development of institutional political agencies enable the administrators (both politicians and bureaucrats) to use the administrative machinery for self-interest.

Another deplorable manifestation of Indian political culture is a sort of 'politics of survival' which has resulted in electoral competition. Elections have become ends in themselves. Money, muscle and mafia powers are used so extensively that the parliamentary democracy is debased as electoral politics. There is not only criminalization of politics, but politicization of the criminal. All parties exploit caste, religion, language, region, ethnicity, etc. to succeed in power politics. This has not only increased divisiveness, but undermined the credibility of the constitutional system of the country. Such divisiveness also ignores or marginalizes other great values as human solidarity, community, a sense of rootedness and so on. We have yet to form a nation and get a large mass of people who due to ignorance and poverty have really no stake in the country, developed into a knowledgeable and virile electorate. Ultimately, it is a growing assertive middle class which will have a stake in the country so as to control errant leaders (Sivaraman). And how can democracy succeed in establishing a 'culture of conscious' where electoral politics leads to social tensions, caste wars, communal conflicts, ethnic assertions and so on? Further when political parties lack inner party democracy leading to politics of dissidence, when election fundings are secured from commercial interests creating opportunities for increased patronage-based politics and when rule of law deteriorates hampering the ability of ordinary citizens to go about their business without hindrance, there is scope for enlarged corruption eroding the quality of democratic values.

THE ADMINISTRATIVE STRUCTURE

A political structure is not complete without its tool, the administrative structure, to carry out its policies and enforce its laws. What was the shape of this structure during the British period? What is it today? The administrative structure which thrived in India during the British period was in the nature of a 'steel frame' with predominant features of : (a) different layers of civil service to have extensive control over administration, (b) superiority complex, (c) aloofness with general public, (d) lack of total transparency, and (e) elitist nature which were reflected in their performance. The behaviour pattern was determined in accordance with the powers that were entrusted to the administration during the British rule. Some of the major characteristics of administrative culture which suited the British rulers were : (i) rigid hierarchical structure with concentration of powers at higher levels, (ii) increased level of regulations, and (iii) impersonal way of operation and rigidity in adhering to formal rules and regulations.

All these were in conformity with the social base of Indian society with its traits of unequal, heterogeneous and feudal social order which were further strengthened with individualistic orientation from the educational system. Further the pattern of development that was initiated during the Second Five Year Plan strengthened the power and privilege of the administrative system. There were several features of the Model of planned development which increased centralisation of economic power with commanding heights of the public sector to accelerate the process of development, control of private sector with permits and licenses to prevent concentration of economic power in the private hands, building of high tariff walls to protect infant industries from foreign competition, controlling prices of essential commodities to provide some benefit to the poor consumers and providing subsidies to give some incentives to consumers and producers. The civil service was chosen as the agency to implement the model.

As for the civil service, the nature of tasks was, as pointed out by Shri S.K. Das, a senior civil servant, congruent with the nature of the command and control bureaucracy that it had been under the colonial rule. Small wonder then that the civil servants in independent India were ardent supporters of the model of planned development and the welfare state since they were among the major beneficiaries. With their active participation in formulation of such plans and support by political leaders, the tasks entrusted to the civil service began to proliferate along with the size and number, though the cycle could only be completed by a downward spiral in the effectiveness with which the civil service could carry out the tasks. Bhambhri in his 'Bureaucracy in India' argues that senior administrators forged an alliance with politicians not only to brighten their own career prospects but also to articulate political views and gain a greater share of social resources. It has been commented by many political commentators that there was close collaboration among politicians, bureaucrats and businessmen in India during the planning era to enable politicians to keep their chair, administrators their power and businessmen their money through licenses and permits.

This shows that in case of India public administration was merged with development administration. There are certain inherent characteristics of public administration under the orthodox and conservative leaderships of senior civil servants with their upper class prejudices which can hardly be expected to meet the requirements of social and economic change that development administration entails. Even in some of the developed countries, administrative culture became an inhibiting factor in the speedy implementation of welfare programmes. We can illustrate the cases of two most important countries like USA and Great Britain whose examples are often cited in comparison with developing countries. Those who have read Peter Principle, they know that in an organisation, an individual will rise to his level of incompetence. This is true of Parkinson's famous dictum that bureaucratic work expands to fill the time available to do it in. Charles Peter in his book, 'How Washington Really Works' concludes that it does not work; Bureaucrats confer, the President proclaims and the Congress legislates, but the impact on reality is negligible, if evident at all.

In "Yes Minister", a number of interesting examples have been given regarding the role of bureaucracy and the relation between bureaucracy and the Minister. It is worth quoting some of these examples to show how bureaucracy controls the Government even in a developed country like Great Britain. One example is 'creative inertia' by which the bureaucracy stalls the programmes of Minister by raising technical, political and/or legal difficulties. Another example is maintaining silence. The bureaucrats observe three types of silence—direct silence by not telling the facts, stubborn silence by not taking any action, and courageous silence which implies that it will not be proper for the minister to know such things. In fact, the bureaucracy increases its authority by maintaining secrecy 'If no one knows what you are doing, then no one knows what you are doing wrong'. Instead of multiplying examples, we can only mention that the bureaucracy have three basic articles of faith. These are: (i) It takes longer to do things quickly, (ii) It is more expensive to do things cheaply, and (iii) It is more democratic to do things secretly. If this is the position of bureaucracy in a developed democratic country like Great Britain we cannot expect better things in a developing country like India.

All this shows that the nature of administrative machinery is insensitive and inflexible. The Development Administration instead of confining itself to general and regulatory functions needs to be developed, adopted or expanded to increase the pace of development which will aim at a sustained and widely diffused improvement in material and social welfare. Sapru in his 'Development Administration' has mentioned a number of elements for Development Administration. We highlight some of the important ones which we consider to be relevant for developing countries.

According to us, the Development Authority is supposed to carry out a number of functions pertaining to : (i) development of human and material resources in a planned and coordinated manner, (ii) if necessary, change existing rules and procedures, in order to achieve certain specified goals set for the administration, (iii) improve the skills and knowledge of development-oriented administrators to respond to the growing needs of the people, (iv) involve the effective participation of people with a view to making the administration people-oriented—people therefore must be given proper training so that they can understand and appreciate the programmes and demonstrate their willingness and ability to effectively participate for the success of these programmes, and (v) it should keep in touch with social realities including grass-root situations and change the programmes as and when required to meet the emerging situations so that programmes do not become obsolete or irrelevant in meeting the basic goals or new challenges that confront in the wake of changing technology or environmental problems.

All these formidable functions require a different approach. The administrators who will be responsible for developmental programmes must play a new role, a catalytic role, a carrier of change instead of continuing only stereotyped functions. Since they have to work with the people who are poor and illiterate, they have to motivate them, mobilise them and build up effective grass-root institutions so that they can get the support and service from these institutions which will ultimately act as agents of change. They must have the capability of adjusting to new circumstances, new ways of life, not as officers to pass orders or make decisions which are binding on others, but to create an environment in which participants of development make joint efforts both in decision-making and implementing programmes. The character of the administrator who exercises authority and the nature of the development officer who participates in development along with others are fundamentally different—one is rigid and authoritarian and the other is flexible and cooperative. In India for the most part service providers do not see the citizens as their clients, but rather as supplicants.

Both R.B. Jain and P.N. Chaudhuri in their book 'Bureaucratic Values' analysing development administration mention that it is (i) flexible in its operation, (ii) pragmatic in nature i.e., it is able to take into account the exigencies of circumstances from a practical point of view, (iii) conducive to open decision-making processes based on dissent and discussions among colleagues, (iv) centred around a client-oriented philosophy, and (v) laden with the human values of service and dignity for all, especially for the weaker sections of the community. All these attributes may seem difficult. But they are nonetheless fundamental to change the nature of developmental authority. In order to imbibe such qualities of head and heart, we do not require only managerial efficiency but also an imaginative and inventive approach, a public spirit which is not subordinated to any pressure group and is capable to respond to the worries and problems of downtrodden. Certainly we are not aiming at the sky, but building some minimum parameters to strengthen its innovational role.

Particularly in case of India we have to change the rule-bound bureaucratic behaviour to improve its publicness so that developmental programmes are implemented with sympathy and understanding. Our senior administrators have enough capability to prepare plans and programmes which can serve the interests of the people. But the system does not respond to changes that are required in development. A developmental goal can succeed only through its instrument of action which serves the needs and aspirations of poor people. A change in the system can be brought about only through better recruitment procedures, sustained training for acquiring requisite skills, change in aptitudes which is oriented to service and improved organisational capacity to meet the challenges of intricacies of development. As Dr. Luther Gulick in one of his lectures in 'New Horizons of Knowledge Series' observed, "The present challenge is not primarily managerial; it is first of all ethical and political, and is aimed at the core of our democratic faith". We may also add that along with professionalisation of administration emphasising management orientation in implementing development programmes, there should be a behavioural and attitudinal change among the administrators and refashioning of the political institutions so that they can control the whims and caprices of individual politicians and effectively contribute for the realization of wider and deeper values. This implies that unless there is a change in power relationships between the administrative authority and people at large, administrative culture of development cannot meet the genuine needs of the people. Status symbols are poor excuses for values.

CONCLUSION

In conclusion we may make a few suggestions for changing the economic system to make it more responsive to the people's needs. If the ultimate aim of development is to enhance the quality of life of the people, as Prof. Amartya Sen observes, economic growth should be helped by the friendliness of the economic climate rather than by the harshness of the political system. In this context we have to consider three main items of agenda. First, policies which will increase the efficiency of the economy. Second, policies which will change the structure of the economy. Third, policies by which benefits of development will reach the weaker sections of the community.

In view of the above agenda, we cannot consider separately either state or market, but one of how much state intervention, what kind of state intervention and by what means. As a general rule, markets must be allowed to function where price signals clearly work in achieving efficiency and state intervention will become necessary in areas where markets do not exist or where they cannot perform efficiently. We have to make a distinction between the supportive role of the state and its repressive role. The supportive role works in the direction of enhancing the effective freedoms of individuals (Amartya Sen).

These freedoms include making public provision for basic education and health care, in setting up social safety nets, in running good macroeconomic policies and industrial competition, in fostering coordination between different parts of the economy, in providing epidemiological, environmental and ecological protection, in improving infrastructure which involves external economies and in developing some of the basic and key industries which require huge investment and gestation period of which is quite long and making the planning process an instrument of social transformation by which more importance is given to liberty and equity rather than concentrating on commodities and things of that sort. This shows that state intervention is not negligible.

But it does imply that repressive measures and interventions which stifle liberty, initiative and enterprise and in crippling the working of individual agency and cooperative action should be avoided by the state. The past experience shows that in many cases government intervention has increased harassment. The approach document of the Eighth Plan submitted in May 1990, stated as follows:

> 'The return to the regime of direct, indiscriminate and detailed control in industry is clearly out of the question. Past experience has shown that such a control system is not effective in achieving the desired objective. Also the

system is widely abused and leads to corruption, delay and inefficiency'.

All this implies we will have both market and government investment in social and strategic sectors to improve the quality of human life and change the economic and social structure of the country which provides more quality, more liberty, less exploitation and greater empowerment of people who are now denied the opportunities of leading a decent and independent life. This is why we have the paradoxical statement 'more market does not mean less government but different government'.

Another area which needs emphasis is the freedom of information. If it is possible to provide for freedom to every citizen to secure access to information under the control of public authorities consistent with public matters, in order to promote openness, transparency and accountability in administration, it will be easier to fight corruption and limit the authoritarian mindset of the bureaucrats and politicians. Not only common people, even many of the intelligensia are not aware of the programmes and policies of the Government that change from time to time. Secrecy in such matters helps the administration to ride roughshod over the people. Even in case of anti-poverty programmes, people who are supposed to get the benefit do not know the privileges that they are supposed to secure. Article 19(1) of our Constitution provides freedom of speech and expression. Freedom of information is obviously a part of the above constitutional provision. A democratic form of government implies that the government should trust the people and make public know all such decisions which affect them. This will enable people to fight injustice, secure benefit from the government which they deserve and shape their own destiny under an environment of a friendly climate.

Access to information technology will not only empower people, it will also provide great benefit for the common man in e-governance. This refers to the use of IT networks for various types of interaction between government and the citizen. Anyone who needs some government permission or certificate like a ration card, a driving license or a certificate relating to land ownership has to go through a procedure which is not only cumbersome but dilatory. These cumbersome procedures also encourage petty corruption, which has become the bane of everyone's life. These problems can be greatly reduced if citizens could undertake these transactions through IT network which can be assessed at any time of the day from the nearest STD booth. This will also help in downsizing administration which has great importance for bringing about better governance, of optimum utilisation of resources of manpower and funds, providing more services to the people and of improving productivity in the offices (Montek Singh Ahluwalia). The Right to Information Act has already been enacted in India, but it is necessary now to ensure that the Act is made a realty.

We may also emphasise the need for reducing over-centralisation of administration in order to fulfil the felt needs of the people. Increased responsibilities of the Central and State Governments have overburdened the governmental machinery. As pointed out in the Third Plan, 'The administrative machinery has been strained and, at many points in the structure, the available personnel are not adequate in quality and number' (p. 277). It was also recognised that the expansion of administrative responsibilities was an important cause of inefficiency and delay. 'As large burdens are thrown on the administrative structure, it grows in size; and as its size increases, it becomes slower in its functioning. Delays occur and affect operations at every stage and the expected outputs are further deferred'. (p. 277)

The same feelings are expressed in the Seventh Five Year Plan. It states, 'there are too many levels of decision making, adding to delay but not necessarily to the quality of decision making. . . . Over centralisation in decision-making is manifested by a large number of meetings continuously taking place at the headquarters. . . . Coordination is one of the major weaknesses in our systems'. It is now felt by planners and emphasised in the Eighth Plan, Ninth Plan and Tenth Plan that developmental activities undertaken with the people's active participation have a greater chance of success and can also be more cost effective as compared to the developmental activities undertaken by the government where people become passive observers. A time has come when it is necessary to make development a people's movement. People's initiative and participation must become the key element in the whole process of development. A participatory planning process is an essential pre-condition for ensuring equity as well as accelerating the rate of growth of the economy.

Now that the 73rd and 74th Constitutional Amendment Acts 1992 have introduced Panchayati Raj Institutions, a participatory process of development may usher in through the involvement of local level representative institutions in formulation and implementation of different programmes. The PRIs have three essential attributes: they have a representative character, act as a responsible administrative agency to the local community and derive the power of freedom in certain matters which are given to them by the Constitution. The success of these institutions would, dependent upon the political will and organised effort by the local representatives, certainly change the economic and political map of India.

In conclusion, we may mention here that poor governance imposes a heavy burden on the economy and society. We all pay a price. But for the poor, the burden is much heavier. They are powerless to resist request for bribes in purchase of public goods for which their dependence is much greater. They often face humiliation from a bureaucracy insensitive to their plight and from police who can harass them even on flimsy grounds. Perhaps the biggest cost of poor governance is, as pointed out by Lateef, that it destroys the credibility and legitimacy of the state in the eyes of its citizens. This is something which India should try to avoid. Otherwise India may do better in the field of economic growth, but may feel worse because of incontestable humiliation both from internal and external spheres.

References

Ahluwalia, Montek Singh, The IT Revolution, *University News*, Vol. 38, No. 21, May 22, 2000.

Chakravarty, Sukhamoy, Development Planning, The Indian Experience, Clarendon Press, Oxford, 1987.

Das, S.K., Civil Service Reform and Structural Adjustment, Oxford University Press, Delhi, 1998.

Dayal, Iswar, Organisation for Policy Formulation in Development Policy and Administration, edited by Kuldeep Mathur, Sage Publication, New Delhi, 1996.

Government of India, Planning Commission Reports.

Kohli, Atul, Crisis of Governability in Politics in India, edited by Sudipta Kaviraj, Oxford University Press, Delhi, 1997.

Kothari, Rajni, State Against Democracy, Ajanta Publications, Delhi, 1988.

Lateef, K. Sarwar, The Governance Challenge, in Tomorrow's India; Another Tryst with Destiny, Edited by B.G. Verghese, Penguin Books India, 2006.

Mathur, Kuldeep, 'Introduction: The Emerging Concerns in Public Administration', in Development Policy and Administration, *op. cit.*

Rangarajan, C., Human Development and Economic Growth, *University News*, August 19, 1996.

———, State, Market and the Economy, The Shifting Frontiers, *EPW*, April 15-21, 2000.

Sapru, R.K., Development Administrations, Sterling Publishers, New Delhi, 1994.

Sen, Amartya, On Development as Freedom, Nikhil Chakravarty Memorial Lecture, *Mainstream*, April 15, 2000.

Sengupta, Arjun, Ensuring Equity, Public Spending as Policy Instrument, *Times of India*, August 21, 1998.

Singh, S.N., Administrative Culture and Development, Mittal Publications, New Delhi, 1997.

Sivaraman, B., The Culture of Democracy and the Politics of Democracy. *Quo Vadis? IASSI Quarterly*, Vol. 15, July-September 1996, No. 1.

CHAPTER

4

The Effect of Economic Growth on Inclusive Development

The economy has already moved decisively to a higher growth phase. We have almost reached a level of 8 per cent per year during the Tenth Five Year Plan. Further, according to the Planning Commission, the growth objective is now more sustainable, and the economy can grow between 8 to 9% on a sustained basis provided there are no interruptions due to either external or internal hazards. All the same, the eleventh plan makes an attempt to restructure the policies to achieve a new vision of growth that will be much more broad-based and inclusive, bringing about a faster reduction in poverty and helping bridge the divides that currently the focus of so much attention. All along the Planning Commission have emphasized rapid economic growth to raise the incomes of the mass of population sufficiently to bring about a general improvement in living condition. And we have also seen that because of sustained economic growth, the rate of growth of per capita income as measured by per capita GDP at market prices grew by an annual average rate of 3.1% during the 12 year period,

1980-81 to 1991-92. It accelerated marginally to 3.7% per annum during the next 11 years, 1992-93 to 2002-03. Since then there has been a sharp acceleration in the growth of per capita income, almost doubling to an average of 7.2 per cent per annum (2003-04 to 2007-08). So also there was improvement in per capita consumption. As can be seen from the Economic Survey, 2009-10, per capita consumption in 2005-06, 2006-07 and 2007-08 increased to the extent of 7.3 per cent, 6.7 per cent and 8.3 per cent respectively. It is only in the next two years, 2008-09 and 2009-10, during the over-all recession in the world economy, the growth of both per capita income and per capita consumption had some set back. However, the growth process has again started improving. Yet, in spite all this, the economic growth has not been broad-based, nor has it benefited all parts of the country and particularly the rural areas.

This raises a number of questions regarding the impact of growth on : (i) employment generation, (ii) poverty reduction, (iii) equity, (iv) improvement in the economic and social well being of the people, and (v) sustainability and/or ecological balance. We will try to answer some of these questions as briefly as possible. Let us first consider the question of employment, because without creation of productive employment opportunities, we cannot reduce poverty. We start with the assumption that economic growth is not a zero-sum game. The demand keeps growing because that look like wants today are needs tomorrow. If you believe human wants and needs are infinite, then there are infinite industries to be created, infinite businesses to be started and infinite jobs to be done, and the only limiting factor is human imagination. When Ricardo was writing, goods were tradable, but for the most part knowledge, work and services were not. There is a difference between idea-based goods and physical goods. If you are a knowledge worker, making and selling some kind of idea-based product, the volume and type of transactions increase and employment opportunities gather momentum. Infosys, for example, received one million applications from young Indians for new knowledge based jobs in the year 2004-05.

However, in spite of this knowledge-based economy, which has been developed in India, employment has not increased in proportion to economic growth or in proportion to increased labour force. Another important factor which has affected employment is structural change in the economy. In the event of liberalization the importance of agriculture has come down. For example, as one of the largest agrarian economies, the share of agriculture in GDP in the year 1972-73 was 41 per cent at 1999-2000 prices and the share in the employment was 73.9 per cent. By 2004-05 the share of agriculture in GDP at the same 1999-2000 prices came down to 20.2 per cent and the share in employment at 56.5 per cent. The latest figures which are recorded in Economic Survey 2009-10 show that the agricultural sector (including allied activities) accounted for 15.7 per cent of GDP (at constant 2004-05 prices) in 2008-09 along with an employment of around 52 per cent of the workforce. On the other hand, neither the industry nor services have provided adequate employment to compensate the loss of agricultural employment. The shares of industry and services in GDP for the year 2008-09 were about 20.25 and 64.05 percentages respectively. The growth of the index of industrial production (IIP) and its major components show that the Indian economy has jumped from agriculture to services bypassing industry. The latest figures which are recorded in Economic Survey 2009-10 show that in 2006-07, the growth of manufacturing which is one of the key drivers of growth and creation of employment opportunities was only 12.5 per cent. The growths of the other two major components, mining and electricity were only 5.4 per cent and 7.2 per cent respectively with the growth of IIP coming to 11.6 per cent. Even though the share of GDP increased in service sector, there was no increase in the absorption of labour force in this sector. It has only the privilege of earning more income for a unit of service. The service sector can easily be identified as an elite sector with enormous income and prestige in the social ladder.

It is also indicated in the Economic Survey that while employment growth during 1999-2000 to 2004-05 accelerated significantly as compared to the growth witnessed during 1993-94 to 1999-2000, from 24 million to 47 million work opportunities, i.e. employment growth accelerated from 1.25 per cent per annum to 2.82 per cent per annum, since the labour force grew at a faster rate of 2.84 per cent than the work force, unemployment rate also rose from 7.31 per cent in 1999-00 on CDS basis to 8.28 per cent in 2004-05. Again it is also noticed that employment in the organized sector accounts only to 7 to 8 per cent while 92/93 per cent is absorbed in the informal sector. According to ILO, the quality of employment in the informal sector is awefully bad, wages are low with insecurity of employment and absence of any social security. It is mentioned in one report that a beggar gets more than some of the labourers in the informal sector.

The most unfortunate part is that many of the industries are substituting technology in place of labour. Eduard Luce in *Finance Times*, London gives some examples to show how some of the industries in India are reducing labour force. The Jamshedpur Steel Plant employed 85,000 workers in 1991 to produce one tonne worth $ 0.8 m. In 2005, the production rose to 5 m tonnes worth about $ 5m while employment fell to 44,000, output increased by a factor of five, employment dropped by a factor of half implying an increase of labour productivity of 10. Similarly, Tata Motors in Pune reduced the number of workers from 35,000 to 21,000, but increased production of vehicles from 1,29,000 to 3,11,500 between 1999-2004, implying a labour productivity increase by a factor four. Stephen Stanley reports that Bajaj Motor Cycle factory in Pune, in mid 1990s, employed 24,000 workers to produce 1 m units of two wheelers. Aided by Japanese Robotics and Indian Information Technology in 2004 it produced 2.4 m units with 10,500 workers—more than double output with less than half of the labour force, an increase in labour productivity by a factor of nearly six. It is not only the private sector where there is substitution of technology in place of labour, many of the public sector units also retrenched labour due to continuous loss in these units.

Due to lack of adequate employment opportunities, increased economic growth in India did not make any significant improvement in the reduction of poverty. The following table shows the extent of poverty in different periods as recorded by NSS studies as per the guidelines of the Planning Commission. The Planning Commission definition of poverty is in terms of consumption of only calories, 2400 units per person per day in rural areas and 2100 calories in urban areas.

Year	Round	Poverty Rate %
1977-78	32	51.3
1983	38	45.65
1987-88	43	39.09
1993-94	50	37.27
1999-2000	55	26.09
2004-05	61	
On the basis of MRP (1999-2000)		22.15
On the basis of URP (1993-94)		27.5

In the mean time however, an expert group appointed by the Planning Commission to review the methodology for estimation of poverty under the Chairmanship of Professor Suresh Tendulkar has made some changes both in methodology and poverty estimates which are different from the recommendations of 61st Round NSSO. The Expert Group in their Report published by the Government of India, Planning Commission, November 2009) has followed the Mixed Reference Period (MRP) and arrived at the new poverty lines after assessing the adequacy of private household expenditure on education and health while the earlier calorie—anchored poverty lines did not explicitly account for these. The proposed lines are in that sense broader in scope and come to 37.2 per cent for all India in the same 2004-05 compared to 27.5 per cent in the previous study based on Uniform Recall Period (URP). Particularly the difference in the incidence of poverty in rural areas between the two studies is wide apart. While the 61st Round NSS study shows poverty level at 28.3 per cent in rural areas and 25.7 per cent in urban areas, according to the Expert Group, it is 41.8 per cent for rural areas and 25 per cent for urban areas. The difference arises because the Expert Group while moving away from the calorie norms has checked the adequacy of actual private expenditure per capita near the poverty lines on food, education and health by comparing them with normative expenditure consistent with nutritional, educational and health outcomes.

Though it is true that the impact of growth on poverty depends on the quality of growth, it is also true that growth by itself tends to reduce poverty. Poverty reduction has been substantial in East Asian Countries which have experienced very high rates of growth. There was very little poverty reduction in India in the 1950s, 1960s and 1970s when the growth of income was meager. The much higher growth rate in the 1980s, 1990s and early part of the 10th plan resulted in a significant reduction in the extent of poverty. Furthermore, poverty reduction has been the greatest in states that have grown faster. There is much less poverty in Punjab (8.4% in 2004-05) and Haryana (14.0% in 2004-05). Poverty is concentrated in the Eastern States of India that have experienced little growth. Also poverty is concentrated among the tribal areas as these have been left out of the economic mainstream.

But the definition of poverty has been questioned by many social scientists. In 1981 Streeten and Hicks considered poverty on the concept of basic needs. Since basic needs were loosely defined, the calorie concept of the Planning Commission continues to determine the poverty level in India. As per NSSO, 61 round, about 260 million people (27.5 per cent) remained below the poverty line whose income was less than Rs. 356.30 a month in the villages and Rs. 538.60 a month in the cities. But in the mean time, the World Bank has revised the concept of extreme poverty, in place of $ 1 per person a day to $ 1.25 per person per day. On the basis of this concept the estimated number of poor in India during 2004-05 was 456 million or 41.6% of the total population. The World Bank has again estimated that extreme poverty in India calculated at $ 1.25 a day would be about 25% of India's population in 2015 and the number would be 313 million. India would be above only sub-Sahara Africa where the corresponding figure would be 37.1 per cent, while in China it would be 6.1 per cent. This shows that our inclusive growth reflects poor achievement despite attaining a growth momentum of as high as 8-9 per cent by the country over the last few years.

Though there are evidences to show that economic growth lowers poverty in many countries, what about income distribution? Does economic growth improve income distribution? After Simon Kuznets' hypothesis that growth initially worsens income distribution and later improves it, a lot of research has been undertaken in different parts of the world to study the inter-relationship between growth and income distribution. Some of the research studies show that the impact of growth on income distribution depends on the factor endowments available in the economy and the growth strategy adopted to increase the rate of growth (Monmohan Agrawal and Amit Shovon Ray). For instance, when Korea initially adopted an export oriented development strategy, the increased exports came from labour intensive industries such as textiles and apparel. Workers in these industries were either earlier unemployed or came from agriculture where their productivity was low. During this phase of development, not only was there income growth, but also favourable income distribution. This falsifies the hypothesis of Simon Kuznets. But later on, when Korean economy shifted from the export of unskilled labour-intensive goods to that of skilled labour-intensive goods, the situation was changed. Wages of skilled labour were considerably higher and, therefore, even though poverty levels continued to decrease, the income distribution actually worsened.

In case of India, there is colossal difference in income distribution between the rich and poor. Human Development Report 2004 shows that the poorest 20 per cent receive 9 per cent of total income while the richest 20 per cent enjoy 42 per cent of total national income. The same report also indicates that there is considerable amount of income inequality in China, Vietnam and Brazil, where along with income growth poverty has been reduced substantially. This shows that poverty reduction is not synonymous with income distribution. The results of a survey by Merill Lynch and Capgenrini (which is reported in the media) shows that one lakh persons each with a personal net worth of more than 4 crores of rupees which makes for a share of 10 per cent of national GDP. Thus, 0.001 per cent of more than a billion in India owns 10 per cent of the national GDP.

Sengupta Committee of the Planning Commission points out that over 22 per cent people who live below the poverty line were not even getting Rs. 9 per day. The Report also indicates that income of 36 big industrial houses amounting to an estimated 8,66,000 crore compared to total central budget of Rs. 4,33,000 crore. The Forbes enlisted numerous billionaires of India. The four richest Indians are collectively worth $ 180 billion—greater than the GDP of a majority of member states of the UN. These four are worth more than 40 richest Chinese combined. We have more billionaires than any country in Asia (even Japan has less) along with 260 million people living below the poverty line. Amit Bhaduri in his 'Development with Dignity' gives a contrast. According to him, more than one in three Indians live in abject poverty, spending less than 1 U.S. dollar a day in terms of purchasing power parity. All this shows that though economic growth may reduce poverty but may not improve economic well-being unless there is proper resource planning for a beneficial growth strategy.

Amartya Sen in 1982 argued that development economics has been discredited because of its very narrow focus on growth and its relative neglect of development which is not synonymous with growth. He stressed that the purpose of development was not merely to generate a higher income: higher income is not an end but an instrument for achieving a better quality of life. He developed the concept of entitlement and capability and increasingly defined development in terms of capability. Entitlement is the link between production and what a person actually consumes. A person's entitlement may be more or less than what he produces. This explains why the relation between per capita income and development in terms of health, education and poverty may be very weak. In fact, even though per capita income in India has increased substantially due to higher level of economic growth, there is great shortfall in social development. India is seen as a wounded civilization—a place of pestilence, malnutrition, illiteracy, poverty and hunger. Capability is the ability of a person to function autonomously. While this may be partly a function of his consumption—what commodities do to the individual or what Sen calls functioning, is also a function of a society's institutional arrangements.

Poverty, ill-health and illiteracy are major constraints to a person's level of functioning and capabilities. Enhancing capability means tackling these debilitating factors. Since we have not so far been able to improve the social sector of the country, India ranks 17th in economic wellness among 23 when economies are compared based on a measure of people's economic well-being (ADB).

We may also indicate here another danger which rings alarm bells for humanity. Scientists studying climate change have set out a stark vision of how the world will change if humanity fails to tackle surging green house gas emissions. Their research studies show how a warming world would threaten billions of people with thirst and malnutrition, endanger more than half of wild life species with extinction and initiate a melting of the Greenland ice cap that could raise global sea levels by more than 22 ft. Such warnings have been heard before but never with so much scientific certainty. For a long time the developing countries including India were thinking that they would not be a victim to such danger since their per capita emissions are much less. For example, India's per capita emissions are 25 times less than the US and 13 times less than EU. But this does not mean that India would escape from the danger. We are now facing the rigour of climate change. Even though per capita emissions are less in India, yet in individual terms relatively inefficient Indian power companies fare badly in comparison to rich country's power generators and emit more carbon dioxide due inefficient use and rising fossil fuel. We have therefore, to make a move to a low carbon growth strategy. Climate change is an international problem and no country, whether developed or developing can escape the danger. As Dr. Rajendra Pachauri has said, climate challenge threatens the environment and unless each and every country makes effort to reduce carbon emissions, there cannot be any sustainable economic or social development. What we are consuming is more than what earth can sustain. Consumption levels are first depleting the world's resources outpacing regeneration.

In conclusion, we may point out that in order to maintain sustainable economic development, reduce poverty, improve equity, entitlement and capability, we have to change the pattern of development and involve the people directly in the process of development. The people should not be passive agents in the process of change. The proponents of development need to urgently produce the micro basis for Human Development. The development debate is mostly concerned with issues of stabilization, fiscal balance and GDP growth. But these really do not help in attaining human development. The approach of neo-classical economics may ensure micro approach and involve people in the process of change.

Another area which needs greater emphasis is how to utilize the rural unemployed for capital formation. If these people can be utilized in some productive enterprises, not only will there be increase in income of the rural unemployed but the pressure of people on agriculture will also be reduced. As long as we do not reduce the pressure on agriculture, agricultural operations will not be a viable proposition. As propounded by economists like Rosenstein Rodan 1943, Nurkse 1953 and Lewis 1954, the policy formulation should be to divert unemployed to higher productive regime which facilitates agricultural growth and provides additional income to the rural poor. The primary focus of development policy formulation is to accelerate the rate of investment, mobilize the underemployed labour force, promote rapid industrialization and determine resource allocation through planning and controls. In this context, we have to point out that many subsidies are given today in India for water or power or fertilizers which are not only regressive as well as ecologically damaging even though they may be politically popular (Meghnad Desai). Such redistribution is always bigger in ambition than in actual transfers and is often appropriated by the not-so-poor who control the transmission channels of aid. We should therefore, make direct investment in both physical infrastructure like roads, electricity, irrigation, etc. which will facilitate capital formation and social infrastructure like education, health, sanitation, drinking water, etc. to improve the capability of the people who are engaged in different types of economic and social activities.

In the sphere of industrialization, we have to give greater stress to manufacturing. The share of manufacturing in GDP has stagnated in India. Only 12.5 per cent of workers is absorbed in manufacturing. The country had the world's seventh largest manufacturing sector at the time of independence in 1947. The rate of growth of value added in manufacturing was 8.5 per cent between 1860 and 1900. Such a sustained rate of growth in the manufacturing sector has not been achieved since independence. Poverty will not be reduced by the growth of services. Even investment in agriculture will not improve economic well-being unless surplus labour force is diverted to other productive enterprises like manufacturing. This would require a growth rate of manufacturing at 12 to 15 per cent with an aim of doubling the manufacturing from the present 40 million to 80 million over twenty years (Desai). China achieved such a rate between 1980 and 2000. There is no reason why India cannot do the same.

What is required is to create an awareness among the political authority for making the necessary change in the economic structure of the country. Improvement in the manufacturing sector will accelerate the process of development both in agriculture and industry and reduce the disparity that exists now in the development pattern of the country. Political will has a major role in the process of change. We guess Media which has now assumed tremendous importance in moulding public opinion can also exercise a definite constructive role in influencing the development policies of the government and at the same time correcting the loopholes that hamper the benefit of development projects.

CHAPTER

5

New Economic Policy, Economic Development and Social Opportunities

Professor D.R. Gadgil in his, "An Approach to Indian Planning" made several suggestions to orient the economy of India to : (a) increase the pace of economic growth through appropriate technology, (b) provide adequate employment opportunities to the labour force so as to improve the living standards of the people, (c) make vigorous experimentation in establishing an efficient and decentralised economy with a view to preventing concentration of economic wealth, (d) control a premature increase of the demand for luxury and semi-luxury goods in order to effectively utilise the resources to meet the basic needs of the people and further, (e) lead to an emphasis on the conservation and development of natural resources all over the country and spreading widely the network of socio-economic overheads which will facilitate a balanced growth. The question which we have to examine whether the New Economic Policy which has been introduced since 1991 can achieve some of the above objectives which were emphasised by Prof. Gadgil.

The New Economic Policy primarily aims at promoting market economy through liberalisation, privatisation and globalisation. It is expected that the market economy through perfect competition and without any government intervention will (a) ensure utilisation of resources with maximum growth of output and services at micro level, (b) upgrade methods of production, improve exports and increase foreign investment with up-to-date technology, and (c) reduce the existing rent seeking opportunities within the country through efficient allocation of resources (due to both internal and external competition) and help in stabilising the domestic price level. Thus liberalisation aims to secure economic advantages of competition.

Impact of Market Economy

However, it may be mentioned here that a competitive economy may increase the rate of growth and per capita income by improving the efficiency of economic organisation, but may not increase the quality of life of people. Amartya Sen in his 'Inequality re-examined' has pointed out that in terms of per capita GNP, South Africa, Brazil, Gabon & Oman have six or more times the per capita GNP of China and Sri Lanka, but these richer countries give their people significantly lower ability to survive premature mortality than do the lower-income countries. Costa Rica, which is also considerably poorer than the above mentioned four countries offers not only a much higher life expectancy than those four, but a life expectancy that is not significantly below those obtaining in the richest countries of Europe and North America. Among the Indian states, Kerala has one of the lower real incomes per head, but its achievements in the field of life expectancy, infant mortality, level of general literacy, and particularly female literacy are not only much better than those of the rest of India, but they have an edge in some fields—especially with respect to women—even over China and Sri Lanka.

Prof. Gadgil also points out that in highly developed and integrated economies, it can be taken for granted that forces of development generated in one place will soon have a decisive impact on other areas and activities. This is especially evident in urban industrial economies. It is not so evident in the rural sectors even of some advanced industrial countries. This implies there is no automatic transmission or spill-over effects of development started in particular locations and activities. Instead of therefore depending entirely on competitive economic growth, the government should initiate development simultaneously in as large a number of locations and activities all over the country so as to distribute the gains of development to different sections of the community. Undoubtedly this dispersal of effort will appear to yield immediately less dramatic results, but it will provide a sounder base for planning in the future and also avoid the accentuation of disparities which is one of the most serious features of the existing situation.

It may also be noted that even in some of the advanced capitalist countries, competition does not exist in the industrial sector. A few firms dominate the economy and determine the manufacturing capacity of the country. In the USA, for example, 100 largest firms accounted for 33 per cent of value added in US economy in 1987. Three market imperfections are found now in the contemporary world. They are : (i) potential development of monopoly power, (ii) the existence of educational and informational deficiencies among the participants in the market, and (iii) free markets, wherever they exist, tend to run counter to the general ethical standards of the larger society. In view of this, we cannot possibly depend upon a competitive market for determining the pattern of production.

Secondly, when we come to market economy, we notice distinct disadvantages for a developing economy. Market demand may not reflect the real needs of people owing to skewed distribution of income. Some of the estimates show that the share in income of the bottom 20% population in India is about 9% whereas that of the top 10% is 27%. If the producers produce, according to market demand, more 'demerit goods' rather than 'merit goods' will be produced. The private economy will not make investment in education, health, sanitation, social security, etc. where social rates of return is much higher than private rate of return. As such, there will be acute deficiency in social opportunities of developing countries. Similarly, certain other goods like national defence, police, fire protection, flood control, etc. cannot be supplied profitably in a free market economy because of free rider problem.

Thirdly, market economy may increase the rate of growth of income, but may not increase employment opportunities or reduce poverty, illiteracy, ill health, child labour or criminal violence. In most of the developed countries, there is not only labour displacement in manufacturing industries, but also in processing the tertiary activities. Private investment may be used to replace men by machines. Between 1980-92, Spain doubled its GDP without creating a single additional job. Even though there were increases in the rates of growth of income in Brazil, as much as one-third of all jobs were suppressed in the manufacturing industries during the nineties. Downsizing also significantly affected the banking sector.

In fact, the link between production and employment is loosening due to (a) technological change in industries, (b) recent advances in office automation, (c) intensive growth taking precedence over extensive growth, (d) diversion of capital from real economy to speculative gain in financial sector which requires less labour, and (e) dominance of the ideology of consumerism which does not allow people to reduce working time inspite of increase in productivity due to improvement in technology. As such there is no scope for additional employment for people who are able and willing to work. How can developing countries manage to provide employment to their growing population if the competitive trends of economic growth does not increase employment opportunities?

Fourthly, some of the capitalist states in developed countries managed to introduce social security system to provide some assistance to the people who were unemployed, disabled or deprived of some of the basic amenities of life. The welfare system worked well so long as they were not being put under too much strain of excessive contribution in conditions of rapid growth and almost full employment. But as pointed out by Ignacy Sachs in his 'Understanding Development', this socially responsive capitalism is showing signs of exhaustion due to a combined pressure of low rates of growth and of a labour-displacing technical process. It is very unfortunate that when the need for social protection is most pressing, they are crumbling under their cost, not to speak of the fact that mere putting of the unemployed on the doles does not shelter them from social exclusion and loss of dignity: work in our societies still has a major socialising function.

Further, in a free market economy, the private sector may not bother to conserve the nature. For the sake of profits, it may destroy forests, over issue mineral resources, pollute air, water and so on. They may not take into account externalities in the form of social costs or social benefits. The producer may charge a price which covers only internalised production costs without taking into account the costs of pollution, destruction of natural resources or adverse impact on health. All this implies that a developing economy cannot entirely depend on a market economy to improve the economic well-being of the people.

We do not mean to say that market is not necessary. Since it accelerates the process of growth, we have to welcome it so long higher rates of growth are not achieved at the expenses of employment, of equity in income distribution and of environmental prudence. We may need more markets, but we also have to go 'more beyond the markets'. What needs curing is not just 'too little market' or 'too much market', but too little market in some areas and too little beyond the market in other areas.

Amartya Sen goes beyond distribution of income and emphasises the need for improvement of basic capabilities, which not only improve the quality of life (through accumulation of human capital i.e., basic education, good health and other human attainments), help in generating economic success which increases the ability to be free from income poverty and choose a life one has reason to value. He thinks that accumulation of human capital should not be conceived as if people were just the means of production and not its ultimate end. The bettering of human life does not have to be justified by showing that a person with a better life is also a better producer.

ROLE OF PUBLIC SECTOR

All this implies that we cannot neglect public sector not only to increase the pace of economic growth, but also to improve the quality of life of people and increase their capability. Even the Asian tigers including Japan and Malaysia had to depend on the strategic role of the government to maintain the tempo of their development. First of all before market reform was introduced in China, Korea and other South East Asian countries, there was a great deal of improvement in basic education, health care, land reforms and many other public actions which helped in improving the quality of life, and increasing the productivity of capital which facilitated market reform to increase the pace of economic growth. Jean Dreze and Amartya Sen in their book 'Economic Development and Social Opportunities' have pointed out that market reform succeeded in these South Asian countries since they had taken a number of measures prior to reform to control morbidity, undernourishment, poverty and to increase employment opportunities by pursuing an active role to improve human capital.

Further, even after liberalisation was introduced, many of these South Asian countries had to depend on Government initiative to develop heavy and strategic industries. In Japan, with government initiative a number of heavy industries such as steel, oil refining, industrial machinery of all sorts and electronics all of which require intensive employment of capital and technology were started to promote rapid industrial development and secure competitive advantage in the international market. Pranab Bardhan in his 'The Political Economy of Development in India' mentioned that 'even in late stages of industrialisation the success story of Japan underlines the imperative of state leadership in restructuring the economy in pace with the rapidly changing technological frontier, in raising and reallocating massive amounts of long-term industrial finance and in underwriting the risks of innovations'. Henry Rosvsky has written that 'Japan must be the only capitalist country in the world in which the government decides how many firms should be in a given industry, and sets out to arrange the desired number'.

Writing on South Korea, Parvez Hasan points out that the Korean economy depends in large measure on private enterprise operating under highly centralised government guidance. In Korea, the government's role is considerably more direct than that of merely setting the broad rules of the game and in influencing the economy indirectly through market forces. In fact, the government seems to be a participant and often the determining influence in nearly all business decisions. Again Edward Mason and associates also point out that the rapid economic growth that began in South Korea in the early 1960s and accelerated since then has been a government directed development in which the principal engine has been private enterprise. The hand of the government reaches down rather far into the activities of individual firms with its manipulation of incentives and disincentives.

We have given the examples of two leading countries who have adopted liberalisation where the state assumed important and paternalistic role, kept the key economic sectors with it and left the rest to private initiative and enterprise. In addition, two other measures which assisted development both in South Korea and Japan were : (i) land reforms (which by increasing agricultural production facilitated the expansion of internal markets), and (ii) maintenance of discipline among workers (which was vital to the pursuit of industrialisation) and among entrepreneurs and firms (which had the effect of ensuring investment of surplus in virtuous circle of growth). And both of these measures were effectively implemented by the state.

This implies that in a developing country like India, the state has to concern itself with three important policy measures. One is economic growth which is concerned with the increasing supply of factors that make for growth and with removing structural and other constraints to growth (i.e. for attaining efficient use of resources to increase output, employment and upgradation of technology), second, the economics of distribution which take some degree of equality in distribution as desirable by no means automatically assured in the process of development and third provision of basic necessities of life like basic education, health, sanitation, social security to improve the quality of life. All these require strategic intervention by the Government (rather than mindless bureaucracy) and cannot be assumed to be taken care of merely by sound macro and micro economic policies as commonly understood.

In the light of experiences of different countries, Panchamukhi makes two important observations. First there is no single universally valid of state versus market. Secondly, the state has to govern the market instead of the state being dictated by the market. Particularly in India, state and market should co-exist in any process of development and the governance of the market will have to be the responsibility of the state.

The co-existence of market and the state becomes inevitable because there has been (i) unnecessary expansion of public sector into non-strategic areas like consumer durables, non-durables and a wide variety of common services to appease workers and middlemen. This opened new opportunities for rent seeking politicians and bureaucrats. In fact, political and bureaucratic control coupled with managerial and workers inertia decreased the efficiency of public enterprises. A number of disturbing features have been observed in the working of public sector enterprises. They refer to : (a) excessive arbitrary power which provided much scope for corruption, (b) insufficient growth in productivity due to too much bureaucratic and political control and excessive use of manpower, (c) poor project management through the help of political and bureaucratic agencies which did not have adequate skill and training to manage the projects efficiently and honestly, (d) very low rate of return on capital investment due to misuse of resources, and (e) inadequate attention to R&D and Human Resource Development. I.G. Patel in his 'Economic Reform and Global Change' points out that market economy had greater public appeal in India for fighting corruption and arbitrary power of the government than increasing efficiency.

It may be mentioned here that the private sector is not an angel. Even one American economist points out, 'A competent, customer driven public sector is necessary, partly to provide services—and partly to keep the private sector honest'. He further adds, 'Even liberals get exasperated at dumb public sector bureaucracies—yet private bureaucracies are neither as efficient nor as self-cleansing as many other champions insist'. Brendan Martin in his 'In the Public Interest? Privatisation and Public Sector Reforms' has made three important observations in respect of private *vs.* public sector. According to him, (a) privatisation of public enterprises is not necessarily in the public interest but in the interest of certain (identifiable) pressure groups and vested interests, (b) the ideology of privatisation is not in the interest of developing countries, and (c) there is a viable alternative, which is possible to attain, by empowerment of the service users (i.e., by decentralisation), by regulation and by genuine competition, by developing management responsibility, in short by restructuring and reforming the management of public services, public utilities, public enterprises.

In India, some of the traditional business houses tend to develop certain characteristics which are not helpful for industrial development. These characteristics can be summarised as follows:

(i) The business houses safeguard their own funds and try to spend public money. Therefore, instead of generating internal resources, they heavily depend upon the assistance of the public financial institutions and capital market. As such they become careless with public funds.

(ii) Industrialists/business houses tend to seek maximum profit in the shortest possible time. Speculation becomes an easy method for the purpose. They do not try to take any risk by floating enterprises where there is need for creativity and innovativeness. Their actions are therefore, more manipulative rather than competitive.

(iii) As such they do not give much importance to research and development. For example, the R&D budget of one American car manufacturer is more than the entire turnover of Indian auto industry. Without such infrastructure, how can the private sector industries improve their efficiency and compete with outsiders?

However, a time has come when it would be desirable for the public sector to shed some less crucial areas of responsibility. As we have already pointed out, the public sector has entered into quite a few areas in which no commercial logic is served nor is there a broader welfare mechanism that is being met. For example, soft drinks, bread manufacturing, luxury hotels, two-wheelers, etc. are not commanding heights. These can be run and sold on commercial basis. But others which are of strategic nature (like defence industries, chemical industries, iron and steel, etc.) and perform social objectives (supplying collective goods like education, health, environment protection, food security, civil and political rights, effective legal system, basic needs of the people, infrastructure, etc.) should be run by the government. Now there are scarcity of funds due to losses of public enterprises. If such commercial enterprises where government is making heavy losses are transferred to private sector, the former can have more funds for enlarging and improving the areas of both strategic and social sectors. And the mechanism of transfer should be worked out in such a manner that there is no human deprivation nor loss of public resources.

Further in order to improve the efficiency of public enterprises, at least two basic conditions should be fulfilled. First, the management of public sector enterprises should be free from government control and should have full autonomy in decision-making. Second, as has been done in Japan and South Korea, the state intervention can be more purposeful if the state can take the responsibility of providing a good deal of infrastructure as well as information facilities. This will not only help the public sector, but also other industries in the private sector. We must remember that when public sector was enlarged, it was enlarged on rather idealistic view of the government. But as our experiences have shown and as pointed out by I.G. Patel in his 'Limits of Current Consensus on Development', the Government is neither omniscient nor omnipotent, neither benevolent nor even impartial. At the same time there is no possibility that the state will wither away, change its essential character or eliminate all political influence from economic policy. So we have to improve some operational mechanism and provide limited field of activity for the government so as to make them more effective. The Gandhian question of 'How much is enough for us' is pertinent in respect of the enlargement of the public sector.

OPENING-UP OF THE ECONOMY

One important element of liberalisation is opening up of the economy or globalisation of the Indian production structure. This globalisation has several features. First, it implies removal of protective methods for enabling foreign producers to freely compete in the Indian market. Second, it allows foreign investment without much restriction along with the inflow of foreign exchange through foreign loans and NRI remittances. Third, it allows substantial reduction in customs duties both for increasing exports and imports.

The principal argument advanced for opening up of the economy is that the Indian economy, sheltered from market forces and denied competition has become inefficient. This has resulted not only in high cost and poor quality of products and services which is not only unfair to the consumers, but has also restricted growth as well. Therefore, there is every justification to release the economy from over regulation both domestically as well as globally. Competition is certainly a good guide, but to become beneficial, it must be between equals or near equals and on 'level playing fields'. A large number of industries in India, in course of a few years, will close down because of competition of industrial products from developed countries and a large number of workers will lose their jobs or their wages dramatically reduced. Particularly small scale industries cannot stand the competition of products of large scale industries of foreign countries which are imported without much restriction. In fact, many of the small industries in India are closed because of competition of foreign products. Further, because of WTO, agriculture in India is facing tremendous crisis. Agriculture which provides main subsistence to majority of the workers cannot compete with agricultural products of industrialised countries where productivity of agriculture is not only higher, but the amount of subsidy received by them is many times more than in India. India cannot provide so much subsidy even though it desires to do so.

The experiences of last several decades show that globalisation has created a number of distortions in both developed and developing countries. First it has widened the income gap both between and within countries. For example, in 1991, the richest fifth of the world's population appropriated 84.4 per cent of world's GNP while the share of the poorest fifth was limited to 1.4 per cent. Within a span of 30 years, the disparity between these two extreme groups went up from 30/1 to 60/1. The Report of UNCTAD 1997 also points out that since the early 1980s the world economy has been characterised by rising inequality and slow growth. Income gaps between North and South have continued to widen. In 1965, the average per capita income of the G-7 countries was 20 times that of the world's poorest seven countries. By 1995, it was 39 times as much. Even in the USA, as the country's economic integration within the rest of the world accelerated after 1970, there was a marked rise in inequality in the 1980s. For example, between 1977 and 1989, the richest one per cent of families in the USA obtained 60 per cent of the after tax gain. Worsening distribution of income was the general rule in Latin American countries during the 1980s, a decade in which the debt crisis brought the full burden of globalisation to bear up on the region. And inequality not only decreased growth due to deficiency in demand but also reduced wages and technological progress.

The Secretary-General of UNCTAD rightly points out that the present modest rates of growth of about 3% per year—some 2 percentage points lower than that achieved during the 'Golden Age' of 1950-71—can solve neither the North's employment problem nor the South's poverty problem. The more so since liberalisation of the world economy has proceeded in a lopsided way, discriminating against areas in which the South can achieve a comparative advantage.

A hundred and sixty years ago, the 'Communist Manifesto' rightly diagnosed capitalism's compulsion to create, dominate and exploit world markets. Globalisation has been advancing since then by ups and downs. Its scope and depth are maximum in the financial realm and in communication. For example, about 40,000 transnational corporations identified by the United Nations dominate in financial globalisation. Lack of adequate international and national controls on huge instant flows of capital around the globe round the clock introduces a structural instability in the world economy, manifested itself through recurrent financial crisis. The Asian crisis is the most recent, but most probably not the last one. The situation is worsened due to the improved communication which facilitates powerful propaganda in favour of globalisation distorting the real picture of the world economy.

It is also seen that globalisation is increasing the extension of market of big powers. Transnational companies are relatively few. Most companies which trade multinationally are national based and maintain a close relationship with their respective governments. Capital mobility is not producing a massive shift of investment and employment from the advanced to the developing countries. Far from being global, the world economy is concentrated among North America, Europe and Japan. About 80% of world trade is conducted between the OECD countries. The group of five of main economies accounts for 70% of foreign direct investment, whose importance is often overstated.

Further globalization instead of increasing inflow of assistance to developing countries has increased outflow of capital from the South to the North. The developed countries are now providing less than 0.25 per cent of the joint GDP of industrialised member countries of OECD. These are very small figures indeed compared to the outflow of capital of the South to the North on account of debt service (420 billion dollars between 1980 and 1992), royalties, dividends, repatriated profits, underpaid raw materials, overpaid imports, international trade conditions being far from equitable.

As pointed out by Prof. Schumpeter, globalisation leads to creative destruction. As capitalist development increases with accumulation of capital, competition forces firms to be creative in order to survive and these firms that are not creative are destroyed. In a world of markets and competition the developed countries are mostly winners and the underdeveloped countries are losers. Creative destruction ultimately leads to closure of industries in underdeveloped countries leading to unemployment of workers, destitution of communities and disempowerment of people.

Another great danger of globalization is that it aggravates environmental degradation. The Western industrial development model (which is generally called fossil-fuel based automobile-centred throw away economy), though increased income, material consumption, level of living and physical mobility to an unprecedented level, cannot sustain for long since it is destroying the Earth's natural system. But such degradation is not confined to developed countries. First globalisation increases consumerism in developing countries which leads to reckless exploitation of the earth. For example, indiscriminate industrialisation has given rise to emission of toxic gases, depletion of ozone layer, threat of acid rain, pollution of air, water and land surface, etc., in fact, nothing is spared resulting in total population.

Secondly, the greater mobility of capital makes it more and more difficult for the government of any country to impose regulations on polluting firms. In the name of free market and competition, the developed countries manage to prohibit the governments of developing countries to regulate private business and productive activities of the public sector. In so doing, it limits people's power to exercise political control over their economic lives. Thirdly, no country can escape from the impacts of ecological stress. There is no international boundary to prevent it. It is seen that industrial wastes escape national sovereignty, they do not show up at customs posts or travel with passports. No country is a self-contained unit, but contingent in actions taken by others.

It is sometimes contended that neo-liberal policies of unregulated international commerce and reduction of state services have been sources of economic growth. But the facts are different. Virtually every country that has achieved some successful economic development from the United States, Germany, Great Britain in an earlier era, to Japan and South Korea in more recent decades—has done with active state intervention in economic affairs particularly with extensive state regulation of foreign commerce. And state regulation has played a major role in promoting industries with substantial technological externalities.

Paul Sweezy has pointed out that it is not globalisation which has increased growth, the very large firms that emerged at the end of the 19th century in the United States and other advanced countries had a tremendous capacity to expand production. In other words, it is not globalisation, but monopoly capitalism which was responsible for unprecedented growth. We can also add that whenever globalisation has been most effective as a foundation for economic growth, a firm institutional basis for international stability had existed. This has been the experience of Asian Tigers and China. And in addition, globalisation has succeeded in generating rapid growth under the aegis of a powerful state—a super imperial power that has been able to regulate international affairs and provide stability that has encouraged business expansion.

CONCLUDING OBSERVATIONS

Experience from other countries including developed industrialised countries like the US and Great Britain suggests that liberalisation, deregulation and privatisation may release socially and morally disruptive forces. Market forces without any regulation may tend to promote a perverse pattern of growth through inequality and unemployment. So long as huge social and economic disparities persist, growth certainly is a necessary but in no way a sufficient condition because the distributive and qualitative aspects of development cannot be over looked. The wealth of any country cannot be measured only by the number of millionaires a country possesses. The country's well-being depends upon the capacity of the largest number of people to satisfy their primary needs. Prof. Kalecki therefore points that equitable distribution of national income and increasing employment of labour force should be seen as a pre-condition and not a fall out of development.

We may also point out that allocative efficiency brought about by market forces may not ensure productive efficiency which depends on many economic and non-economic factors. The economic factors influencing productive efficiency are: (a) size of capital stock and infrastructure, (b) improvement in the quality of human resources, and (c) structural change in the economy. It is often said that capital-output ratio is exceedingly high in small scale industries where it is supposed to be low. The main reason for this high capital-output ratio is on account of very low labour productivity due to lack of improvement in the quality of human resources. If these above factors are lacking, manipulation of exchange rate cannot improve the competitive advantage of the producers.

The non-economic factors are no less important. As stated by Prof. Kaldor, 'A study of the dynamics of economic growth leads, beyond the analysis of economic factors, to a study of psychological and sociological determinants of these factors'. In other words, attitude to work, the spirit of adventure and efficiency of the government are as important as economic factors. Macro-adjustment is, therefore, a necessary condition, but not a sufficient condition for productive efficiency.

Further no country can entirely depend on foreign aid or investment to pursue a pattern of development which can meet the internal needs. The integration of internal economy with world economy through the instrumentality of TNCs will not necessarily lead to rise in productivity across all the sectors of the economy. It will benefit productivity-wise only those industries where TNCs bring in investments. And clearly the choice is their and not of the host countries. This means there must be inward economic orientation to tackle the major problems of the country. Prof. Amartya Sen therefore rightly points out that the impetus of foreign investment and high technology industries in India will benefit only a small segment of the economy, and will not tackle poverty or unemployment. Multinational investment will be confined to enclaves with limited linkages.

This does not imply that we should neglect fiscal consolidation. There is no harm in borrowing, both internally and externally, to finance investment if the cost of such borrowing is less than the rate of return, and if the burden of the debt remains within limits. But in India, loans in most cases have been utilised to meet non-developmental expenditure and therefore, the burden of public debt has become precarious. The main reason for growing fiscal deficit in India is increased revenue deficit. Whereas upto 1983, there was no revenue deficit, now it constitutes almost two-thirds of fiscal deficit. Avoidance of a revenue deficit should therefore be the basic element of prudent fiscal management. If economic reform in

India can tackle these micro economic issues of efficiency, we can have a sustained economic growth without any debt trap.

Another issue which has created a great deal of controversy is whether we should rely on export promotion or import substitution. As I.G. Patel observes, there is nothing to choose, in itself between import substitution and export promotion. Both provide employment for domestic resources. Both generate external economies and learning by doing whether production is for the home market or for the foreign market. Both augment the supply of foreign exchange, whether by saving it or by earning it. In the initial stages of development in India, import substitution considerably helped the economy to establish a number of basic industries which provided the necessary framework for accelerated development. We have now come to a stage where we can pursue both import substitution and export promotion to meet the basic requirements of the economy, import substitution to develop capital goods industries and export promotion to secure adequate foreign exchange to correct adverse balance of payments.

What we see in India is that liberalistion clearly has made the Indian private corporate sector vigorous and willing as well as able to take on global competition. Some of the corporate magnates of India have not only made investments in developed countries, but also acquired some of their business concerns. But the major part of the economy is outside that sector. There is some ripple effect through links with the informal sector, but vast masses of our population remain left out, mainly because of the underdeveloped physical infrastructure (particularly roads and electricity) and social infrastructure (basic education and public health). It is true that global recession has hurt India less than the west, but in general global competition, as pointed out by Bardhan, has wiped out some of the low productivity firms and people employed there have gone out and crowded the informal non-traded sector. Some of the adverse economic effects of globalisation in India are due to lack of social protection like unemployment benefits and lack of adequate education and skill formation which can help in job adjustment. In

Scandinavian countries where workers enjoy social protection and high skills, they welcome globalisation.

Several measures are needed to be taken in India to fortify against the adverse effects of globalisation. Globalisation has come to stay and no country can remain outside the international arena. Now that India has made considerable improvement in its economy, it has necessary potential to ensure a number of economic and social measures which can change the nature of the economy. We have pursued growth for a long time. As Prof. Amartya Sen has suggested, we should end our obsession with growth and try for equity since we have enough potential surplus which can cover minimum social services for the poor like food security, health benefits and basic education provided we are able to minimise corruption, improve operational efficiency of public sector enterprises and other governance failures. India's growth pattern has been mostly capital intensive and skill intensive sectors (software, business processing, pharmaceuticals, vehicles and parts among others), who do not employ too many people (Bardhan). Such a pattern of growth is not sustainable either economically or even politically. We therefore, suggest the following measures to reorient our economy towards more labour intensive products and processes both in agriculture and manufacturing so as to create more employment opportunities, ensure economic growth with equity and at the same time offset some of the weakness of NEP.

1. Since more than 50% of the workers work in agriculture and the total aggregate agricultural income is being gradually reduced, steps should be taken to increase the productivity of agriculture with greater amount of investment by the public sector which may facilitate irrigation, consolidation of holdings, evolution of new technology for dry land agriculture and so on. Public sector investment in agriculture which was about 16.1% in 1980-81 at 1980-81 prices came down to 6.1% in the year 1995-96 (G.S. Bhalla). Capital formation at 14% of GDP at present in the sector is improving with public sector

taking the lead, even though it is still considerably short of taking growth to 4% levels. Additional investment may be done by cutting down some of the inessential subsidies where there is a lot of leakage and which does not serve any social purpose. At least five additional measures should be taken to improve the productivity of agriculture. First, land redistribution which has been neglected due to green revolution should be expedited to counter the widespread landlessness in rural areas, which continues to frustrate prospects of poverty alleviation through productivity increases. Second, there should be improvement in delivery systems of inputs so that the small and marginal farmers in villages can be able to get them in time. Further, new inputs like biomass resources should be popularised to prevent degradation of land. Third, facilities like irrigation which have been created at heavy cost should be fully utilised along with field channels so that there is no wastage of water resources. As canal irrigation is now difficult, more emphasis should be given to water harvesting structures to increase additional irrigation facilities. Fourth, there should be diversification in cropping pattern so as to provide additional income to the farmers. Fifth, new research facilities should be created to evolve new technology which would rectify the weakness of green revolution and effectively utilise dry land with new crops.

2. Agriculture alone cannot improve the overall development of the rural economy. We have therefore to start a number of small industries in rural areas. While choosing small industries, special emphasis should be given to agro-based industries. Agro-based industries should supplement and complement both agriculture and industry. Agro-based industries are those industries which are supported by agriculture in the form of supply of agricultural raw materials. They also support agriculture by way of supplying inputs. Thus the complementarity between agriculture and industry enables the economy to use

the by-products of agriculture and improves the technological base of agriculture apart from the fact that the whole process brings about a transformation in the rural economy. The establishment of agro-based industries also opens up scope for location of a number of other small scale industries that are more or less ancillary to agro-based industries.

It may be mentioned that surplus labour from rural areas migrates to urban areas and creates in most cases slums. This is a kind of export of poverty from rural areas to urban areas. The opportunity cost of urbanisation of the rural inhabitants is very high compared to the modest outlays required to improve rural industries. A balanced rural-urban configuration provides greater scope for the establishment of an equitable society with productive employment and prevention of environmental pollution.

3. Another area which is most important in developing rural areas is improvement of infrastructure which facilitates economic growth and expansion of human resources that increases the quality of life of people. Economic growth alone may not reduce poverty, ignorance, disease and destitution. Basic education, good health and other human attainments are not only directly valuable as constituent elements of our basic capabilities but also generating economic success of a more standard kind, which in turn can contribute to enhancing the quality of human life and elementary freedom (Amartya Sen). All these can change the vicious circle in which we now live to a virtuous circle. It is sometimes contended that public borrowing crowds out private investment. May not be true in all cases, particularly public investment in social and economic infrastructure is often necessary to stimulate private investment.
4. Most of the allegations against the government refer to creation of redundant or even fake employments in public institutions at all levels. Overstaffed bureaucracies, exorbitant privileges of the upper

strata of public servants allied to poor performance generate a negative image for the government. Some of the excesses of the government can be curbed mainly in two ways. First, many of the commercial enterprises which are now handled by the public sector should be entrusted to the private sector. This will improve the quality of the government. Second, many of the local responsibilities should be transferred to local bodies. Local bodies enlarge the scope of decentralisation, enhance democratic character of the government, improve the effectiveness of development programmes through people's participation and reduce corruption as the programmes become transparent. What we require is the improvement in quality of the government, and not the quantity of government.

5. Finally our development must not endanger the natural systems that support life on Earth: the atmosphere, the waters, the soils, and the living beings. This implies that economic development should not cross the limits of the carrying capacity of our planet. And at the same time, sustainable development should make provision for supplying essential needs of the poor which include a secure and adequate source of income, adequate shelter, health, education, security and amenities. This implies that it requires a change in the content of growth, to make it less material and energy intensive and more equitable in its impact. These changes are required in all countries as part of a package of measures to maintain the stock of ecological capital, to improve the distribution of income and to reduce the degree of vulnerability to economic crisis. 'Our Common Future' hence emphasises that, 'In essence, sustainable development is a process of change in which the exploitation of resources, the direction of investments, the pattern of technological development and institutional change are all in harmony and enhance both current and future potential to meet human needs and aspirations'.

The foregoing analysis suggests that both the government intervention and market economy will have to go side by side to increase economic growth along with human development. The real issue is not whether government intervention should continue or not, but what form of government intervention should be there so that the failure of both government machinery and market mechanism can be reduced with the attainment of social objectives with minimum social cost.

References

Bardhan, Pranab, The Political Economy of Development in India. Oxford Indian Paper Backs, New Delhi, 1998.

———, No Indian Left Behind—An Interview with Pranab in *India Today*, Special Issue, 1975-2010, December 27, 2010.

Bhalla, G.S., Political Economy of Indian Development in the 20th Century—India's Road to Freedom and Growth, Presidential Address in 83rd Annual Conference, *Indian Economic Association*, December 30, 2000.

Gadgil, D.R., An Approach to Indian Planning, *IASSI Quarterly*, October-December, 1999, Vol. 18, No. 2.

Dreze, Jean and Sen, Amartya, Indian Development, Selected Regional Perspectives, Oxford University Press, New Delhi, 1997.

Misra, B., Economic Profile of India, APH Publishing Corporation, New Delhi 1997.

———, Capitalism, Socialism & Planning, Oxford & IBH., 4th Edition, New Delhi, 1988.

Patel, I.G., Economic Reform and Global Change, Review Article by Arjun Sengupta in *Economic and Political Weekly*, December 16-22, 2000.

Sachs, Ignacy, Understanding Development People, Markets and the State in Mixed Economies, Oxford University Press, New Delhi, 2000.

Sen, Amartya, Inequality Re-examined, Oxford India Paperbacks, Seventh Impression, New Delhi, 1999.

———, Development as Freedom, Oxford India Paperbacks, New Delhi, 2000.

CHAPTER

6

Economic Development and Social Ethics

CHANGE IN ECONOMIC CONTOUR

Since the beginning of fifties, we have been trying to increase the pace of economic development through an organized effort of planning. Not that we have not achieved anything. There are several areas where there have been steady progress. It is not necessary to make a quantitative analysis of the progress achieved on different fields. In many fields change is visible and there is a psychological impact on change. All the same there are many areas where our efforts are far from satisfactory. We are still struggling to abolish poverty, unemployment and inequality: the major economic maladies that raise their ugly heads in spite of different measures designed in different plans to tackle these maladies. Planning for economic development has therefore, to be continued, continued in a more systematic and well designed method so as to effectively utilize the potential resources available to the community to tackle these maladies, raise the living standards of the people and open out new opportunities for a richer and more varied life.

BIG GAP BETWEEN OUTLAY AND OUTPUT

Another area which needs emphasis is effective implementation of the programmes that are launched to increase the pace of development. As the Prime Minister once said, there is a big gap between outlay and output. We think this is one of the major stumbling blocks in the attainment of desired progress. There are several fields in which remedial action can be taken to improve the effectiveness of the programmes. One major defect of planning is proliferation of a number of projects without adequate funds to complete them on time. It is often seen that a project which is supposed to complete within a period of 5 or 6 years takes almost 20 years for completion with escalation of costs to the extent of 12 or 15 times. Therefore, it is necessary to select a few important projects on priority basis and provide the required amount of funds for their completion on time.

Second, it is also seen that in many of the anti-poverty programmes, quite a substantial amount of funds is siphoned off by the agencies, which are entrusted with the job of implementing such programmes. Two things can be done here to avoid leakage of such funds. If the local authorities are entrusted with the responsibility in organizing such activities, there will be better transparency in sanctioned amount of funds and the process of implementation. This will prevent leakage to some extent. Further very often many infructuons programmes are taken up which do not assist the poor nor provide them with any productive assets which can help them to maintain their livelihood without further aid. If the projects are selected in consonance with the wishes and ability of the poor, it will go a long way in increasing the worthwhileness of the projects. Finally, there is need for monitoring such programmes by some outside agencies whose credibility is more or less recognized by most of the people. Many other suggestions can be given, but at least if these few precautions are taken, we can improve efficiency, economy and effectiveness to a great extent.

INTEGRATION BETWEEN ECONOMIC DEVELOPMENT AND SOCIAL WELL-BEING

While considering the problem of economic development, we have to consider the broader social environment that is a part and parcel of economic development. The development of resources should not be viewed in a narrow technical sense, but in the sense of improvement of human faculties and the building of an institutional framework, as mentioned in the very First Plan, adequate to fulfil the needs and aspirations of people and at the same time preserve the natural ecosystems for the physical and psychological well-being of people. Economists have produced a large literature on how to increase growth, but like the sorcerer's apprentice, have not considered the need to stop the process at some point where it is necessary, (Herman Daly). Yet, by a short chain of reasoning from the laws of diminishing returns and diminishing marginal utility, it is clear that growth in physical commodities and in population will eventually begin to cost more than either is worth. The relevant challenge is not to torture the nature by attempting the impossible task of perpetual growth, but rather to learn how to maintain the highest level of living that can be universally shared and ecologically sustained over the long-run.

All this means we should not like Alice and Red Queen in 'Alice in Wonderland', keep on circulating without any particular direction. According to them, "It does not matter where we are going so long as we get there quickly". Such purposeless travel does not sustain the society nor improve the quality of life. There are many options which are available to maintain a steady-state economy without sacrificing social and human values and preserving ecological balance. We limit our analysis to five guidelines which we consider most important in the process of change. These guidelines are:

(i) Restoration of Social Values in Economics,
(ii) Improvement in the quality of Institutions,
(iii) Sustainable Development,
(iv) Empowerment of the People, and
(v) Improvement in Quality of Life.

(i) Restoration of Social Values in Economic Development

India's economic development is attributed to the high degree of mistrust and dishonesty, erosion of values (Fleix Raj). According to a Transparency International Survey (2004), the corruption level in India is 91 in the list of 146 countries. India stands out as one among 30 most corrupt countries in the world. The Black Economy is estimated to be about 40 per cent of the GDP which is worth 12 lakh crore today. The economic change has produced such an adverse effect on social values that one cannot secure any facility from the government without making any payment in bribe. It is now called speed money. It has found out that Indians pay a whopping Rs. 267 billion in bribes (2003) annually with the health sector perceived to be the most corrupt with people being made to pay for what they are entitled to.

The politicians, bureaucrats and governments in India are involved in scams and scandals. In fact, corruption has now become a part of life. If somehow, you are caught, you can get rid of the crime by paying a bribe. On the one side, since corruption manifests itself at the highest political level, others do not hesitate to secure some ill-got money. And further, our legal system has made life too easy for criminals and too difficult for law abiding citizens. A touch here and a push there, and India may become ungovernable under the present constitutional set-up (Nani A. Palkhivala).

The alarming rise in the incidence of corruption and crime has also an important economic aspect. Even though India has not yet attained a take-off stage in the process of development, there is a tendency on the part of the influential to strive for acquisitiveness leading to disruption of social values. Globalization has greately contributed to the pursuit of materialism to such an extent that inspite of colossal poverty, unemployment and inequality, our young men, who are supposed to be motivated by certain ideals, are making reckless effort to live a life of luxury without caring for any traditional social norm. And Jean Dreze in Time Magazine writes, "The so-called middle class in India (read the upper class) has become rich beyond its members' wildest dreams. They have literally translated themselves to the 'First World' without applying for Visa".

A time has come when we should try to restore social values in the process of development which result in a strong human bond by creating some effective public institutions that restore higher degrees of trust, honesty, accountability and transparency. Such a change will save the country from dishonour and disgrace. Civilization is an act of the spirit and the promotion of that spirit can control the banality of evil and improve public good.

(ii) Improvement in the Quality of Institutions

We have already pointed out that there is a big gap between outlay and output. Different governments (Centre and States) have established a number of institutions to implement different programmes of development. We have already mentioned some of the leakages that take place in the implementation of these programmes. The quality of these institutions can be known when we consider their impact on development.

H.G. Wells has observed that human history is becoming more and more a race between education and catastrophe. This shows the importance of education. That is why in the common minimum programme, it is emphasised that about 6 per cent of GDP should be allotted to education. But nobody bothers how the money allotted to education is utilised. We have a wonderful institution called Sarva Shiksha Abhiyan. Year after year huge amount of money is pumped into this organisation. Yet, in a recent speech the Prime Minister, Dr. Manmohan Singh deplored the fact that the dropout rate under the scheme was over 50%. A survey by Pratichi in West Bengal showed that barely 7% of children could write their own names after five years of schooling. The PROBE report revealed massive absenteeism in government schools.

At the secondary level, we have vocational education which does not provide any technical education to meet the demands of economic development. Economic development provides great opportunity for new skills for the young people to manage the process of development. We are opening different types of vocational education without necessary equipment or qualified teachers. In higher education, our gross enrolment for the relevant age has come to only 10 to 12%

whereas it is almost 50% for the developed countries. But what is most distressing is that there is no attempt to improve the quality of higher education. Education as we understand it today implies duster, blackboard, chalk, teacher, classroom, text book, examination, grades certificate etc. and is based on the way we learned in schools and colleges 50/60 years ago. Today, learning is, collaborative, multidisciplinary and take place faster than ever before. New technology of the web, internet and high speed computing offer us new learning models (Sam Pitroda). Most of the young who attend our colleges and universities must understand and appreciate the new technique of knowledge and adopt it for the improvement of the modern economy. That is what is desired for the improvement of higher education. We have not made any attempt to modernise education even though we are trying to modernise our economy.

Take another example. The budget increases the allocation for the National Rural Employment Guarantee Scheme almost to the extent of Rs. 40,000 crore per year. Rajiv Gandhi had once pointed out that only 15 paise in the rupee got through to the poor. Economists like Dr. Mahendra Dev and Ajit Ranade put it at 21 paise in the rupee. This shows the amount of waste in poverty alleviation programmes. NSSO surveys give us rural poverty ratios for different periods. These surveys show that there is little connection between rural employment schemes and poverty. Very often bogus claims are made that rural employment schemes build durable assets that increase rural prosperity. If so, decades of rural employment schemes should have provided a pucca road, school building and health clinic in every village. We know the deplorable condition of all these assets.

The Union Budget from time to time has increased the allocation for Integrated Child Development Services and augmented the number of anganwadis. That sounds wonderful, but a survey by Sukhatme and others showed that one third of anganwadis do not function at all, one-third function only part of every month and just one-third function fully. What will be the benefit of additional anganwadis if the existing ones do not serve their purpose.

We all emphasise the importance of public distribution system. The system is strengthened from time to time with special emphasis on the Antodaya scheme. Yet one study of Eastern UP by Kripa Shankar shows such high leakage in the public distribution system that it takes Rs. 20 of government spending to get Re. 1 to the poor. A UNDP study in the same UP found that there were no sales to BPL families in three out of four villages studied. Estimates of diversion to the open market range from 40-83%. A study based on NSS data suggests that in UP 98% of rural households make no PDS purchases at all.

We do not go on multiplying examples. All that we want to emphasise is that the institutions which have been created to serve the people must do their duty. If these institutions are inefficient and ineffective and follow corrupt practices with impunity, economic development cannot help any social purpose.

(iii) Sustainable Development

We have discussed in great detail the meaning and need for sustainable development elsewhere. All that we can mention here is that sustainable development involves more than growth. It requires a change in the content of growth, to make it less material and energy intensive and more equitable in its impact. These changes are required in all countries as part of a package of measures to maintain the stock of ecological capital, to improve the distribution of income and to reduce the degree of vulnerability to economic crisis. 'Our Common Future' hence emphasises that, "In essence, sustainable development is a process of change in which the exploitation of resources, the direction of investment, the orientation of technological development and institutional change are all in harmony and enhance both current and future potential to meet human needs and aspirations".

Such sustainable development has greater relevance now since the present pattern of development has started destroying the life support system both for the present and future generations. As a result of reckless exploitation of earth due to indiscriminate industrialisation and agricultural development we have come to a stage where there is rise in emission of toxic gases, depletion of ozone layer, threat of acid rain, pollution of air, water and land surface etc. in fact nothing is spared resulting in total pollution. The increase in chemical industries and application of chemical fertilizer, pesticides and insecticides in agriculture are causing the depletion of ozone layer which acts as a blanket of earth to filter out the harmful rays of the sun causing a great danger to the humanity. If the ultra-violet rays of the sun reach earth, there will be incidence of skin cancer, increase in temperature of earth which could melt polar ice-cap (already started). The climate change is so severe now that the scientists are worried how to reduce green house gas (GHG) emissions.

The Kyoto mission is now busy in preparing a programme to tackle environmental degradation and preserve the life support system. At least in our country we should try to adopt a few important measures like : (a) population control, (b) environmental sustainable technology, (c) improvement of awareness among the people through sustained education and health programmes, (d) prevent consumerism, and (e) involvement of people to promote eco-friendly development. If a sustained effort is made to achieve the above guidelines, we may succeed to some extent to restore the past ecological damage and insulate the country from the damage as a consequence of future development.

(iv) Empowerment of People

One of the major concerns that has been agitating the minds of social scientists is the failure of the development strategy in reducing poverty and improving the quality of life of most of the people in the country. The strategy of development which has been formulated in India connotes a movement from poverty to prosperity. It is a cumulative process, which is supposed to bring out a continuous improvement in the process of change, both physical and human, increasing the gains of real development and providing facilities for percolating such gains to the poorest of the poor. As we have already said we have made quite a lot of progress in different fields. But because of political and administrative hurdles, our progress has not been as good as it should be.

In 'Emerging Concerns in Development Administration' we have discussed in great detail the characteristics of political and bureaucratic system in India. Instead of repeating all these, we can only highlight a few important points for illustration. It is acknowledged by most of the sensitive citizens in India that the country's democratic polity has deepened the class schism. As Justice P.B. Sawant remarks in a judgement, the ruling elite seems oblivious of the elegance of the concept of social and economic democracy. Instead, those in power are interested in perpetuating social and economic inequalities for their benefit. Beyond the right to vote and the right to contest elections, political democracy confers no other right on citizens. In the absence of social and economic democracy, even the rights to elect and get elected remain on paper for a majority of people. And further with growing social and economic inequalities, the right to vote itself may be manipulated while the right to contest polls has become the preserve of a wealthy few.

What is worse and dangerous is the theory going round that corruption needs to be condoned to some extent as elections involve huge expenditure. People must realise that they cannot and should not expect anything in return-apart from what they may share with others as citizens—for voting for a person. In such a democratic set-up, the country's public life can hardly be clean and safe. Refering to politicians, justice Sawant remarks: "It appears that for the last some decades now, a tribe is growing fast which looks upon public office as a source of pelf and power".

What Justice Sawant says with regard to politicians, the same trend is noticed among most of the bureaucrats: they also consider public office as a source of pelf and power. Three important characteristics are visible in the administrative culture of India and these are: (i) rigid hierarchical structure with concentration of power at higher levels, (ii) increased level of regulation, and (iii) impersonal way of operation and rigidity in adhering to formal rules and regulations. As we have discussed elsewhere senior bureaucrats have forged an alliance with politicians not only to brighten their own career prospects but also to articulate political views and gain a greater share of social resources. It has been commented by many political commentators that there is close collaboration among politicians, bureaucrats and businessmen in India during the planning era to enable politicians to keep their chair, administrators their power and businessmen their money through licenses and permits.

All this implies that we have to change the administrative culture to make it more responsive to the people's needs. If the ultimate aim of development is to enhance the quality of life of people, as Prof. Amartya Sen observes, economic growth should be helped by the friendliness of the economic climate rather than by the harshness of the political system and arrogance of bureaucratic culture. Many suggestions can be given to improve the character of development. But we emphasise one aspect which is considered to be the most important to improve the quality of administration. At present, there are too many levels of decision-making, adding to delay but not necessarily to the quality of decision-making. Over centralisation in decision-making weakens the process of coordination. It is now recognised by planners that developmental activities undertaken with the people's active participation have a greater chance of success and can also be more cost effective as compared to the developmental activities undertaken by the government where people become passive observers. Further, a participatory planning process is an essential pre-condition for ensuring equity as well as accelerating the rate of growth of the economy. It is therefore, necessary to empower the Panchayati Raj Institutions by transferring to them both functions and resources. A time has come when the PRIs must become the cutting edge of our three-tier political structure and the focal point of democratic decentralization'.

(v) Improvement in Productive Capacity and Quality of Life

The most pressing problem in development pattern of the country is not only to increase the rate of growth of income, but at the same time provide opportunity to each and every Indian to realize his or her full creative potential and improve his or her economic well-being. It has been mentioned in the Tenth Plan that the development process must be viewed in terms of the efficiency with which it uses an economy's productive capacities, involving both physical and human resources, to attain the desired economic and social ends and not just material attainment. In view of these two over riding objectives, we emphasise three important areas that need greater attention. They are: (a) Agricultural Development, (b) Improvement in Infrastructure, and (c) Acceleration of Social Sector.

Agriculture is the mainstay of the Indian economy. Though more than 50% of the labour force is working in agriculture and 60 per cent of the population is dependent on agriculture for their livelihood, the annual growth rate of agriculture has been terribly erratic. Of the total GDP, the share of agriculture now comes to 15 to 16 per cent. We cannot reduce poverty, unemployment or underemployment in rural areas unless there is improvement in the productivity of agriculture, diversification of cropping pattern and higher investment in agriculture to increase irrigation facility, create water harvesting structures and develop environmental friendly agricultural technology which can be applied by small and marginal farmers without much cost. Agricultural development must be viewed as a core element of the plan, since growth in this sector is likely to lead to the widest spread of benefits especially to the rural poor.

In addition there is also need to develop rural infrastructure so as to start a large number of agro-based industries in the rural areas. This will reduce the pressure of population on agriculture by diverting some surplus population from agriculture to these industries. Further, there will be scope to effectively utilise the by-products of agriculture in these industries. A number of recent studies have indicated that the rate of growth of rural incomes and reduction in rural poverty are strongly influenced by the provision of rural road connectivity. In addition, agricultural productivity requires other forms of rural infrastructure like irrigation, power, credit, transport facilities, etc. In fact, development of infrastructure is an essential prerequisite for economic development of any country. As has been pointed out by Dr. V.K.R.V. Rao, "The link between infrastructure and development is not a once for all affair. It is a continuous process and progress in development has to be preceded, accompanied and followed by progress in infrastructure, if we are to fulfil our declared objectives of self-accelerating process of economic development".

Finally to improve the quality of life we should make more investment in social sectors like education, health, sanitation, social security etc which will provide the basis for equity, efficiency and sustainability of economic well-being. Education is a training of mind which provides the right kind of leadership for social and economic improvement. Improvement in health will improve the capability of one to stand the strains of life. Provision of social security will enable the poor and destitute to lead a life of decency and dignity. In sum, improvement in social sector increases Human Development Index (HDI) which is aimed at increasing the people's skills and capacities and widening their choices to live a long and healthy life and effectively participate in the process of economic development and promote social values.

Economics should not be viewed only for increasing the material standard of living of the individuals, but as a means to establish higher social values. As Gandhiji said, 'I do not draw any sharp distinction between economics and ethics. Economics that hurts the moral well-being of any individual or nation are immoral and therefore, harmful'. In fact, India needs an economic system based on self-respect which must fulfil certain basic human values. And these human values imply simple rules of conduct and action for living together, that is, social living for natural benefit.

References

Aiyar, S. Anklesaria (2005), Outlays Versus Outcomes, *Economic Times*, March, 17.

Daly, Herman, On Limiting Economic Growth in Dennis, L. Meadows (Edited 1977), Alternatives to Growth, *The Woodlands Conference*, USA.

Misra, B. (1977), Economic Profile of India, APH Publishing Corporation, New Delhi.

Misra, B. (1999), Emerging Concerns in Development Administrtion, *IASSI Quarterly*, Vol. 18, No. 2.

Our Common Future (1987), The World Commission on Environment and Development, OUP.

Palkhivala, Nani A. (1982), The State of the Nation, *Illustrated Weekly of India*, November 21.

Raj Felix (2005), Social Values-II, ,March 15.

Sawant, P.B. (2005), Justice Sawants' Report on Arrogance of Power of Ministers and a Social Crusader, *Times of India*, March 18.

Tenth Five Year Plan, Vol. 1 (2002-07), Planning Commission, Government of India, New Delhi.

CHAPTER

7

Food Security in India

MEANING OF FOOD SECURITY

There has been a considerable change in the meaning and concept of food security. Till the seventies, food availability and stability were considered to be the major components of food security. Most of the developing countries therefore, aimed at attaining self-sufficiency in foodgrains. The World Food Programme has now broadened the concept and has pointed out that food security has multiple dimensions that relate to demographic, nutritional, economic and social causes. The principal four areas which have been emphasised in the Report include: Availability, Access, Utilisation and Vulnerability. Broadly the meaning of these components are given below:

(i) Food availability derives from agricultural production which includes food crops, cash crops and livestock produced in a sustainable environment which should not exhaust common property resources so that needs of the future generation are not jeopardised. It may be mentioned here that increased production is necessary to meet the requirements of both present and growing population. According to the latest estimate, the human race which numbered 4400 million has increased to more than 6 billion by 2000. By the year 2000, the annual increase in population has come to be about 95 million in contrast to 80 million in 1982. In India while the population was 683.33 million in 1981 has increased to 1200 million in 2010. The more the increase in population, the greater is the need of food production. If internal production does not meet the required demand, there may be need to import food grains to meet the domestic demand along with inter-regional transfer of foodgrains to meet the deficiency in any particular region. But as far as possible imports of foodgrains should be avoided, unless it becomes inevitable, since imports lead to unemployment and poverty in a developing country.

(ii) Food access refers to the ability of households to secure food at a reasonable price. One of the major factors in most of the developing countries is their colossal poverty. Food access therefore, includes adequate purchasing power in relation to price of food in market place. When we talk of food, we do not only mean the availability of cereals or calories, but also basic needs such as shelter, clothing, education, health programme, etc. In income poverty, we only consider the availability of calories which enables a person to derive certain minimum energy requirement to maintain his/her livelihood. But that does not help one to lead a healthy and decent life. Accessibility should therefore, include basic needs.

(iii) Food utilization does not only depend on availability of food or the capacity to purchase such food that provides minimum energy, but includes many other non-food factors which help absorption of food materials and improve the economic well being of the people. Amartya Sen and Jean Dreze point out, "It is a mistake to view hunger in terms of food deprivation only: the capability to be nourished depends crucially on other characteristics of a person that are influenced by such non-food factors as medical attention, health services, basic education, sanitary arrangements, provision of clean water, eradication of infectious epidemics and so on" (Dreze, Sen 1989). According to World Food Programme, a household may still remain malnourished even though it has enough food. Utilization depends on three other factors like : (a) nutrition practices (which include dietary practices, child care, nutrition knowledge depending on female literacy), (b) metabolic absorption (which requires safe drinking water, sanitation, adequate health services to prevent infectious diseases and such other factors which enable a person to effectively absorb food), and (c) intra-household distribution to prevent gender discrimination. Gender discrimination is not only confined access to food, but also access to health care, primary education and command over resources. Even though income poverty is eliminated, social bias against women and girl children deprives them of many of the basic facilities of life. On the basis of these considerations, Dr. Swaminathan defines food security as follows:

"Sustainable food security involves strengthening the livelihood security of all members within a household by ensuring both physical and economic access to balanced diet, including the needed micro-nutrients, safe drinking water, environmental sanitation, basic health care and primary education".

(iv) We guess this quotation covers all the three aspects we have analysed above except vulnerability. Vulnerability refers to natural calamities like flood, drought, cyclone, etc. Such transitory food insecurity may deprive many people in a particular region to get adequate food and other basic needs for a long time if immediate steps are not taken to meet such tragedies. In some regions such calamities occur frequently and in some others these are infrequent.

Whether these are recurrent or non-recurrent, villages or families who are affected by such disasters undergo tremendous hardship to meet their daily requirements. Whether such suffering is temporary or not, adequate preparedness should be made to provide livelihood necessities that are required in the region and if there is destruction of residential buildings, dislocation of communication or water supply, failure of crops or deterioration of life system, steps should be taken to repair them as early as possible so that such disasters do not dislocate the life pattern of the entire region.

CAUSES OF FOOD INSECURITY IN INDIA

1. Inadequate Availability of Foodgrains

Though the rate of growth of overall GDP was only 3.5 per cent per year from 1950-51 to 1980-81, in the eighties and nineties, the rate of growth of income was a little more than 6% per year along with some increase in per capita income. In the ninth plan, the rate of growth of income was 5.5 per cent and in the tenth plan, it was increased to a little less than 8 per cent per year. The rate of growth of GDP at factor cost since 2005-06 to 2007-08 at 1999-2000 prices increased at more than 9 per cent per year. It was only in 2008-09 and 2009-10 that the rate of growth came down to 6.7 per cent and 7.2 per cent respectively due to economic recession. It is estimated that during 2010-11, the rate of growth of income would be more than 8 per cent. Because of increase in growth, per capita income also increased to 7.6% in 2005-06, 7.9 per cent in 2006-07 and 8.1 per cent in 2007-08 and all at 2004-05 prices. It is only in 2008-09 and 2009-10 that per capita income came down to 3.7 per cent and 5.3 per cent respectively. Because of increase in per capita income there was also increase in per capita consumption, with 7.3 per cent in 2005-06, 6.7 per cent in 2006-07 and 8.3 per cent in 2007-08. In the last two years, 2008-09 and 2009-10 for which figures are given in Economic Survey 2009-10 (p. 5, Table 1.3) per capita consumption came down to 5.4 per cent and 2.7 per cent respectively. While there was considerable improvement in economic growth and per capita income and consumption both in ninth plan and tenth plan, growth of agriculture was almost negligible, 2.0 per cent in ninth plan and 1.8 per cent in tenth plan (An Approach to the 11th Five Year Plan, Table 1, Macro Economic Indicators, p. 3).

Production of foodgrains which responded to the green revolution in seventies and eighties, has more or less stagnated at 230 to 233 m tonnes in normal years since there is a fatigue in new technology. Per capita availability of foodgrains which was about 460 grams per day in early sixties has come down to 440 or less than 440 grams per day. And per capita availability of pulses which is the main source of protein has come down from about 64-70 grams to about 33 grams during the same period. It is often claimed by developed countries that foodgrain prices have soared because of more demand from China and India due to increase in their GDP. But as a matter of fact, it is completely invalid since aggregate and per capita consumption of foodgrains have actually fallen in both countries. The National Sample Survey also shows a secular decline in consumption of foodgrains. On account of the vast inequality in land holdings and income, there is low level of food consumption among the poorer sections of the community who are awefully large. Fourteen per cent of the rural population consists of agricultural labourers who do not find work for more than 200 days a year. According to the NSS, the number of days of employment of rural agricultural labourers is declining, from 224 days in 1993-94 to 209 days in 2004-05. In addition, there is also considerable inequality in the country. According to Human Development Report, 2004, the richest 20% of people in the country are getting more than 42% of GDP whereas the poorest 20% are getting only 9 per cent of GDP. The Sengupta Committee Report also points out that more than 70 per cent of workers in India are getting hardly Rs. 20 per day. When we talk of food security, we have to ensure adequate supplies of food and needed purchasing power to buy the necessary food, which in turn means that employment, remuneration and livelihood issues are important.

Because of unemployment, poverty and low level of wages of most of the workers, the purchasing power of vast majority of people is inadeque to purchase adequate amount of food for their livelihood. What is worse is that in India, agriculture has been more or less neglected. Neither has there been adequate investment in agriculture to increase its productivity, nor to improve agricultural research so as to evolve some new technology in place of the old one which has created a number of hazards in agricultural development. Excessive use of ground water and over use of chemical fertilizer along with insecticides and pesticides have damaged water resources and deteriorated soil quality which have adversely affected productivity of land. It is reported that due to excessive extraction of ground water in Punjab, Haryana and Western UP, the ground water table is receding by one metre every three years. Though the technology in green revolution was size neutral, it was not resource neutral. And therefore, small and marginal farmers whose numbers were large, could not afford to apply the technology to increase the productivity of land. In addition, the impact of climate change has created poor harvests in many food crops. No attempt has been made to change the cropping pattern to escape from such exigencies.

We cannot also depend on foreign supply of foodgrains as they are trying to divert land from food crops to other crops which can produce biofuels as an alternative to petroleum. For example, in 2007, the US diverted more than 30 per cent of its maize production, Brazil used half of its sugar cane production and the European Union (EU) used greater part of its vegetable oil seeds production to make biofuel. In addition, global food market is also volatile. We have therefore to try to increase food production so as to avoid imports from outside. This means national food security requires increasing domestic production of food, so that the country is not dependent upon imports. We may also point out here that the green revolution depended to a great extent on irrigation. Canal irrigation probably may not be of much use in future agricultural development. The cost of irrigating one hectare of land through canals is almost Rs. 1 lakh. State irrigation works are also running under huge losses where 70 per cent of the expenditure goes only in maintenance. Under the given constrains, conservation of surface water and construction of water storage should get top priority. However, more attention should be given to research to produce some type of food crops which are suitable for dry land areas.

All this implies that national food security can be successful if we can increase domestic food production so that the country does not depend on imports. We can highlight three main areas here to increase domestic food production. First to enhance investment in agriculture so as to increase the productivity of land. There is not much scope to increase the area of crop land and therefore, increase in productivity is a major concern. In order to increase productivity, not only there should be increase in irrigation and other inputs required for cultivation of different crops, but also to develop new technology which can facilitate cultivation of viable crops which can be produced in dry land. In fact, lack of investment and also attention to relevant agricultural research and extension have denied farmers, access to necessary knowledge to improve the productivity of land or to change the cropping pattern. Second, the cost of cultivation in most cases has increased because of lack of institutional credit. Agriculture which directly supports more than half the population gets only 12 per cent of the bank credit. In fact, 60% of the rural savings is diverted by banks to the urban areas. Many farmers are forced to opt for much more expensive informal credit networks that have increased their costs. Government have to guarantee adequate credit to the farmers at a concessional rate so that farming becomes a lucrative job. In addition small farmers face many hurdles in procuring necessary inputs which are required for increasing production. Most of the measures initiated by the state governments to facilitate convenient supply of inputs have not proved successful. If Panchayati system is entrusted with the responsibility of distributing such inputs, there may probably be some improvement in this field. Finally in order to avoid instability in food prices, speculative activities in foodgrains have to be curbed both in the present and future markets. Generally in case of scarcity of domestic commodities and rise in international prices, speculative activities become rampant. Only prevention of hoarding may not succeed unless speculation is banned in all essential commodities.

2. Poverty

On the basis of above characteristics, we may discuss the problem of food insecurity in India. Chronic food insecurity is primarily associated with poverty. High poverty levels are synonymous with poor quality of life, deprivation, malnutrition, illiteracy and low human resource development. That is why, eradication of poverty has become a major component of Indian planning since the Fourth Five Year Plan. Many attempts have been made to study the poverty line on the basis of calories, 2400 calories in Rural and 2100 calories in Urban areas. As per NSS study, poverty ratio by URP method at all-India level was 36 per cent in 1993-94 and 27.5 per cent in 2004-05. This shows that there is decrease in poverty line between 1993-94 and 2004-05. But the study of Deaton and Dreze shows that there is an increase in poverty line between 1983 and 2004-05 as shown in Table 1.

TABLE 1
Percentage of People Getting less than 2400 Calories in Rural and 2100 Calories in Urban Areas

Year	*NSS Round*	*Rural*	*Urban*	*All India*
1983	38	66.1	60.5	64.8
1993-94	50	71.1	58.1	67.8
2004-05	61	79.8	63.9	75.8

Last three columns refer to the findings of Deaton and Dreze.

There are a number of other studies where the concept of poverty is not defined only on the basis of calories. Tendulkar Committee for example while moving away from calorie norms has validated by checking the adequacy of actual private expenditure per capita near the poverty line on food, education and health by comparing them with normative expenditures consistent with nutritional, educational and health outcomes. The findings of the Committee are given in Table 2.

Instead of analysing other studies, we can mention here that inspite of aggregate income growth during the last two decades, there is stagnation in nutrition indicators along with decline in per capita calorie consumption. This implies that pervasive hunger may have got worse rather than better (Jayanti Ghosh).

TABLE 2
Poverty Head Count Ratio (%)

Year	*Rural*	*Urban*	*Total*
1993-94	50.1	31.8	45.3
2004-05	41.8	25.7	37.2

The study of National Family Health Survey (NFHS) 2005-06 shows that 46% of children below 3 years are under weight, 33% of women and 28% of men have a Body Mass Index (BMI) below normal, 79% children aged 6-35 months have anaemia as do 56% of ever married women aged 15-49 years and 24% of similar men and 58% of pregnant women. Very little change from the previous NFHS study in 1998-99. What is worse, according to NSSO large survey of 2004-05 the average daily intake of calories of the rural population has dropped by 4.9% from 2153 Kcal to 2047 Kcal from 1993-94 to 2004-05 and by 2.5% from 2071 to 2020 Kcal in urban areas. The average daily intake of protein by the Indian population decreased from 60.2 to 57 grams in rural India between 1993-94 and 2004-05 and remained stable at around 57 grams in the urban areas during the same period. Both in respect of poverty and mal-nutrition, we have given aggregate all-India average figures. But there is great variation between different states. One illustration in respect of State Hunger Index 2007 shows that while India's scores come to 23.30, the scores in Punjab and Madhya Pradesh come to 13.63 and 30.87 respectively. States like Orissa, Chhattisgarh, Bihar, Jharkhand have all high scores meaning thereby that people in these states are deprived of many basic amenities of life.

Further, there is a decline in the economic entitlement of the poor to ensure food security not only due to poverty but also due to market dependence and changing consumption pattern. There is a change in consumption pattern in favour of costly superior cereals and non-food crops dictated largely by availability than by choice. After green revolution, there is a change in the production pattern in favour of superior cereals instead of coarse grains. Second, there is a decline in the purchase of such food and non-food items by the poor due to increase in their prices. Thus there is increase in malnutrition of the poor, particularly more so of women and children. And such malnutrition is more severe in poorer states. A National Sample Survey shows that malnutrition in India is a bigger problem than even hunger.

In order to meet the requirements of balanced diet to the people, steps should not only be taken to increase agricultural production, we have also to see who grows the food and what kinds of food are grown, the linkage between farm, off-farm and non-farm activities, and who is getting income from these activities. Since food security implies nutritional security, it is desirable to see what types of food increase the nutrition of the people. This means there should be diversification of agricultural production along with improvement in the productivity of agriculture, animal husbandry, fishery and forestry. If we emphasise only crop production, we exhaust common property resources by limiting human carrying capacity of the earth.

Linkage between farm, off-farm and non-farm activities will provide additional employment to the labour force and increase their income which may help them to sustain their livelihood. Because of financial constraints, many small and marginal farmers extend their cultivation very often to marginal land and forest areas which create environment degradation. Under such resource constraints, what is important is to identify and popularise varieties which can give maximum yields with available resources. A certain degree of resource neutrality can be introduced by substituting non-monetary inputs to purchased inputs (Swaminathan). Though green revolution has provided a number of benefits, some major difficulties have been noticed in its sustainability. Therefore, additional research should be oriented to improve the productivity, profitability, stability and sustainability of major farming systems in India.

3. Increase in Production may not Attain Equity if there is Lack of Purchasing Power and Other Constraints

It may be mentioned that increase in food production may not ensure equitable distribution of foodgrains. Amartya Sen has challenged government food management systems by pointing out that surplus and starvation co-exist in countries where the focus is on production. Equitable distribution may be affected by lack of purchasing power, infrastructure constraints, market imperfections and government regulation. If per capita income is considered as an index of purchasing power of a particular person, per capita income in many states is much lower than All India average. The availability of appropriate infrastructure services is a pre-condition to rapid agricultural production, nay economic development. Some of the infrastructure sectors like power, roads, irrigation, etc. which help agricultural development require high upfront and long gestation periods. Many of the poorer states in India have not been able to provide quality infrastructure services as a result of which they have not been able to adopt advanced technology for improving food or non-food production. Lack of infrastructure development has stood in the way of market unification.

The government regulation has also affected the price level of cereals. The relative cereal price which showed a decline in the seventies and eighties registered a rise in the nineties. An increase in cereal price significantly reduced the calorie intake of the poor as is brought out by available food price elasticity estimate which shows that for the poor, the food (calorie) price elasticity is numerically large (R. Radhakrishna). Though the programmes like PDS have a major role to play in the context of food insecurity due to market imperfections and inadequate delivery system, the recent large increase in procurement prices and the subsequent upward revision in the central issue prices have had an adverse impact on the efficacy of PDS in helping the poor to secure food at a price which they can afford to purchase with their low level of income.

4. Deficiencies of PDS

The PDS in case of India has not been able to protect food entitlements of the poor. It has been pressurised to increase procurement prices which to some extent has given incentive to the producers to produce more in some regions in India, but it has failed to stabilize consumer prices. Protecting food entitlement generally encompasses large scale employment schemes to provide a social safety net both for the urban and rural poor. But some of the empirical studies show that PDS has a severe bias in the inter-regional distribution of PDS supplies, poorer states generally are found to be neglected in receiving adequate supplies of foodgrains. One of the reasons for this is lack of effective initiative on the part of the state governments of the poorer states to actively participate in PDS by providing required assistance for operating the system due to their severe financial crunch. It is also observed that the net gains from the PDS in India seem to be more in favour of non-poor households; large parts of rural India have so far benefited little from the PDS (Krishnaji & Krishnan).

Critics also point out that centralised food management systems are prone to corruption, inefficiency, wastage and misallocation of resources. Due to lack of competition and appropriate incentives, PDS entails very high cost at all stages, from production through distribution. Because of such centralisation, the delivery system entails high cost and results in abnormal delay for which its impact on the access to food becomes negligible. Compared to many other anti-poverty programmes, PDS has been found to be the costliest. The subsidy paid to the FCI for distribution of foodgrains has increased from Rs. 9200 crore in the year 1999-2000 to about Rs. 60,000 crore in the year 2009-10 while the quantity of foodgrains actually distributed has not changed much. One of the studies of PDS show that only 25 per cent of foodgrains actually reach poorest 40 per cent of the population. Further, since procurement and issue prices are high, the PDS is not able to release all that it purchases and is compelled to maintain a high buffer stock which results in an abnormal increase in the carrying cost. It is estimated that the excess stock over the minimum norm involves an additional central government expenditure which comes to about half of the carrying cost. Two other major difficulties are also noticed in PDS for which there is colossal wastage of resources apart from misappropriation of funds which has become a part of all economic activities. First, because of lack of storage capacity, almost 18 million tonnes of foodgrains, i.e. about 30 per cent of total stock procured are stored in open allowing these to be rotten while almost 230 million people go hungry in the country. Further it is alleged that the shopkeepers who are entrusted with the responsibility for providing rationed food to the consumers do not derive adequate profit from such transactions. Their transportation and porters' charges are said to be more than their profit. Since there is difference in price fixed for distribution of rationed commodity and their open market, they manage to sell a large portion of the allotted quota in the open market and derive huge amount of profit with the connivance of the regulators who can easily be purchased with a bribe. As such, public distribution system does not attain the objectives for which it is designed.

Now therefore, there is a move to ensure 'Food Security' by enacting an Act in the Parliament. Different proposals are considered to make it more effective and provide adequate amount of food regularly to the deserving poor people of the country. The National Advisory Council (NAC) headed by the President of the Congress has recommended legal entitlement to subsidised foodgrains to both 'priority' and 'general' households, covering at least 72% population in phase I starting 2011-12 and 75% in the phase II in 2013-14. According to the NAC proposal, the foodgrains requirement would be 74 million tonnes upon completion of final phase in 2014. However, the Prime Minister's expert panel on Food Security Bill has pointed out that it will not be possible to implement NAC recommended food entitlement for either of the phases due to non-availability of foodgrains.

The expert committee has suggested legal entitlement to 46% of rural and 28% of urban population which it said are the same as NAC recommended 'priority' households. This captures not only the poor but also some at the margin. In the NAC proposal food requirement would be 74 million tonnes upon completion of final phase in 2014 while the total food grains availability with the government in 2011-12 and 2013-14 are likely to be 56.35 million tonnes and 57.61 million tonnes, respectively based on the current production and procurement trends. According to the panel recommendations, the grain requirement will be nearly 52 million tonnes in 2014 and the subsidy will be Rs. 68,539 crore and if outgo on other welfare schemes and maintenance of buffer stocks included, the total subsidy will be Rs. 83,000 crore. At present the government provides 35 kg of foodgrains to 6.52 crore families below poverty line (BPL) through ration shops. Wheat is provided at Rs. 4.15 per kg and rice at Rs. 5.65 kg.

There are also other proposals to make food security more effective. One such proposal by Jayanti Ghosh is that in "hierarchical and discriminatory societies like India, where social and economic power is unequally distributed, it requires no imagination to realise that making scarce good (cheap food) supposedly available only to the poor is one of the easiest ways to reduce their access". The working of food assistance as provided through ration shops illustrates clearly that such assistance only to a few cannot be successful. Therefore, it is desirable that food security should be universal as to make it more effective and attempt should be made to increase food production through increased productivity of agricultural output. Second, it is evident from NSSO and NFHS surveys that the proportion of the population that is nutritionally deprived is significantly larger than the 'poor' population, and in many cases they are not completely overlapping categories either. As we have already seen, the percentage of population getting less than 2400 calories in rural and 2100 calories in urban area comes to 75.8 (Deaton and Dreze). So, there is no justification in equating poverty and hunger and it will be therefore, more desirable to make food security more comprehensive. A comprehensive or inclusive food security may be operationally more effective with food stamps. There will be no scope for counterfeiting of such stamps. The only problem which may arise in universal food security is additional funds. At the present level the food subsidy comes to almost Rs. 60,000 crore. It is estimated that different kinds of subsidies and exemptions in taxation come to more than Rs. 4 lakh crore. The Budget document of 2010-11 indicates that the total tax arrears under no dispute were more than Rs. 46,000 crore and under dispute about Rs. 71,000 crore at the end of 2008-09. Then there is huge amount of Black Money both in India and abroad which is equivalent to our GDP, if not more. If a part of it can be recovered and also a portion of other funds which have been mentioned above can be diverted for utilisation of Food Security, there will be no difficulty in regard to funds. All that is necessary is to increase the production of agricultural commodities by increasing the productivity of land. If adequate investment is made in agriculture along with research, we do not think there will be any problem in successful implementation of food security.

5. Effect of Other Assistance Programmes

Since budgetary cost of PDS is excessively high due to (a) considerable leakage of benefits to the non-poor, (b) incomplete coverage of the poor population, and (c) the inefficiency of the Food Corporation of India (FCI) which handles a crucial portion of the PDS, alternative options are needed for ensuring food security (Suryanarayan). We therefore, have a number of food assistance programmes to improve nutritional security. They refer to : (a) supplementary feeding programmes for children and nursing women, (b) school feeding programmes, (c) food for work programmes, and (d) disaster emergency relief measures. Though some of these programmes have provided some benefit, malnutrition is still a major problem in the country. Many of the studies also show that : (a) these programmes are not well coordinated nor properly targeted, (b) food assistance is too meagre to meet the basic needs of the poor, (c) there is lack of proper supervision for which there is a great deal of misutilisation of resources, (d) food provided sometimes does not meet the requirements of the people, and (e) particularly in case of disaster emergency, food assistance is not given on time. The results of these studies show that there is plenty of scope to improve the operational efficiency of the programmes so as to make them cost effective, and link assistance and relief with the development programme of the country along with more participatory and decentralised approach.

According to World Food Programme, even though India has 20 per cent of the world's children, it has 40% of its malnourished children. WHO figures also show that low birth weight and underweight are common among children in India. These two not only perpetuate inter-generational malnutrition, but also constitute conditions for chronic diseases in adulthood. Generally in a patriarchal society excessive demands are often made on women for which they face a lot of unfair treatment. Their poor health leads to malnutrition of children. They are also easily susceptible to many kinds of diseases. The Dietary

Energy Supply (DES) to make one healthy is estimated to be 2800 calories. But per capita calorie intake on average in India is only 2071 (1993-94). Most of the states have less than the prescribed DES to make one healthy.

ASSISTANCE SHOULD BE DEVELOPMENT ORIENTED

Though there should be increase in production to meet the growing requirements of people, we cannot avoid assistance in one shape or other to improve the economic and social well-being of the poor. But the assistance for the sake of reducing malnutrition, improving educational facility or creating employment opportunities should not be only welfare-oriented but development-oriented. To make such programmes effective, the following measures will have to be taken:

(a) The proposed measures should provide sustainable benefit to the target groups and create some sort of investment that pays back overtime. A development path is sustainable provided it creates some assets which not only help the present generation but also future generation. In other words, efforts are to be made to create some beneficial assets which should be maintained and operated in an effective manner so as to secure inter-generational equity. These assets should pertain both to physical and social assets to create more income and improve the quality of life.

(b) Such measures of assistance should be taken which receive the support of the people. If the public perceives that the benefits accrue only to a selected few who do not deserve such assistance, support for such programmes will be inevitably eroded. In many anti-poverty programmes, there is a great deal of misappropriation of funds. Even though huge amount of funds are allotted for different types of anti-poverty programme, there is not much improvement in the quality of life. The economic and social position in India as depicted in Human Development Report, 2009 shows that there is still a long way to go.

India's Position in Human Development, 2007

HDI	*GDP per capita (PPP US $)*	*Life Expectancy at birth (years)*	*Adult Literacy (% aged 15 years and above)*	*Combined Gross enrolment Ratio in Education (%)*
2007	2007	2007	1999-2007	2007
0.612 (134)	2753	63.4	66.0	61.0

India is generally compared with Brazil, Russia and China—they are all a part of BRIC and each one of them has much better position than India. All this implies, there is considerable scope to improve the developmental needs of assistance measures.

(c) The institutional capacity should also be capable to achieve declared objectives. Many good programmes have failed to secure desired objectives by weak implementation, lack of government commitment, or limited resources spent on achieving them. Very often programmes are drawn by political motives rather than helping the poor to derive any benefit. Another major drawback which is noticed is that a large number of projects are run simultaneously making it difficult to monitor them effectively. Such multiple programmes become so unmanageable that even when there are serious disasters, the delivery system does not reach the people when they need it most.

On the basis of the above analysis we may suggest that assistance for improving food security should shift from appeasing hunger towads development of human faculties. And to make such programmes operationally efficient, local self-governments should be entrusted with many such programmes which will facilitate more participatory approach, enhance cost effectiveness and improve timeliness of the delivery system.

Further these measures have become more imperative due to the onset of globalisation. The small and marginal farmers who dominate the Indian agricultural scene cannot compete with the products of developed countries. If there is self-sufficiency of foodgrains in India today this is due to weak purchasing power of the poor classes. A time has come when India should make more investment in agriculture, diversify its products and try to get a foothold in world market. This would be possible if India could accelerate cost reducing technology and put pressure on developed countries in collaboration with other developing countries to open up their markets for agro-processed products. The challenge is severe, but not unmanageable.

References

Dev, Mahendra, S. (ed.) (2001), Social and Economic Security in India, Institute of Human Development, New Delhi.

Dreze, Jean, Amartya Sen (1989), Hunger and Public Action, New York, Oxford University Press.

Ghosh, Jayanti, The Political Economy of Hunger in 21st Century India, *EPW*, October 30-November 12, 2010.

Government of India, Economic Survey of different years.

Government of India, Planning Commission, Report of the Expert Group to Review the Methodology for Estimation of Poverty—2009 (Tendulkar Report).

Krishnaji, N. and Krishnan, T.N. (ed.) (2000), Public Support for Food Security, The Public Distribution System in India, Strategies for Human Development in India, Vol. 1, Sage Publications, New Delhi.

Radhakrishna, R. (2001), Food Security : Emerging Concerns (pp. 102-21) published in Social and Economic Security (ed) by S. Mahendra Dev *et. al.* Institute for Human Development, *op. cit.*

Rao, C.H. Hanumantha and R. Radhakrishna (1997), National Food Security : A Policy Prospective in India, quoted from R. Radhakrishna, *op. cit.*

Swaminathan, M.S. (1996), Sustainable Agriculture, Towards Food Security, Konark Publishers Pvt. Ltd.

Suryanarayana, M.H., Food Security and Calorie Adequacy Across States : Implications for Reform in Public Support for Food Security, *op. cit.*

Tendulkar, Suresh D. (2000), Planning and Market in Indian Development Process, *Artha Vijyana*, September.

World Food Programme, Enabling Development Food Assistance in South Asia (2001), Oxford, New York.

CHAPTER

8

Health Care System in India

INTRODUCTION

There is no doubt that India has made several improvements during the last six decades of its planning. Not only is there a structural change in the economy, there is also a spectacular increase in the rate of growth of the economy in spite of a rising tide of uncertainty in global finance. Today there are a host of statistics that demonstrate our modest yet substantial success. To mention only a few, we can indicate some of the changes in the life pattern of the people. For example, Indians live two and a half times longer than they did at independence, they eat on average a third more than they did and their diet has become infinitely more varied, they are on average seven times better off than they were in 1947 and the proportion of Indians below the poverty line has fallen from more than half to almost one-third. However, the dualities that exist in the country is so enormous that one wonders whether all these changes can improve the image of India.

When we consider the economic wellness of India, it is found by an ADB study that India is ranked 17 among 23 when economies are compared based on a measure of people's economic well being. According to an International Comparison Programme (ICP) in Asia and the Pacific purchasing power parity preliminary report, China and India account for 64 per cent of total real GDP of the 23 economies participating in the study. However, if the size of these economies is adjusted by population, China and India drop down 10th and 18th positions respectively in the full GDP comparison. Similarly, China ranks 15th and India 17th when economies are compared based on actual final consumption of households (AFCH). AFCH is a measure of what households actually consume comprising what they purchase and what they are supplied for individual use by the government. The economic well-being of population is obtained by comparing household consumption expenditure per capita.

A recently released report by the UN and ADB (Asian Development Bank) points out that India is a laggard in meeting some of the millennium development goals (MDGs) identified in 2000. The MDGs include eradication of extreme poverty and hunger, achieving universal primary education, promoting gender equity, reducing child mortality, improving maternal health and combating HIV/AIDS, malaria and other diseases. For a country that is growing at 8 to 9 per cent per year, there is no reason why India's social indicators should be embarrassingly poor even when compared to other middle income countries. In this paper instead of discussing all the different aspects of social sector, we confine our analysis to Health Care System in India—its Problems and Concerns.

PERFORMANCE OF OUR HEALTH INDICATORS

Table 1 gives some of the indicators of existing position of health parameter in India. The table shows that in respect of mortality rates, we have still a long way to go to improve the quality of life.

When we compare India's health parameters with some of our neighbours, we find that while life expectancy at birth (years) in the years 2000-06 is 72 in China, 70.8 in Sri Lanka and 63.6 in Pakistan, it is only 62.9 in India. In respect of mortality rate under five (per 1000 live births) in the year 2005,

TABLE 1

Sl. No.	Parameter	Current Level
1.	Crude Birth Rate (per 1000 population)	22.5 (2009)
2.	Crude Death Rate (per 1000 population)	7.3 (2009)
3.	Total Fertility Rate per Woman	2.6 (2008)
4.	Maternal Mortality Rate (per 100,000 live births)	254 (2004-06)
5.	Infant Mortality Rate (per 1000 live births)	50 (2009)
6.	Child (0-4 years) Mortality Rate (per 1000 children)	15.2 (2008)
7.	Life Expectancy at Birth	*2002-06*
	Male	62.6
	Females	64.2
	Total	63.5

Source : Economic Survey, 2010-11, Table 12.12.

while it is 27 in China, 14 in Sri Lanka and 73 in Bangladesh, in India it is 74. Same difference is also found in infant and maternal mortality rate. According to UNDP Human Development Report 2007-08, while infant mortality rate (per 1000 live births) in 2005 is 23 in China, 12 in Sri Lanka and 54 in Bangladesh, it is 56 in India. Similarly in respect of maternal mortality rate (per 100,000 live births) in 2005, while it is 45 in China, 58 in Sri Lanka and 320 in Pakistan, it is 450 in India. All this shows India is substantially worse than China, Sri Lanka and Bangladesh, let alone richer developing countries like Brazil, Mexico, Thailand and Turkey.

The World Health Organization (WHO) constructs an indicator of 'Healthy Life Expectancy at Birth' (HALE) which adjusts the normal life expectancy measure for years of serious illness/injury predicated from the data. By this measure, HALE for a girl baby in India in 2002 was only 54 years, compared to 65 in China, 68 in Mexico and 71 in the U.S. On a direct measure of health service delivery, immunization coverage of one year old for DTP, India scores particularly badly, even in comparison to Pakistan and Bangladesh. Perhaps most shocking, 46 per cent of young children in India are (according to National Family Survey-3 for 2005-06) underweight for age, compared to 6 per cent in China, 20 per cent in Indonesia, 31 per cent in Pakistan and 27 per cent in Nigeria.

Perhaps even more disquieting are the trends in the key indicators of health care of kids under five. According to latest global report card, over 53 per cent of children in India under five years—that is 67 million-live without basic health care facilities. This includes access to parental care, skilled child birth, immunization and treatment for diarrhoea and pneumonia. The report brought out by a reputable global NGO—Save the Children—compared 55 countries. And India which is proud of its robust growth, ties with Ghana and Eritrea for the 27th rank. According to the study, 66 per cent of the poorest children in India receive negligible or no health care whereas the figure stands at 31 per cent for those who are well-off. Again what is more shocking is that over a million children die annually before they turn a month old.

One disturbing fact the report throws up in the gender survival gap which is widening. Between the ages of one and five, for every five boys who die, eight girls die. The report cites less money spent on girls' health compared with boys as one of the major reasons for the survival gap. For instance, in Punjab the expenditure on medical care in the first two years after birth for boys is 2.3 times higher than that of girls. Many Indians might be adopting modern life styles but mindsets remain largely medieval.

If we look at health indicators of different states, we also notice wide differences between different states. Just to take the example of infant mortality, Orissa, UP, Rajasthan and Madhya Pradesh define the bleak end of health parameters while Kerala and Tamilnadu provide the beacons of hope. Infant mortality rate in Orissa for example, is more than five times higher than in Kerala and two times higher than in Tamilnadu. This enormous difference defines a great challenge for improvement in lagging states. But such improvements won't happen by themselves. Sustained effort has to be made to increase the pace of development, provide employment opportunities for all those who are able and willing to work, improve both physical and social infrastructure so as to upgrade educational (to improve the mindset) and health services (to reduce a number of avoidable diseases).

RURAL HEALTH SERVICES

It is even admitted by the government that rural health services have not yet come to cater to the needs of the people. There are several reasons for which the health status of rural areas is dismal. Beside government, Indian health care system also includes a private sector and an informal network of providers of health care operating within an unregulated environment with no controls on what services can be provided by whom, in what manner and what cost, and no standardized protocols to help measure the quality of care. Second, failures at the government level are also linked to non-availability of resources for public health system. Public health expenditure has declined from 1.3 per cent of GDP in 1990 to 0.9 per cent of GDP in 1999. Out of pocket expenditure on health is more for curative services in the country. There is little expenditure on preventive and promotional health.

The Economic Survey 2007-08 indicates even though there has been a steady increase in health care infrastructure in rural areas, there is a shortage of 20,903 Sub-Centres, 4,803 Primary Health Centres, and 2,653 Community Health Centres as per 2001 population norm. According to Survey almost 50 per cent of the existing health infrastructure is in rented buildings. Poor upkeep and maintenance and high absenteeism of manpower in rural areas have also eroded the credibility of the health delivery system in the public sector.

The government believes that the National Rural Health Mission (NRHM) which has been launched will ensure quality health care in rural areas. Achievement of health objectives really involves much more than curative or even preventive medical care. There is a need for a comprehensive approach which encompasses individual health care, public health, sanitation, clean drinking water, access to food and knowledge keeping in mind the socio-cultural complexities of different regions. If NRHM aims at covering all these aspects mentioned above, it may somehow make an effort to reach Millennium Development Goals.

FINANCING OF HEALTH CARE IN INDIA

Health financing centers primarily on the ways how to improve sustainability, equity and access to health services. It is acknowledged by most of the enlightened citizens that health care system in India is not performing well. It is mainly due to the fact that an adequate and well managed financing of public health system remains an elusive goal in India. Several factors like insufficient funding, inefficient use of resources, lack of incentives for health workers to provide quality care, inequitable distribution of health resources between urban and rural areas and between poor and better-off populations.

We propose to discuss three aspects of health financing in this paper—government budget financing, household out-of-pocket spending and health insurance. The government health spending in India has been low in both absolute (real value) and relative (share of GDP) terms for several decades when compared with other lower income countries. However, though it was increasing at the nominal rate of only 5 to 6 per cent every year during 2000-01 and 2004-05, it has now started to increase at 15-20 per cent per annum due to increase in the rate of growth of income. Because of this acceleration, the share of government health spending which was 0.89 per cent of GDP has increased to 1 per cent in 2006-07. Though there is increase in the spending of both the Centre and the States, health spending at the Centre has increased from 25 per cent in 2001 to 30 per cent in 2006-07. However, in spite of all this increase, government spending is still quite low, comes to about Rs. 400 per capita. There is a commitment now to increase government health spending to 2-3 per cent of GDP over the next five years along with some new initiatives to improve results. The NRHM which is launched by the GOI will provide an opportunity to implement new approaches such as decentralized financing, local planning and community involvement, which are expected to change the performance of health programmes and facilities, improving access, quality and efficiency.

The share of private expenditure on health services has been increasing in recent years due to increase in income and expansion of educational facilities. As per NSSO study (60th round), private expenditure on medical and health services within total private consumption has come to 6.5 per cent in 2005-06. Both the volume of services consumed privately as well as its cost has been rising. The NSSO report states that the average medical expenditure per hospitalized care of treatment has increased substantially from Rs. 3,202 in 1995-96 to Rs. 5,695 in 2004 in rural areas and from Rs. 3,921 to Rs. 8,851 in urban areas over the same period. The maximum rise has taken place for the private hospitals in the urban areas, accounting for 62 per cent of hospitalization cases. Such out-of-pocket (OOP) spending on health is one of the major sources of impoverishment in the country. It is estimated that 3.3 per cent of population is getting impoverished on account of high health expenditure incurred in private sector hospitals (due to decline in utilisation of public facilities in most cases). Health spending averaged 11 per cent on non-food expenditures and almost 5 per cent of total annual expenditures of households. Almost 40 per cent were reported to have taken loans to incur such expenditures and nearly 10 per cent sold assets resulting in intergenerational poverty.

Then there is the question of health insurance. It is especially useful for reducing the large financial risks accompanying high cost events like serious surgeries. There can also be group insurance to meet the health needs of some members of the group. Health insurance funds can also be utilized to develop well managed purchasing mechanism which can provide facilities to improve quality and efficiency in health service. However, it is difficult to organize such health insurance among poor people though it is most useful for them. It is reported that only around 10 per cent of the country's population is covered under some risk pooling mechanism. Government is now funding several health insurance efforts focusing on the poor. NRHM also provides subsidies to states for health insurance pilots.

HEALTH CARE SYSTEM—SOME ISSUES AND CONCERNS

What is needed in health care system is that there should be improvement in sustainability, equity and access to health services. In this context, we propose to discuss three issues. The first issue is whether we can rely on a market driven allocation of resources for health care in India as in case of many other goods and services. We do not think health partakes the characteristics of other goods. It is neither a pure private good nor a public good. To a certain extent it is excludable—the introduction of user fees for health care services could potentially exclude many who cannot afford to pay these user fees. At the same time it is not a non-rival good, where one person's use of health service does not reduce the amount available for the use of others. It can therefore, be taken as a 'merit good' where both private and public sector can operate together.

But there are many cases where market operation in health may create social hazards. First, there are strong externalities in health. There are cases where private and social benefits/costs diverge considerably. For example, if one individual does not get immunized, it may create social cost for others. Where the marginal private net benefit is less than social marginal net benefit, market operations do not succeed. In such cases, there is need for public intervention. Second, demand for health is not the same as per demand for other goods. Nobel Laureate Kenneth Arrow has emphasized that the relation between patients and their physicians involves agency, trust, information and professionalism. In many cases patients depend on their physicians to their own demand for health care. Since there is a great deal of difficulty in such cases, the patient is not free to decide the quantity of health care services to be purchased as in other cases. Third, there is also uncertainty regarding the cost and quality of health care. The provider has the knowledge and information in such cases—sometimes these may be correct or in some cases these may be incorrect, depending upon the expertise and integrity of the provider. If the diagnosis fails, the quality of health care may lead to disaster. All this implies that health care should not be left to unregulated market mechanism.

Though we have argued that health care should not be left entirely to the market forces there is no guarantee that increase in public resources will automatically benefit the poor. It is often noticed in many low income countries that the rich disproportionately capture the benefits of government expenditure on health. One problem is inadequacy of resources allotted to social sector. But the second problem is a deeper one – which reflects political and institutional weaknesses. If the resources are not specifically oriented to benefit the poor, an increase in aggregate resources for social sector may not help the poor. We have different social groups in the country. There are some social groups who do not have access to many benefits of development. In such cases an allocation will be typically deemed pro-poor, if, say the bottom 20 per cent of the population receives at least a 20 per cent or higher share of total governmental expenditure spent on health. Again, if services provided are of poor quality then a poor programme may look good in paper, but may not serve the needs of the poor who have greater health needs than the rich.

Another danger that looms large in social problem is inequality of income arising from jobless growth. Globalisation has increased the rate of growth of income in some sectors, but has failed to increase adequate employment opportunities. According to Amit Bhaduri though India is experiencing a growth rate of some 7 to 8 per cent per year in recent years, the growth in regular employment has exceeded just one per cent. This means most of the growth, some 5-6 per cent of the GDP, is the result not of employment expansion, but of higher output per worker. As a result, there is a distortion in the distribution of income in the country. As per one study of Radhakrishna (2008), the share of national income of the poorest 20 per cent of the population in India is only 8.2 per cent. Since Eleventh Plan aims at an inclusive growth, it is essential that specific provisions should be made to provide basic facilities to the poor so that they can get some benefit from economic growth. It is not only a case of health provision, but also of other basic necessities of life.

This implies that there should be a change in the pattern of growth. Otherwise, such mechanism of growth, will reinforce 'cumulative causation' as described by Gunnar Myrdal, the mechanism by which growing inequality drives growth and growth fuels further inequality. The political economy of health implies that changes in the economy, as suggested by World Bank, should take three forms: a prescription for labour-intensive growth; investing in the poor via the development of human capital—chiefly investment in health and education; and finally the promotion of safety nets and targeted social programmes. Since growth by itself does not reduce poverty nor prevents stagnation in health services, there is an implicit recognition that overall change in the programmes of development is necessary to protect the poor from the consequences of structural adjustment.

Operational Problems

As we have seen, public health in India is ridden with all the ills of poor governance. India is as per Times view, one of the worst performers in its ability to secure access to health. At the most basic level, a mere 28 per cent households have access to improved sanitation and over 200 million still have no access to safe drinking water sources. Women continue to die at child birth, children's nutritional status has stagnated in the last five years and immunization rates continue to falter. Public spending on health care, at one per cent of GDP is among the lowest in the world. There is therefore the need to bring about some radical changes in the health system to make it more effective to cater to the needs of the people. The following suggestions are offered to improve the health system and reduce the yawning gaps that exist in the health sector.

1. Under the Eleventh Plan, the Health Ministry has envisaged setting up of six AIIMS—like institutions and upgrading 13 existing medical institutes. It has also planned for 60 new medical colleges and 225 new nursing colleges, to be established in the public-private partnership mode. According to Planning Commission the country has a shortfall of six lakh doctors, 10 lakh nurses and two lakh dental surgeons. This has led to a dismal patient-doctor ratio in the country. The overriding requirement in the country is for increasing the supply of human resources from specialists to paramedical personnel. India also has a very low turnout of personnel with post graduate qualifications. The above institutions should be immediately established in suitable locations along with adequate facilities so as to reduce the yawning

gap that exists between privileged few and millions neglected citizens of the country.

2. One of the major difficulties in some of the medical institutions which have been already established is that they do not have adequate funds nor do they have trained workers. First, most of them were set-up incredibly slowly and no attempts were made to improve their operational efficiency. If any one goes to a general hospital, one will see flies and bugs chasing the patients, the clothes of the nurses are dirty, latrines are filthy, phenyl and medicines are not available, dogs and cats compete with the patients for beds and the worst of all, the patients do not get any, attention if they are poor. Sanitation is never considered as an important issue in the hospitals. The Central Government had set-up a National Rural Health Mission (NRHM) to provide effective health care to the most backward villages. However, government review of NRHM shows tardy progress in strengthening of hospitals at taluk levels due to lack of standardization of medical facility. Now in the line of NRHM, the Central Government has proposed to establish a National Urban Health Mission (NUHM) to monitor and improve the health of 220 million people living in urban slums in 429 cities and towns. It was to be launched mid-2008, but the Rs. 8,000 crore mission is yet to become functional. The programme promises to start a medical insurance scheme under which 5.5 crore of the 22 crore people would get an insurance cover of Rs. 40,000 to Rs. 50,000 for basic medical care and out-patient facilities in private and government hospitals. For the remaining population, the government would just pay the first instalment of Rs. 600 per person a year.

3. India's ban on tobacco consumption in public places does not have much effect in the country. In theory, only about 12 states in the country have banned tobacco consumption in public places, but they do not take any effective measure to control the

smokers. It is estimated more than 57% male and 10.9% females consume tobacco in one form or other. Around 14-15 per cent children are consuming tobacco. More than 10 lakh people at present die in India every year due to tobacco consumption. It is understood that round about 40 per cent of disease burden is associated with some form of tobacco. Unfortunately, the government is not serious to control this abuse as it is more, as Dr. Reddy suggests, addictive to tobacco than the individual. Unless this attitude changes the control measures will never be effective.

4. Along with disease-eradication, general nutrition and health care should be promoted through preventive measures. The West made the connection between bad food and bad health pretty late. People turned towards preventive health care only after unforeseen spikes in illness related to diet and life styles. In fact, the focus on preventive health care is critical if we are to avoid the mistakes made by the west in health policy. But instead of broader and preventive solutions, we have all kinds of one-point national health programme. They aim at specific diseases or have extensively narrow view agenda such as 'post-partum care'. Most of these programmes fail to achieve even their modest goals and are isolated from each other. Such policy measures need to be changed as early as possible.
5. Somehow or other there has been growing sense among political class that health care is not a priority for voters. Wild horses cannot, as pointed out by Nandan Nilekani, drag politicians to endorse something they do not find popular support for this. Even now there are many areas where superstitions dominate the mindset of the rural people. For instance, parts of North India had a small pox deity called Sitala—the white bodied one, mounted on ass and vaccinations for the diseases were considered a direct insult to the goddess. Such fatalistic attitude of the poor helps the Indian Government to get away

with indifferent approach to health. Unless public awareness is improved, it is doubtful whether political authority in India will attach sufficient importance to health care. We guess this can be done only by enlightened citizens of India.

References

Acharya, Shankar, 2007, Government and Health, *Economic Developments in India*, Vol. 116, Academic Foundation.

Berman & Ahuja, Rajeev (2008), Increased Health Care Spending in India: Opportunities and Risks, '*Health for Millions*', February-March and April-May.

Bhaduri, Amit, 2008, Predatory Growth, *EPW*, April 19-25.

Government of India, *Economic Surveys*, 2007-08 and 2010-11.

Nandan, Nilekani, 2008, Imagining India, Ideas for the New Century, Penguin Books.

Rao, Mohan (2008), The Political Economy of Health in the Second Phase of Globalisation in *Health for Millions*, March and April.

Roy, Amit Shavon (2008), Financing of Health Care in India: Issues and Concerns, *Health for Millions*, February-March and April-May.

Tandon, Ajay (2007), Measuring Government Inclusiveness: An Application to Health Policy, *Asian Development Review*, Vol. 24, No. 1.

Times of India (2009), Suffering from Chronic Apathy, dtd. 03 April.

CHAPTER

9

Economics of Corruption

MAGNITUDE OF CORRUPTION IN INDIA

Corruption in India has become a part of life. It has become so common and so many people are involved in this that nobody takes any serious note of it. It has become as common as poverty, hunger and squalor. It was generally said that India is a rich country but its people are poor. Now many social scientists have changed the epithet and point out that India is a poor country, but its people are not. This does not seem to be unreasonable when we analyse the disclosures by Global Financial Integrity (GFI), a Washington-based think tank which states that an estimated $ 500 billion (Rs. 22.5 lakh crore) have been spirited out of India and deposited in banks overseas. This financial flows cover the period from 1948 to 2008. India's GDP comes to $ 1,300 billion. This means nearly 40 per cent of our economy has been stolen and stashed in foreign banks and that by Indians. According to Supreme Court, this is 'pure and simple theft of national money—a mind boggling crime'. It is surprising that when India takes loans for its development it does not lay claim to this mind boggling amount of money its citizens have hidden abroad.

A disclosure by Rudolf Elmer, a former Swiss-banker (information given to the founder of Wikileaks) shows that in 2000 offshore accounts, many companies and individuals have been successful in evading domestic taxes to the extent of $ 1,000 billion by stashing away their money in tax havens. There are some Indians and Indian companies in this list. In recognition to this threat of national economies, G20 in their meeting at their London Summit of 2009 of which India is a member, agreed to take action against non-cooperative jurisdiction, including tax havens. On this basis many European countries have already signed tax information exchange agreements with so-called tax havens and collected some money from offshore evaders. India has not yet signed a single Tax Information Exchange Agreement to bring back black money from abroad.

What is most unfortunate is that this overseas capital is flying back to the Bombay Stock Exchange and increasing speculative activity without improving the real economy. We have in India colossal poverty and malnutrition, high illiteracy, infant mortality and many such disabilities which have reduced India's international status inspite of rapid economic growth in recent years. If we could make some effort to recover the stolen money, we can successfully implement some of the social improvement measures like Food Security, Right to Education and Right to Information which are in the programmes of the Government. Apart from the stolen property of $ 500 billion which travels outside, there is some underground black money in India. India's underground economy is estimated at $ 640 billion, which comes to almost one-half of our GDP. The major problem of India's black money is that it is not only finding safe havens in foreign banks (and more particularly to Swiss banks which have a clause not to disclose the names), but the real issue is that the same money is used for illicit trade of drugs, arms and even terrorist activities, all of which destabilise India's economy. As a matter of fact all this black money has been acquired through criminal and illegal activities.

We have in India almost 400 billion people who are below the poverty line. As we have already said there are many other social disabilities in India in the field of primary education, coverage of health programme, improvement in nutritional level of children and women and many other social features. If the black money which is stashed away can be recovered and utilised for the improvement of social sector, India's prosperity will be better appreciated in international field along with the improvement in life pattern of Indian people.

Scams are not a new thing in India. We may cite a few examples which created a lot of stir in political circles and slowly and gradually died down with some adjustment. Since many eminent politicians, businessmen and public servants were involved in such crimes and were associated in one way or the other with the political authority, no action was possible except some prolonged commotion. And all of them managed to escape with impunity. We may mention a few such cases to indicate the amount of money involved in crimes. These are: Telgi Scam (Rs. 43,000 crore), Satya Scam (Rs. 24,000 crore), Bofors Scam (Rs. 64,000 crore), Fodder Scam (Rs. 950 crore), Howala Scandal (Rs. 810 crore), IPO Scam (Rs. 61 crore), Securities Scam (Rs. 4000 crore), UTI Scam (Rs. 32 crore), Mutual Fund Score (Rs. 1350 crore), Madhu Koda Scam (Rs. 4000 crore), and Bhansali Score (Rs. 1200 crore). These few cases will give some idea how India's scarce resources have been used in scams—these are an intrinsic part of the Indian socio-economic political land-scape—every few years we have an outbreak of them as regularly as floods, droughts and natural calamities causing great damage to India's economic and social framework.

But in the last 2 or three years, the mega scams and scandals that dominated national life and rocked Parliament show how the country is looted by influential politicians, administrators, bureaucrats, military officers and many others who determine the destiny of the nation. We have a unique politician, A. Raja, the Telecom Minister who flouted all rules to grant spectrum licences to select companies, which to quote the CAG, cost the country Rs. 1,76,645 crore. Ring Master, Raja even clung on to power for 400 days after 2G allotments were challenged in court. Being close to Karunanidhi, he considered himself so big that he did not care for the advice of the Prime Minister. His body language and manner in which he interacted with the media indicated that the power had gone to his head. Being close to Karunanidhi, he considered himself too big to be questioned. We have Ashok Chavan, the Chief Minister of Maharashtra who bent laws to get flats for politicians, bureaucrats and army officers in a housing society meant for Kargil heroes and their widows. Though the cost of one Adarsh apartment was Rs. 6 to Rs. 8.5 crore, money paid for each was Rs. 60-85 lakh. Chavan's declared annual income in 2009 was Rs. 24.61 crore but in realty he owned assets worth hundreds of crores. In 2003, the Indian Olympic Association had estimated that the Commonwealth Games would cost the country Rs. 1,620 crore. By 2010, the bill had risen to Rs. 11,800 crore. With other additional expenditure, the games expenditure to be around Rs. 30,000 crore, making the sportive event most expensive. CBI sources say that Rs. 665 crore spent on overlays, around Rs. 200 crore was stolen. In fact, Suresh Kalmadi had played only money game. The Chief Minister of Karnataka B.S.Y. allotted prime land to his family members at throw away prices, flouting all rules against the advice of BDA and Urban Development Department. In this context we may mention that former Commissioner of IPL, Lalit Modi, according to BCCI involved in financial bungling amounting to Rs. 473 crore. The BCCI complains that Modi misused its money using up taxi bills of Rs. 40 lakhs. The country has got used to the idea of corrupt politicians, greedy businessmen and high rank bureaucrats but it was shocked to learn that officers of the rank of generals and admirals were involved in purchasing Adarsh flats at a concessional rate hiding their income. It has gone so far, that the armed forces earned the unsavoury nick name, the 'Harmed Forces' and the Medical Profession has not also escaped from corruption. Dr. Ketan Desai, the President of the Medical Council of India was dismissed on grounds of brazen corruption that highlighted the venality present in the medical education sector. The LIC Housing bank loan scams highlighted the continuing corruption in financial services sector. The very institutions designed to check corruption have themselves become subject of controversy. An affidavit in the Supreme Court (SC) alleges that eight of the last 16 Chief Justices of India are corrupt, the jury is still out on two more. The Central Vigilance Commissioner (CVC) himself has been challenged in a public interest litigation in the SC questioning his integrity as well as the manner of his selection for his job. All this shows that no sector of public life is immune from corruption.

All these thefts and crimes have declined India's social and ethical values so much so that India is now considered as a super corrupt country inspite of its magnificent achievement in economic growth and IT sector. A study conducted by the global corruption watchdog, Transparency International (IT) in 2005, shows that more than 50 per cent of Indians had the personal experience of paying bribes or using power brokers to get work done in a government office. State borders which see most of the commercial traffic in India are frontiers of corruption. TI estimates that truckers pay about Rs. 22,500 crore in bribes annually to policemen and excise officials. A recent report indicates that nearly a trillion dollars of India's wealth has been stashed in shady overseas bank accounts. The TI in their 2010 report points out that India ranks 87 in the corruption level among 178 countries. The disease of corruption has spread all over the country. What is most unfortunate is that even the poor are forced to pay to get what is their right-availing benefits under various schemes such as MGNREGS, PDS, Indira Awas Yojana and many others. According to India's corruption study 2008 conducted by IT India, those living below the poverty line paid Rs. 900 crore in bribes to avail basic and need-based services in 2007. Many of these incidents do not make news because these are not reported to the authorities as it is taken for granted that nothing will come out of these complaints. On the other hand, those who make complaints, face unnecessary harassment. And as such corruption has become a part of life.

CAUSES OF CORRUPTION

There are many reasons why corruption has become so common in India. In a survey of literature of 'Economic Analysis of Corruption' by Toke S. Adit in 'The Economic Journal', November 2003 mentions what Jains says, that corruption is an act in which the power of public office is used for personal gain in a manner that contravenes the rules of the game. This is a general rule applicable in most cases. In addition there are many other conditions which give rise to the persistence of corruption. Some of these are mentioned below:

1. *Discretionary Power*: The relevant public official must possess the authority to design or administer relations and policies in a discretionary manner. During the entire planning era discretionary power was the norm which many officials used for their own advantage. It is even said that corruption can be efficient enhancing. If an entrepreneur is interested to start an industry, instead of waiting for a long time for the disposal of his application, pays some bribe to speed up the bureaucratic procedure (greases the wheels) which enables him to start the work without much delay. It is even said that corruption introduces competition for (scarce) government resources with the result that services are provided more efficiently than they otherwise would have been. The licences are allocated on the principle that those who are willing (and able) to pay a high bribe are served first. This implies that whenever the power of sanction of licence is delegated to a bureaucratic or political authority, the chances of corruption are greater.
2. *Economic Rents*: The discretionary power must allow extraction of (existing) rents or creation of rents that can be extracted. The licence system creates rents because the would be entrepreneurs are willing to pay a bribe to get hold of a licence. The extraction of rent proliferates when the rules and regulations are so ambiguous that one cannot easily comprehend them. In such a case, it becomes easier on the part of officials to interpret the rules and regulations to secure some rent. Another factor which perpetuates corruption is lack of transparency in government decisions. Even though there is no secrecy in most of the government files, the secret element is used to

secure some rent. Further, when a large number of individuals in one organisation or society are involved in corruption, the cost of eliminating corruption becomes too high. All these people share the booties and have a common interest in concealing information. It is sometimes said that an efficiency wage or remuneration reduces corruption. It may, it may not. In such cases, efficiency wage may reduce the number of corrupt acts, but those who continue may demand higher bribes as per their status and position in the society.

3. *Weak Institutions*: If the institutions are weak, the incentives embodied in political, administrative and legal institutions must be such that officials are left with an incentive to exploit their discretionary power to extract or create rent. Inefficient regulation and corruption are two sides of the same coin. One of the institutions which is considered to be an antidote is democratic form of government. In democracy it is said that the control system via conscious public opinion, alertness of the opposition parties and the independent judiciary may restrict the collusion between bribe givers and bribe takers for the prevalence of corruption. However, if democracy does not have firm roots, the institutions of control may be weak, the grabbing hand may find much scope to increase rent in the economic system.

   Take the case of India which has the largest functioning democracy. The ingenuity of scams in India even during the new millennium has increased so much corruption that thousands of crores of rupees have been used for personal aggrandisement. Many such people and agencies have not only squandered away public money for their personal benefit, they have also concealed quite a lot of such black money in foreign banks. All such black money has created so much distortion in the economy that as FAO has estimated over 300 million people in India go to sleep every night without a square meal.

4. The legal system is so weak that dishonest persons manage to escape from punishment (even when some influential people are found guilty and put in prison cells, they are provided with the comforts of a five star hotel) whereas honest persons sometimes become victims to even crucial murder. The three cases that come out recently, one in Bihar and two in Maharashtra show how mafias control the economic system. In Bihar when there was misappropriation of funds of Prime Minister's road connectivity, Satyendu Kumar Dubey, an engineer informed the Government and even wrote a letter to the Prime Minister, but before any action could be taken to prevent such misuse of funds, he was brutally murdered. In Maharashtra, the officials of Public Service Commission including the Chairman were found recruiting government servants in the year 2002 on receipt of bribes. Please remember even a Chairman of PSC was a party to the scandal when a young Tehsildar (age 28) exposed the scandal, he was also brutally murdered. Where do you stand, when Chairmen of PSCs, Vice-Chancellors of Universities and Judges occupying the prestigious posts of Governors indulge in such scandals? The third gruesome murder of Additional District Collector, Yashwant Sonawane by Oil mafia in January 2011 when he was trying to prevent oil adulteration shows how corruption is rampant in oil sector and how politicians and officers of Maharashtra are involved in such cases. We have only mentioned three cases of the new millennium, but there are thousands of such cases in different parts of the country.
5. Another source of corruption is election. Political parties and even individual candidates try to purchase votes by offering different kinds of freebies to woo the voters. We have now examples of Tamilnadu Assembly election (2011). Tamilnadu is now facing a debt of Rs. 1 lakh crore accumulated over the last five years. The bill for the fresh round of

> promises could reach Rs. 2.5 lakh crore. The Chief Minister, Mr. Karunanidihi is promising free mixers and grinders to women voters, his rival Jayalalitha is offering a free fan, wet grinder and mixer. If Karunanidhi is doling out laptops for all students, Jayalalitha has matched this with a promise of free laptops to class 11 and 12 students irrespective of caste and economic considerations. Both promise bus passes of those above 58 years old and financial aid to married women. Party politics is at play even while deciding the sops.

While political parties are offering freebies, individual candidates cannot escape from this competition. Some of the individual candidates have made most unbelievable offer of a Nano Car to each and every voter if they are elected. We do not know whether the Election Commission could prevent such corrupt practices as an offence under the Representation of People's Act. But even if the Election Commission intervenes it cannot control freebies which are distributed by candidates to the voters. It cannot have watchmen in each and every village to guard such unlawful activity. As a matter of fact freebies have become a common affair in election. Politicians pay bribes and once elected take money out of the exchequer, meet their own expenses and further sell patronage and extort money in the name of political activity. But they pocket a large part of the collection and pass on the rest to the party and the workers they employ. Indian democracy is thus funded by corruption.

REMEDIAL MEASURES

We cannot of course sacrifice democracy to prevent corruption. If the political institutions are controlled by a dictator, corruption also increases unabated. In case of Philippines under the Marco regime, corruption became epidemic and state resources were appropriated for private ends. We have also the example of Tunisias' dictator, Zine al-Abedine Ben, whose wife and family controlled 30 to 40 per cent of the country's economy and owned assets in every sector from banks and insurance to transport, tourism and property while amassing an estimated $ 10 billion. Not to be out done, there is Hosni Mubarak who has been President for the last 30 years in Egypt and whose regime has been associated with crony capitalism and repression. His family has amassed an estimated $ 41 billion including a London town house worth $ 14 million and a six-floor Georgian mansion where the Presidents' son Gamal reportedly deposited the 97 pieces of luggage with which he flew from Egypt. Such examples are numerous. The question which bothers us, is there any scope to control the grabbing hand? We can suggest two or three remedies which may be of some use to control this malady. One is the vigilance of people. It is said that eternal vigilance is the price of liberty. All those who have read Charles Dickens' novels, they may be aware of the fact that there was a time when wide scale corruption was prevalent in England. One example will be sufficient to illustrate the point. Oliver Twist when he was in a charity house, money sanctioned for his maintenance was grabbed by the Managers and his assistants of Charity House. But now there is tremendous improvement in social ethics. Even a great economist like Hugh Dalton had to resign when there was partial leakage of his budget. Unfortunately, there is tacit acceptance of corruption in India. Persons branded for massive corruption are lionised and invited to inaugurate academic conferences, schools, hospitals and bridges. Unless there is social ostracism of such persons, there is no scope to control corruption.

Second, many things depend on leadership of politicians. If honesty and integrity of the leaders are above board, they can create a congenial atmosphere for enforcing rule of law. A big push is necessary. Hongkong is a bright example of this big push. Corruption was enormous in Hongkong police in the beginning of 1970s. An Independent Commission was set-up with widespread power to investigate and prosecute corrupt officials. And corruption was effectively eliminated within a decade. In the first decade of Indian independence, the level of corruption was minimum. The political leadership and the bureaucracy played an important role in changing the economic and political scene of India even at a critical time.

Another area in which more work has to be done is decentralisation of power. If the political and economic powers are concentrated in a few hands, they can misuse the power to extract public funds for their own benefit. Decentralisation of economic and political power increases the empowerment of people which enable them to control the monopoly power of a few who are at the helm of affairs. Political institutions, economic policies and vigilance of the people may to a great extent, control corruption, though may not eradicate it altogether. These are basic principles on which the success of democracy depends. In addition, we need to have some administrative measures to effectively control corruption.

It is necessary to improve the efficiency of institutions and agencies created to control corruption. Most of the institutions or agencies are ineffective to enforce anti-corruption laws. Take the case of Central Vigilance Commissioner (CVC). He has independent power only in theory. Before inflicting any punishment against a senior officer, he has to take the advice of the government. And such advice is not a routine matter. It depends on the position of the officer, his rank, his influence and the support he gets from other influential cabinet ministers. We have also a CBI though independent is completely under the control of the government. Before starting an investigation or before prosecuting an officer or a politician, the CBI has to take permission of the government. Such permission depends very often on the status of man. The anti-corruption machinery is equally handicapped in states in enforcing laws. Further, the anti-corruption laws are highly inadequate. For example, if someone is convicted of corruption and suffers a jail term, on his release he can enjoy the bribe money. There is no provision to confiscate his ill gotten money.

There is an attempt now to enact a Lokpal Bill to effectively control corruption. But the Bill which had been drafted had neither the powers to initiate enquiry into a case directly, nor could it accept a complaint from the public. If the Lokpal conducts an enquiry against a politician or a minister, it does not have the power to take action. It will forward the report to the Speaker and Prime Minister. If the enquiry is against a Minister, the Prime Minister will decide whether any action will be taken. In a coalition government, the Prime Minister's power is limited as we have seen in the case of A. Raja. Now a new Committee has been appointed with Government and Civil Society representatives to draft an effective bill with meaningful operational powers. This will be placed before the Parliament for approval. We have to wait to find out the provisions of the Lokpal Bill.

Fraud is not only confined to only influential citizens or politicians, but also is common in case of companies. Many corporate houses do not have systems to counter potential frauds. After Satyam scandal, it has now become a common knowledge that even efficient business concerns may be tempted to fall a prey to easy money and indulge in frauds to accumulate personal and family wealth. What is necessary is to give the anti-corruption institutions operational freedom in their functioning and enforcing accountability at all levels. Most of the time frauds, scams happen because of the weak enforcement of laws and that is also the reason why the guilty can evade penalty.

Many social scientists have suggested for the appointment of two new institutions to deal with both demand and supply side of corruption. They call for the creation of an integrity commission and another a centre of integrity studies (CIS). The CIS would be a think tank to: (a) monitor and report levels and trends in corruption, (b) identify and publicise best practices in reducing corruption in India and overseas, and (c) periodically assess effectiveness of integrity commission and other anti-corruption watchdogs.

The integrity commission will develop its own agenda but be guided by the study reports of CIS. The integrity commission mandate should be to reduce corruption at all levels, in all areas of public life and all over India. It should be chaired by the Prime Minister and have the same status as Planning Commission. It can have a Vice-President. It will be better to have the speaker as Vice-President. The other members of the Commission would be persons of impeccable honesty and integrity comprising of men of academic and judicial background, members of Parliament and representatives of business community. It should be a small body consisting of eight or nine members which can be cohesive and take decisions without prolonged debate. An effective statutory body with the PM at its head may probably have greater scope for implementing decisions without much litigation. One of the greatest difficulty in crime detection in India is inordinate delay in court decisions. If the integrity commission can detect crime and inflict punishment without much delay it will have a great service to reduce the level of corruption in India.

CHAPTER

10

Sustainable Development—Problems and Challenges of 21st Century

DEVELOPMENT CONTRADICTIONS

The accelerating pace of change in the 20th century in different fields of economic and social activity though brought about wondrous changes have created a number of baffling challenges. On the one hand there has been tremendous improvement in the economy. For example, during the century, the global economy has expanded from an annual output of $ 2.3 trillion in 1900 to $ 39 trillion in 1998, a 17-fold increase. Income per person, mean while, climbed from $ 1500 to $ 6,600, a rise of just over four-fold, with most of this rise concentrated in the second half of the century. In fact, economic growth has allowed billions of people to live healthier with more productive lives and to enjoy a host of comforts that were unimaginable in 1900. That is why, growth has become the goal of every society, a kind of religion or ideology that drives each society (Lester R. Brown & Christopher Flavin).

On the other hand, while one-fifth of humanity lives better than the Kings of yore, another one-fifth still lives on the very margin of subsistence, struggling just to survive. According to Brown and Flavin, an estimated 841 million people are undernourished and underweight, 1.2 billion do not have access to safe water, 1.6 billion are illiterate and 2 billion do not have access to electricity. Forbes Magazine estimates that 225 richest people in the world now have a combined wealth of more than $1 trillion, a figure that approaches the combined annual incomes of the poorest one-half of the humanity. Indeed, the assets of the three richest individuals exceed the combined annual economic output (measured at the current exchange rate) of the 48 poorest countries. This shows that the income gap between the rich and poor is widening. Further, while each country is trying to increase its economic growth, some countries are making adequate progress while others are lagging behind.

Similarly, in the field of technological development, there has been spectacular change in the 20th century. It can be said as a century of technological progress. The change has enabled us not only to increase production of agricultural and industrial commodities, but enabled us to explore other planets in our solar system and to travel to moon. Astronauts now routinely orbit the Earth in 90 minutes and discover many secrets of the Earth which were unknown to mankind. Robots in some of the advanced countries are not only doing some arduous jobs and relieving men and women from physical torture, but also helping mankind to bring about new innovations in the process of change. The outgrowth of information age with the increase in telephones, televisions and computers has been so rapid that there has been a death of distance as described by the Economic Editor Frances Cairncross. The emergence of antibiotics in the field of biology has not only controlled many infectious diseases, but also increased longevity of life. In fact, technological progress in the century has been remarkable.

And the most fascinating thing is the Internet which has become a dominant infrastructure. It is the mechanism by which all things will be connected in near future. Scientists have gone so far to say that within a few years, appliances like cars, washing machines, dish washers, microwave ovens, refrigerators and toasters will become smarter with the help of intelligent chips inside them and will start processing information as directed by users through Web (Vidyasagar). No one knows how life will be when all these appliances at home get the power of the 'human'.

But on the darker side, the 20th century has also been the most violent in human history, thanks in part to technological 'advances' such as the airplane, automatic weapons including atom bombs. Some 26 million people were killed in World War I and 53 million in World War II; combined with other war deaths since the century began, the total surpasses the war casualty figure from the beginning of civilization until 1990.

Another challenge which has emerged in the western industrial development model (which is generally called fossil-fuel-based, automobile-centred throwaway economy), though increased income, material consumption, level of living and physical mobility to an unprecedented level, cannot sustain for long since it is destroying the Earth's natural system. Take the case of increased consumption. Industrial development through technological change has increased consumption of several renewable and non-renewable resources destroying the environmental support systems. For example, in 1900, only a few thousand barrels of oil were used daily. By 1997, that figure had reached 72 million barrels per day. There is also a vast increase in the use of materials, including growth in the use of metals from 20 million tons annually to 1.2 billion tons. Production of plastics largely unheard of in 1990 reached 131 million tons in 1995. The human economy now draws on all 92 naturally occurring elements in periodic chart, compared with just 20 in 1900.

And all this with a population of about 6 billion in 1999. The total population of the Earth which was about 1 billion in 1825 has now reached more than 6 billion. The United Nations projections show that it would be about 10 billion during the next century. If the western model becomes the global model, what will happen to the increased demand? At present we have about 501 million cars. If for example the world has one car for every two people in 2050, as in the United States today, there would be a demand for 5 billion cars. Given the congestion, pollution and the fuel requirements of current 501 million cars, it is difficult to imagine the effect of 5 billion cars on environment. If petroleum use per person were to reach the current U.S. level, the world would consume 360 million barrels per day, compared with the current production of 67 million barrels. Even with regard to the consumption of foodgrains on the basis of American standard, ten billion people would require about 9 billion tons of grain. This would be the harvest of more than four planets at Earth's current output levels (Brown and Flavin). All this implies that the present pattern of development would destroy the life support system both for the present and future generation. The following analysis shows the impact of development on environment.

IMPACT OF DEVELOPMENT ON ENVIRONMENT

The fossil-fuel-based automobile centred, throwaway economy which is now pursued leads to reckless exploitation of earth. For example, indiscriminate industrialization has given rise to emission of toxic gases, depletion of ozone layer, threat of acid rain, pollution of air, water and land surface, etc., in fact, nothing is spared resulting in total pollution. The increase in chemical industries causing the depletion of ozone layer which acts as a blanket of earth to filter out the harmful rays of sun is a greater danger to the humanity. If the ultra violet rays of the sun reach earth, there will be incidence of skin cancer, increase in temperature of earth which could melt polar-ice cap. As a result of this melting, all the cities, towns along with the seacoast will submerge in water with great devastation to human civilization.

Some of the recent developments in pollution cause great harm to mankind. Take the case of chemical spill into rivers, lakes and oceans which has polluted water in different parts of the world. To take just a few examples. The chemical spill that occurred in November 1, 1986 in Basle plant of Sandoz in that beautiful country of Switzerland when 30 tons of highly toxic chemicals spilled into the river Rhine, killed a million fish and forced several towns along the upper 200 miles of the river to take emergency measures to secure alternative sources of drinking water. Experts believed at that time that it would take upto 10 years of the Rhine to recover from these toxic effects. Again the toxic effects of Bhopal tragedy killed hundreds of people and handicapped many more. The Iraq and Iran war and subsequent Iraq and allied war spilled chemical substances in the neighbouring seas killing thousands of birds, fishes and sea animals and deprived millions of people getting pure drinking water for years together. The explosion of atomic plant at Chernobyl in the erst-while Soviet Russia contaminated milk even in third world countries. Milk sent out from Dutch to Philippines after two months of the explosion was found to possess radioactive elements.

It is true that industrial revolution has heralded an era of tremendous prosperity, huge quantities of manufactured goods and many other blessings. But at the same time, it has created serious threat to the environment. As already pointed out, the destruction of protective ozone layer, global warming, air pollution and the resultant acid rain have decreased tropical forests. As the world's largest user of sulphur rich coal, China is witnessing forest damage due to air pollution which causes acid rain to fall on 14 per cent of its land mass. And other adverse effects like spilling of the oil by tanker load, spewing of harmful gases into the atmosphere, pouring of poisonous fluids into the rivers, lakes and the sea . . . all these have heaped almost every possible abuse upon our planet Earth.

Even agriculture which is a part and parcel of nature has damaged nature to a considerable extent due to mismanagement of agriculture. We can cite a few examples from India to show how environment has been badly affected due to indiscriminate use of pesticides, improper use of land, excessive use of ground water and so on. India's land area is rapidly turning barren and it is estimated that about 1 million hectares of crop lands and grazing lands are badly affected due to lack of proper maintenance. The per capita availability of agricultural land which stood at 0.48 hectare in 1951 has probably been reduced to 0.14 hectare in 2000 A.D. No notice is taken that land is a non-renewable resource.

Irrigation dams due to lack of proper drainage have created water logging at different parts of the country. It is estimated that the menace of water logging (and consequent Salinization of the soil) has already affected atleast 13 mh of good agricultural lands and threatens many more. Due to extensive denudation and soil erosion, the siltation of reservoirs which represent a highly valuable and irreplaceable potential for irrigation, power and flood control is taking place at much higher rate than was envisaged. It is understood that on an average, every hectare loses 20 tonnes of top soil a year. Again the flood prone area has doubled over the last 10 years from 20 million to 40 million hectares. And millions of people have been displaced and uprooted apart from the fact that the productivity of irrigation dams is not fully utilized and investment cost for creating irrigation potential is almost galloping from one plan to another.

This shows that canal irrigation instead of becoming a blessing has turned into a curse and allows our renewable resources of water to damage our non-renewable resource of land. In fact irrigation and power projects have given birth to powerful engineering interests (which include equipment manufacturers and contractors) backed by decision-makers who have more than the public interest in view while conceiving of the expenditure intensive projects. As Simon Kuznets has pointed out the development sequence goes from science to technology and then to engineering.

In many parts of Bengal arsenic contamination in ground water has assumed alarming proportions due to intensive digging of tube wells both for drinking and irrigation purposes. Probably such overuse has disturbed the underground geological balance which has resulted in arsenic contamination of water creating skin diseases, conjunctivitis, liver enlargement and diseases of upper and lower limbs. It is also found by a study of Delhi University in Ludhiana District that ground water extraction is 30 per cent higher than replenishment. As a result water tables are falling at the rate of one metre a year.

The green revolution which has increased the productivity of land to a great extent in Punjab, Haryana and Western Uttar Pradesh pulls out more plant nutrients, from soil than it puts back. In these parts of the country deficiencies of plant nutrients in the soil are the highest. Many farmers have already started applying zinc. In addition, because of application of pesticides in high yielding varieties, the air, water and soil are polluted which threaten the livelihood of rural people. These agricultural chemicals leave behind residues in food and produce ill effects when the concentration exceeds a safe tolerable level. The International Development Research Centre (Ottawa) has claimed that every year about 10,000 people die and another 4,00,000 suffer from various effects of pesticide poisoning in the developing countries. And India accounts for about one-third of pesticide poisoning in the Third World. Even though the coverage of crops by pesticides in India is barely 25 per cent of total cultivated land, the residue problem has become quite alarming.

Forests which provide us with our basic needs of life like food and shelter and influence the environment through the supply of clean air by absorbing carbon dioxide and other harmful gases which are by-products of industrialization, are being rapidly destroyed in different parts of the world. In India, of the 67 mh, which are officially notified as 'Forest Land', not more than around 28 mh possess good natural forests (with a crown cover of at least 40 per cent). Such forests are being lost at the rate of at least 1.5 mh per annum. Since independence about 4.3 mh are lost on account of irrigation projects, industries and power projects only. Other reasons which cause the loss of forests are extensive felling of trees for fuel wood, economic requirements which necessitate exploitation of the forests for profit, shifting cultivation and other unscientific and inappropriate agricultural/horticultural practices. Indiscriminate mining activity has also destroyed several million hectares of good crop and forest lands. Besides, the reckless discharge of industrial wastes and atmospheric pollution are also damaging extensive forest areas. According to UNEP of the World's 5200 million hectares of agricultural dry land, 69 per cent is being desertified. The land degradation is caused by over cultivation, over grazing, deforestation and poor irrigation practices.

The loss of forests not only increases pollution and creates acid rains, but also reduces water supply and aggravates floods; forests work like speed breakers to the surface run off and absorb the water to be released later on in the form of streams. It is estimated that the country's total precipitation in the normal monsoon conditions works out to 400 mh metres. Out of this only 150 mh metres reach the soil, and out of this only 40 mh metres reach the ground water which is used for irrigation and drinking purposes all throughout the year. The loss on account of surface run-off comes to about 180 mh metres. This implies that forest cover in a water shed is the cheapest and best method of water storage in space in a country where the whole economy revolves around the monsoon. In addition, because of deforestation, ground water table in many parts of the country is going down leaving the poor persons' dugwell high and dry. In many other parts the water table is going down creating serious problems of water logging.

EFFECTS OF URBANISATION

Economic development and industrialization are closely associated with urbanization. In fact, industrialization leads to urbanization. The adverse effect of urbanization on ecology and environment can be seen just by visiting Delhi, the capital of India. The World Health Organisation (WHO) has already classified Delhi as one of the 10 most polluted cities in the world, in the same league as Mexico City where better-off citizens routinely look at pollution metre before deciding if it is safe to step out of their homes without a gas mask. Delhi is following suit speedily.

The Central Pollution Control Boards' study of the quality of air at Shahdara area in 1987 and in 1992 shows that in the former, suspended particular matter (SPM) was around 250 micrograms in cubic metre air. Five years after, this had jumped to somewhat over 350 megm/cu.m. These are average figures, particular points can be more worse. The same level of pollutants is also seen in many other parts of Delhi. And the levels rise significantly in summer, during the day. Every day in Delhi, it is estimated, around two and a half million kilograms of pollutants—carbon monoxide, lead, sulphur dioxide, nitrogen oxide and so on are added to the air. The majority is due to emissions from motorized vehicles. And while our air lungs are continually being constricted, the quality of air in our cities worsens every day.

A report in the Delhi Legislative Assembly says that till December, 1993, 63 per cent of Delhi's air pollutants came from vehicular smoke, 29 per cent from industries and 8 per cent from domestic fuels. Thus vehicles are identified as the primary polluters. The report warns that by 2000 A.D. vehicles would be responsible for a whooping 72 per cent of the pollution. Hardly surprising considering Delhi's two million vehicles outstrip the 1.96 m in Bombay, 0.65 m in Calcutta and 0.63 m in Madras. And further, one motor vehicle is added to Delhi's roads every five minutes, or a colossal 1,20,000 per year.

In fact, Delhi is now becoming a gas chamber. According to the Draft Regional Plan 2001, prepared by the National Capital Region (NCR) Planning Board, Delhi, people are suffering 12 times more than the national average in respiratory ailments and 30 per cent in Delhi's population suffer from the same disease. Child patients have more than doubled between 1991 and 1993 with one out of every 20 kids being asthmatic. Overall, the ailment accounts for 29 per cent of the respiratory tract infections between ages 5 and 16.

A Times of India study (21st May 1994) also shows that Delhi's roads are becoming a living nightmare. Driving in the free-for-all Delhi traffic is more than just a daily headache. It is a stress factor. For those susceptible to hypertension or who have suffered angina trouble, traffic conditions can cause blood pressure to increase. In the last few years many men in their 30s are suffering from heart attacks and in this group, driving stress contributes to over all stress. And worse the endless breaking, weaving of cars, cutting in, snarl-ups, honking and lack of discipline on roads hinder the recovery of those who have had heart attacks. Further, people often develop migraine while driving in heavy traffic or stomach muscles and feel exhausted both emotionally and physically. One lady says she is 'shattered' after a long drive home. And another says, 'it is a miracle you come back home safe'.

Delhi's water supply is also polluted due to the discharge of industrial effluents into the river Yamuna which is the main source of water for the city. It is not only a question of industrial effluents, even factories along with the people in the neighbouring areas are used to dumping their wastes to the river contaminating everyone's drinking, washing and cooking water. Many slums and shanties which crowd close to the river allow their sewage water to seep into the river, the water of which is used without treatment by the large sections of the community. They therefore, suffer from high incidence of diseases linked to poor sanitation and contaminated drinking water (diarrhea, dysentery, hepatitis and typhoid) which are usually endemic, and major causes of illness and death, especially among children.

What we have said with regard to Delhi is more or less true to most of the other cities of India. 'Our Common Future' shows how economic development in different parts of the world has created environmental stress. While economic growth has led to improvements in living standards in some parts of the world, it has been achieved in ways that are globally damaging. Much of the improvements in the past has been based on the use of increasing amounts of raw materials, chemicals and synthetics, and on the creation of pollution that is not adequately accounted for in figuring the costs of production processes. These trends have had unforeseen effects on the environment. Thus today's environmental challenges arise both from lack of development (in many poor countries) and from unintended consequences of some forms of economic growth.

THE IMPACT OF CLIMATE CHANGE ON ENVIRONMENT

There is no longer any doubt that the adverse effect of production pattern has increased global temperature which has changed the climate all over the world. Unless we reduce the amount of global warming gasses we release into the atmosphere, we cannot control the aberration of the climate change. It is estimated that global temperatures have been rising since 1750 as a consequence of economic activity. Today America emits 20 tonnes of carbon dioxide per capita, whereas Europe 10 tonnes, China between four and five tonnes and India between one and two. It is said that unless we take some action to reduce the emission of green house gases, temperature will continue to rise another one to six degrees Celsius by the century (Levin). Even a one-degree increase in temperature will limit fresh water availability and cause coastal flooding in much of the world, but economic, social and environmental damages and dislocation will become much more consequential if global temperatures increase by two or three degrees.

A report released in November 2010 by the government's Indian Network for Climate Change Assessment has said that by 2030, the average temperatures in India will rise by 1.7-2.2 degree Celsius and extreme temperatures by 1.4 degree Celsius in comparison to the 1970s. The hot summers and warmer winters will lead to substantial changes in agricultural production, water flows and cause dramatic changes in country's weather. The report further adds that in all the regions of the country rainfall will increase, with central and north western Himalayan regions suffering the brunt of the highest increases. Worse, the high rain fall days (extreme rainfall events) in the country are bound to increase. The 7800 km coastline will face its own problems with sea levels along the coast rising at the rate of 1.3 mm/year and the intensity of cyclone expected to increase, though the frequency would reduce. The report also mentions that severe droughts will see a moderate to extreme increase in the Himalayan region and floods will intensify by 10-30 per cent in all the regions of the country. All this will change the cropping pattern in different parts of the country.

It is not only a case of India. Climate change is human kinds' most pressing challenge. The global warming gases released into atmosphere, the heating they cause will melt the world's glaciers, create both droughts and floods, drive many people from their homes as sea levels rise and threaten the world's ability to feed itself. All the same, no serious attempt has been made so far to stop it. There are several reasons for this. One is the dis-information made by fossil fuel companies that fossil fuel energy does not create much climate change. If there is any attempt to replace fossil fuel energy, the investments made by such companies will lose their value. Second, since fossil fuel energy has been convenient to increase the rate of growth of income, there is a great deal of bargaining between developed and developing countries not to reduce the use of such energy. That is why government's meetings in

Copenhagen and Cancun are proposing only a fraction of the cuts needed to prevent disaster. Further, since the matter has been left to the governments and public awareness is feeble as science and the policies needed to deal with manmade climate change are inherently complex, public protests demanding action have been small and muted (George Monbiot). However, a time has come when global warming has to be kept with an acceptable range, by reducing carbon emissions balancing both efficiency and global equity to save the human race.

This shows that pollution control is not a luxury. It is necessary both in developed and developing countries. When some people point out whether a poor country can afford to worry about pollution, we should ask in turn whether we can afford to ignore it. Before we discuss the methods of sustainable development, we want to clarify two points. First, the environment must be protected from avoidable pollution, destruction and exploitation from all sources. Economic development does not mean destruction of nature: it is a part and parcel of nature. In other words, the pattern of development should be in harmony with nature. A cleaner environment would not only result in greater productivity but would also lead to sustainable development. Destruction of environment is bound to increase the costs and create impediments in the way of development. All natural resources have to be conserved and developed by ensuring their efficient, equitable and sustainable use. People have to be educated on the need to preserve and protect our natural habitat and environment.

Second, the polluters should be compelled to take measures to prevent pollution. Though the polluters pollute the atmosphere, the costs of pollution are paid by the public. There might, therefore, be a dangerous tendency to considering costs for pollution control as an external diseconomy as it becomes necessary to spend money to clear the air before others can use it. While it is easy to calculate the cost pattern, it is not so while attempting to consider the benefits that accrue when measures are taken to control a particular pollution problem. Therefore, whoever pollutes the air or water, must be held responsible to prevent it or to pay for the cost incurred in preventing the pollution. In Germany for example, the government is planning a massive tax restructuring, reducing income taxes and raising energy taxes to economise the use of fossil-fuel.

MEANING OF SUSTAINABLE DEVELOPMENT

The World Commission on Environment and Development in 'Our Common Future' defines sustainable development as development that meets the needs of the present without compromising the ability of future generations to meet their own needs. It contains within it two key concepts:

(1) The concept of 'needs', in particular the essential needs of the world's poor, to which overriding priority should be given. These needs include a secure and adequate source of income, adequate shelter, health, education, security and amenities.
(2) The idea of limitations imposed by the state of technology and social organization on the environment's ability to meet present and future needs. A minimum sustainable development must not endanger the natural systems that support life on Earth: the atmosphere, the waters, the soils and the living beings. This implies that economic development should not cross the limits of the carrying capacity of our planet.

These two concepts imply that sustainable development involves more than growth. It requires a change in the content of growth, to make it less material and energy-intensive and more equitable in its impact. These changes are required in all countries as part of a package of measures to maintain the stock of ecological capital, to improve the distribution of income and to reduce the degree of vulnerability to economic crisis. 'Our Common Future' hence emphasizes that, "In essence; sustainable development is a process of change in which the exploitation of resources, the direction of investments, the orientation of technological development, and institutional change are all in harmony and enhance both current and future potential to meet human needs and aspirations".

The authors of Worldwatch Institute, Washington while defining sustainability point out that 'an economy is environmentally sustainable only if it satisfies the principles of sustainability-principles that are rooted in the science of ecology. In a sustainable economy, the fish catch does not exceed the sustainable yield of fisheries, the amount of water pumped from underground acquifers does not exceed acquifer recharge, soil erosion does not exceed the natural rate of new soil formation, tree cutting does not exceed tree planting and carbon emissions do not exceed the capacity of nature to fix atmosphere CO_2. A sustainable economy does not destroy plant and animal species faster than new ones evolve'. All this implies that bounties of nature are to be nurtured and used sparingly for the benefit of all.

NO NEGATION OF DEVELOPMENT

This broad perspective does not imply that economic development should be neglected particularly in developing countries where there is colossal poverty and unemployment along with inequity and insecurity: economic development has to assume a major role in the policy programmes of these countries. Even while defining sustainable development the Brundtland Commission makes this clear: 'Sustainable Development seeks to meet the needs and aspirations of the present without compromising the ability to meet those of future. Far from requiring the cessation of economic growth, it recognizes that the problems of poverty and underdevelopment cannot be solved unless we have a new era of growth in which developing countries play a large role and reap large benefits' (WCED, 1987:40).

What about developed countries? Would sustainable development require that at least these countries give up the objectives of economic growth henceforth and be content with their present standard of living? No, the development of these countries has not improved the quality of life of all the people. From the point of view of Human Development Index (HDI), not only the developing countries lack a number of economic and social amenities, many of the developed countries also suffer from inadequacy of social goods which promote cultural and social values. The HDI is a composite of quality indicators such as literacy and life expectancy, as well as income based on purchasing power parity. Though this concept is a broader measure than GDP, it is not all comprehensive. It does not include the vast array of variables that determine social welfare and human well being. Even on this index, the USA is ranked thirtieth after Norway, Australia, Canada, Sweden, France, Switzerland, Japan and five more countries (Human Development Report, 2009). Again while defining sustainable development; the Brundtland Commission is equivocal about growth needs of the North. It says, 'Meeting essential needs depends in part on achieving full growth potential and sustainable development clearly requires economic growth in places where such needs are met. Elsewhere, it can be consistent with economic growth, provided the content of growth reflects broad principles of sustainability and non-exploitation of others' (WCED 1987:44).

And the ranking of developing countries in terms of HDI is terribly low. Take the case of India. India is 119 on UNDP index among 169 nations (2010). If we include a number of other social indicators like human rights, job creation, environmental protection, human security etc., the ranking of India will be still lower. More or less the same situation prevails in most of the other developing countries. All this suggests that, neither the developing countries nor the developed ones can neglect economic development to improve the quality of life. Particularly in India, where 40% of the population is still illiterate, infant mortality is as high as 53 per thousand (2008), almost 37 per cent of Indians lives in poverty (2004-05) and 22 per cent is chronically undernourished (FAO-2010), India has to make substantial effort to fulfil the basic necessities of life of people. Hence the pattern of development should encompass increase in per capita income, improvement in quality of life with economic and social amenities and reduce the wide disparities that exist across regions.

TOWARDS SUSTAINABLE DEVELOPMENT

The environmental difficulties that confront us are not new, but they have become enormous as a result of the growing demand on scarce resources, indiscriminate use of such resources and increased level of pollution that have taken place because of such unbalanced development. Previously our main concern centered on the effects of development on the environment. But today since environmental degradation is eroding the potential for development, we should be more careful regarding the pattern of development. Economy is not just about the production of wealth, and ecology is not just about the protection of nature; they are both, as mentioned in 'Our Common Future' equally relevant for improving the lot of human kind. We have already crossed the thresholds of nature and there is a limit beyond which we cannot go.

Hence we have to reorient our economy so as to establish a sustainable society which conserves natural resources, promotes equity, establishes environmental harmony, improves economic efficiency and increases local self-reliance. Unless we develop an ethical basis for human survival, our technical solution for improvement will not only damage our environment but also create a wide gap between the two sets of people, some affluent and a vast multitude of others who are on the verge of subsistence. The issue is not growth versus no-growth, but what kind of growth and where. Converting the economy of the 21st century into one that is environmentally sustainable represents the greatest investment opportunity in history, one that dwarfs anything that has gone before. In fact, the 21st century should be a century of environment in contrast to a century of lopsided growth that preceded it.

Though environmental challenges confronting us today are greater than ever before, we have potential to meet these challenges. Action can be taken in several fields to protect nature and at the same time improve the economic well-being of different sections of the community. For example, in order to preserve the life support system for the entire humanity, we have to find out the main causes which are responsible for environmental degradation and inequitable distribution of income and welfare. These are: (1) population explosion and its impact on poverty, (2) environmental degradation technology, (3) inefficient use of economic resources, (4) consumerism, and (5) lack of global effort in improving the pattern of development. A few important areas are only indicated here to promote eco-friendly development.

(i) Population Control

Population explosion has become a major source of environmental degradation. In the year 1993, some 91 million people were added to the world's population, bringing the total to 5.5 billion. In 1999, the population had come to 6 billion. By about 2005, the population of the world has probably reached the figure of 6.7 billion. India's population in 1999 came to 1 billion. In 2010, it comes to 1.2 billion. It is estimated that by 2050, population of India would come to more than 1.6 billion. This huge growth of population increases the demand on scarce resources and the pollution generated by the rising living standards of the relatively affluent. But poverty itself creates further environmental stress. Those who are poor and hungry will often destroy their immediate environment in order to survive. They will cut down forests, their livestock will overgraze grasslands, they will over use marginal land and encourage large families as an insurance against high mortality. The consequent destruction of environment and the pressure exerted by population on natural resources lead to further immiserisation. The cumulative effect of these changes makes poverty itself a major global disaster. We have now a demographic fatigue in many parts of the world which is likely to increase further if the population of the world in the 21st century becomes 10 billion. Therefore, one of the major problems in improving environment and ecology and to protect nature is to reduce the rate of growth of population particularly in Asian and African countries where it has assumed a dangerous proportion.

As pointed out by Paul Kennedy in his 'Preparing for the Twenty First Century', the poor countries must give more serious attention to control population because the poor are not only one of the important agents of ecological degradation, but because developing countries like India cannot simply cope with the task of providing employment, health care, education, etc. to an ever increasing population. He has suggested to ensure a decrease in fertility rates by introducing cheap and reliable forms of birth control. The three key elements in any general effort to reduce the growth of population are education, empowerment of women and enlightened political leadership.

(ii) Improvement of Healthy Technology

In respect of technology, we can either have high Tech/ Super Industrial Society or a Sustainable Development Society. A high-tech society assumes that (a) sophisticated technology can increase production and guarantee a good quality of life, (b) carrying capacity of the earth is unlimited, and (c) such a society presupposes unlimited resilience in life support systems to keep on absorbing the continued shocks of pollution and eco-degradation. But the experiences of development in different parts of the world show that all these assumptions are wrong.

First, a high-tech society may increase production but may not reduce poverty, unemployment or inequality. It may create a dual society in which a few may have abundance of wealth and a vast majority may suffer from deprivation. If we provide a computer for every household in the next century, but also wipe out half of the world's plant and animal species, that would hardly be an economic success. And if we again quadruple the size of the global economy but half of the world's population suffer from starvation, we will not be able to declare the 21st century a success. And it may not also improve the quality of life.

Second, it is not correct to say that the carrying capacity of the planet is unlimited. Take the case of energy. It was once conceived that fossil fuels which create instability in climate and increase air pollution can be substituted by nuclear power. But nuclear power has failed to live upto its promise and is being challenged on economic grounds in most of the countries where it is produced. After continuing without interruption since mid fifties, growth in nuclear power has come almost to a halt in 1990. To a large degree this is also on account of the impossibility of safely storing nuclear wastes over unimaginable stretches of time. According to Einstein, there are only two things which are unlimited, the Universe and human stupidity. This stupidity has to be stopped.

Third, there is no guarantee that a high-tech society will be able to support the life support system. As we have already noted, the major atmospheric problems facing our planet today are global warming and the destruction of the protective ozone layer, air pollution, acid rain and the resultant forest destruction. All these are cumulative effects of increasing industrialization. It may also be noted that environmental degradation involves a loss of capital and incurring of social costs which are not usually taken into account in the process of valuing goods and services.

(iii) Efficient Use of Natural Resources

The guiding principle in case of a sustainable society is to satisfy the needs and not greeds of the people, ensure comfort, not luxury and above all bring about equity with social justice. The twin goals of sustainable development are : (a) restoration of the past ecological damage, and (b) insulation of the country from the damage as a consequence of future development. The latter must entail minimum risk to environment. Each type of development entails some risk. To accomplish both restorative and preventive strategies we have to improve the efficiency of energy use, increase the forest area, reduce wants, increase awareness, provide power and authority to the village units so that they can take the responsibility of protecting the environment.

It is sometimes pointed out that if the local people are given a free hand, they will make a reckless use of natural resources. Take the case of forests. If local people are given a free hand in forests, they will destroy the forests. Paul Kennedy has given the example of Ethiopia where forty years back 30 per cent of the area had forest cover which has now shriveled to a mere 1 per cent. Even though sometimes free individual choice leads to reckless use, it is impossible, as pointed by Nandkarni, to conserve a natural resource against the will of the local people. It can be done only by conceding their right to the natural resource base of their economy and then by compensating them adequately for their sacrifice involved in conservation and for creating alternative opportunities of livelihood.

Sustainable development does not only mean prevention of pollution and control of depletion, but also aims at ecological improvements, reversing of degradation and economic use of resources. Let us take the case of agriculture. If we entirely depend on fossil fuels, borrowed capital, chemical fertilizers and pesticides to modernize agriculture, all these will decrease soil productivity, deteriorate environmental quality and threaten human and animal wealth. It is, therefore, suggested that sustainable agriculture should encompass (a) rotation of crops, (b) application of crop residues, manures and other organic materials to the soil, (c) integrated pest management which may involve disease resistant crop varieties and biological controls, and (d) increase in forest area to improve the quality of air and prevent desertification which is increasing in different parts of the world. Though organic farms have lower crop yield than the conventional farms, their operating costs are lower by about the same cash equivalent. As a result, the net incomes from crop production on the two types of farms are about equal every year.

Further, organic farms have two more advantages. First, it provides healthy soil which is a hospitable world for growth. Air circulates through it freely and it retains moisture long after a rain. Second, the cultivation of legumes fixes nitrogen in the soil and thus increases soil productivity. It follows from this that biology and ecology rather than chemistry and technology should govern agriculture so as to prevent ecological degradation and improve economic use of resources. And again, to protect the environment from further degradation, there should be at least 30 per cent land under forest cover. Two things are important in this field: Large scale plantation in wastelands and to increase water supply through low cost conservation measures. Both of which are complementary to each other, provide a positive externality through which benefits of the gain are shared by many.

Similarly, if there is efficiency in improvement of energy use, it would reduce carbon dioxide emissions which cause global warming. In industrial societies, about one-third of the energy is used at home. Yet, much of that energy is wasted due to poor insulation. If insulation could be improved, a lot of energy can be saved. Massive savings in energy could also be made in transport, which at present accounts for one-third of energy used in industrialized societies. Although cuts could be made through improving the efficiency of cars, energy use in transport could be reduced more effectively by improving public transport, a measure that would also improve the quality of life in cities. Another third of the energy is used in a modern society in power industry; in developing world, the figure is closer to 60 to 70 per cent. There is plenty of scope to save energy by evolving new sources of energy and through recycling the basic industrial materials.

New sources of energy which can reduce emissions is greater use of natural gas in place of coal or oil. Because combustion of natural gas produces almost no sulphur and far less nitrogen oxide than coal or oil. Ultimately the transmission from fossil fuel to renewable energy economy based on solar, wind, geo-thermal and small scale hydropower will dramatically reduce air pollution. Even new compact fluorescent bulbs in place of incandescent bulbs can provide the same light but using only one-fourth as much electricity. Replacing a throwaway economy with a reduce/recycle economy is probably more suitable for sustaining a healthy development.

Recycling of basic industrial materials also saves quite a lot of energy. For example, recycling paper uses a third less energy than producing paper from trees, while recycling iron and steel brings an energy saving of between 60-70 per cent. Improving the efficiency of power generation could also save large amount of energy. Sixty per cent of the energy generated by conventional power stations (both nuclear and fossil fuel) is lost directly into the atmosphere through cooling towers. Combined Heat and Power (CHP) systems allow that waste heat to be captured and used to provide hot water and space hitting for the local. However, there is a physical limit to the number of times any product can be recycled. Some of the original material is always lost in reprocessing. Further if we reduce the pollution from cars by half, but double the number of cars, we shall be back to square one. Though we cannot avoid cars, more emphasis should be given for the use of bicycles, trains and public transport which poor people can easily afford and create less pollution. This means, we should bring about wider changes in society that would enable us to move away from an expansionist economy to one that maximizes the conservation of resources. It is estimated by some of the scientists that the use of materials can be reduced by a factor four without reducing the level of production. Indeed the Organization for Economic Cooperation is investing ways to reduce the use of materials in modern industrial societies by 90%.

Particularly in case of developing economies there is need to reorient its growth strategies in such a way that they do not initiate the historical growth strategies of the North but adopt clean technologies so that less pollution is generated per unit of GDP. Though per capita CO_2 emissions may be less in terms of national average in low income countries, they generate more pollution per unit of national income. The CO_2 emission per million dollars of GDP in 1989 as high as 670 tons of carbon in India and 1547 tons in China, compared with only 186 tons in high income countries (World Bank, 1992: 204). The poor countries have to shift from dirty to clear technologies and at the same time adequate growth opportunities for the poor to rise above mere subsistence.

(iv) Prevention of Consumerism

While eco-friendly and sustainable technologies are important as is population control, we cannot save the planet only through these methods. We have to consider reducing material needs, if anything is to be left for future generations. The report titled, 'People and Environment' World Resources, 1994-95 indicates the extent of consumerism that exists between different parts of the world. With regard to India, it is found that upper income group which constitutes 1.5 per cent (roughly 12 million people) of its population—accounts for about 75 per cent of the total consumption of electricity, petroleum and machine based household appliances. The report further points out that the urban population of India accounts for 39.6 per cent of total consumption, whereas 60.4 per cent of the total consumption is by the rural population.

Compared to a person in a developing country, one in an industrialized country uses 10 times as much energy, three times as much fresh water and 19 times as much aluminium.

The average consumer of a rich country uses 2000 kg. of average grade coal a year; while one in a poor country uses 400 kg a year. Compared with India, the US consumes 4.5 billion metric tons of natural resources or 18 metric tons per person with less than one-third of the population of India. Among other comparisons, the US consumes 12 times the amount of petroleum and three times as much iron ore compared to India.

This increased consumerism is also sustained on the ground that it will increase production, create more employment and make life happier and easier. But it is forgotten that consumerism increases the rape of the earth and creates more inconvenience than convenience. For example, when more cars are multiplied to meet the increased demand for faster commuter travel in our cities, diminishing returns are set in with a vengeance. You buy a car to get to work faster, but because thousands of others do the same, the cars get in one another's way, and Traffic slows down to average speeds below 10 km an hour. Traffic congestion, air pollution and fuel extravagance become the common features of most of the mega cities. This shows that unbridled consumerism will undermine even the most concerned efforts to safeguard the planet through eco-friendly technology and family planning. Hence, we can say that judicious use of diminishing resources like fossil fuels, development of alternative energy sources, coupled with population control, improvement of forest area and a less consumerist attitude, could actually make it possible for everyone to have a comfortable if modest life style and save something for the future generation to live a decent and dignified life.

We may also mention here that if the rich cannot maintain restraint and curb their consumption, there is nothing to prevent the poor from aspiring to achieve the standards of the rich in an ecologically disastrous race. It is true that there are conflict of interests between different groups. Nandkarni has given the example of forest produce—some are interested in minor forest produce and firewood for self-consumption, some others convert forest land into crop lands and some commercial groups try to exploit the timber from forest to secure more profit. Thus, there are livelihood interests and commercial interests and though both damage the environment, commercial interests damage much more than livelihood interests. If no reconciliation can be brought about by voluntary effort, state has to intervene to prevent the destruction of environment.

(v) Need for International Co-operation

We may also point out here that each country will have to design its development according to its social, cultural and economic milieu. Yet, irrespective of all these differences, sustainable development should be seen as a global objective. No country can develop in isolation from others. Hence, there should be an international understanding to manage the economies of different countries jointly so as to attain sustainable development.

Particularly there is need for international agreement to control global warming. As yet there does not seem to be any consensus about how the level of CO_2 emissions and other green house gases have to be stabilized or reduced. The developed countries seem to prefer freezing the allocation based on existing levels which Pearce has called 'grandfathering'. Such an approach would be extremely unfair to developing countries whose levels of CO_2 emissions are significantly lower than in developed countries even after taking into account larger population in the former. As per World Bank's 'World Development Report' (p. 204), the average emission in 1989 in low income countries was 0.32 ton of carbon per capita (0.21 ton in India) while it was as high as 3.26 tons per capita in high income countries. In the USA, the figure was as high as 5.34 tons. As mentioned earlier, per capita emission has increased almost four times both in developed and developing countries. That is why the Centre for Science & Environment (CSE) states in the RIO conference: 'The South needs ecological space to grow, which has already been colonized by the North. The poor are not even using a small fraction of their legitimate share of the global commons like the atmosphere thus permitting the North to pollute over the last century at little cost and build up its economy and industrial base extremely cheaply and rapidly' (CSE, 1992: 266).

The CSE statement therefore suggests to grant equal rights to all individuals on earth to the use of the atmosphere to certify the extremely inequitous position in the international ecological economic order. The granting of equal rights is consistent with the principle of equity and democracy. It is imperative that the international community should rise, as it must, to the challenge of securing sustainable human progress, otherwise ecological imbalance will create terrible catastrophe for the mankind.

REFERENCES

Brown, Lester and Others: Environment Who Cares, The World Report on Environment, *Economic Times*, 6.6.1994.

Brown, R. Lester, State of the World, A World and Others: Watch Institute Report on Progress Towards Sustainable Development, Prentice Hall of India Private Limited, New Delhi, 1989.

Brown, R., Lester and Flavin, Christopher, State of the World, Part I and Part II, *Young Indian*, Feb. 6, 1999 and Feb. 13, 1999.

D'Souza, J.B., Breathing: Easy, World Report on Environment, *Economic Times*, 6.6.1994.

Gold Smith, Edward and Others: Solution for Survival, *The World Report on Environment*, 6.6.1994.

Jain, Sashi, Dying of Consumption, Slowly, *Economic Times*, March 27, 1994.

Kennedy, Paul, Preparing for the 21st Century, Fontana Press, London, 1994.

Khoshoo, T.N., Towards a Sustainable Society, *Times of India*, March 1, 1994.

Levin, Richard, C., How to Stop Global Warming, *Economic Times*, 22.9.2008.

Misra, B., Political Economy of Development, Ajanta Prakashan, Delhi, 6, 1993.

Monbiot, George, The Truth about Climate Change is buried under Jargon *Times of India*, 6.12.2009.

Nandkarni, M.V., Political Economy of Sustainable Development, Review of Development and Change, Jan.-June, 1996, *Madras Institute of Development Studies*.

Our Common Future: The World Commission on Environment and Development, OUP, 1987.

Times of India: Every Breath You Take, April 16, 1994.

Vidyasagar, N., Informing Appliances to Talk Smart, *Times of India*, 29.11.1999.

World Bank, 1992: World Development Report, 1992—Development and Environment, Oxford, Oxford University Press.

CHAPTER

11

Prospects of Restructuring Higher Education

COLONIAL LEGACY

Though in the last 60 years, there is some improvement in higher education, with a large increase in Universities and Deemed Universities (from 30 to 500), Colleges (from 750 to about 24,000), our GER (Gross Enrolment Ratio) is very low, only 12.4 per cent, which is only one-half of the world average, and one-third of even the average for developing countries. Until 1999, India and China both had GER of about 6 per cent. In the last ten years, we have moved to 12.4 per cent but China has moved to 22 per cent (Narendra Jadhav). This does not augur well for a country like India which is hoping to become an economic super power. Without a substantial increase in access, India cannot make a noticeable change in higher education. Union HRD Minister, Kapil Sibal, therefore, points out that the task in higher education in the country is daunting as more Universities and Colleges are needed to achieve the increased gross enrolment ratio of 30 in the higher education by

2020. According to him India requires 800 Universities and 40 to 45 thousand Colleges to be built in 10 years. And if we look at the quality, it is far from satisfactory. Consider the research output. Until 1984, India and China were producing the same number of research papers in international journals. Today, according to Jadhav, China is producing five times more research papers than India.

It is true that the higher educational system in India has produced a few outstanding academic people equipped with scientific and technological capability, but by and large, the higher education is neither quite relevant nor effective to meet the challenges of the 21st century. Even Kothari Commission in its report (in the later part of sixties) pointed out that there is a general feeling in India that the situation in higher education is unsatisfactory and even alarming in some ways, that the average standard has been falling and that rapid expansion has resulted in lowering quality. During the British period, higher education remained an integral element of colonial underdevelopment. Apart from the fact that it did not serve Indian interests, there were a number of other distortions for which it was called dysfunctional. The elements of higher education which dominated the British period may be described as (a) low level of enrolment, (b) liberal nature of education, (c) concentration of higher education in and around selected port centres which served as a suction mechanism for exploitation, and (d) denial or unfair deal to most of the weaker sections of the community.

Though there were different motives in introducing higher education, it can be generalized that the colonial rulers used this device to create a set of educated people who can assist the government to perpetuate its rule in India and insulate the local people against the tides of modern industrial and scientific culture. Macaulay once said, "We must at present do our best to form a class who may be interpreters between us and the millions we govern, a class of persons, Indians in blood and colour but English in taste, in opinions, in morals and in intellect". And, as a matter of fact, a number of Indians who served the British were thoroughly denationalized, looking with contempt everything that was Indian. But the very same education gradually created an awakening in the country which developed a spirit of self-respect and national consciousness. Today it is recognized that education is not only an important element in improving high intellectual standards, but also to provide right kind of leadership for social and economic improvement and strive to promote equality and social justice by reducing social and cultural differences through diffusion of education.

NEED FOR INTELLECTUAL ADVENTURE

Radhakrishnan Commission has pointed out that Universities are the homes of intellectual adventure. This implies that the Universities would seek and cultivate new knowledge, engage vigorously and fearlessly in the pursuit of truth and to interpret old knowledge and beliefs in the light of new needs and discoveries. The intellectuals who come out from the Universities should give up the fatal obsession of the perfection of the past, that greatness is not to be attained in the present, that everything is already worked out and all that remains for the future ages of the world is pedantic imitation of the past. When they are hypnotized by our own past achievements, when all their efforts are to repeat a past success, they become fetish worshippers. If our cultural life is to retain its dynamism, they must give up idolatory of the past and strive to realize new dreams. This does not mean that they should blindly give up the great values of our past nor should they cling to beliefs simply because they are ancient. They should accept so much of ancient thought as is sympathetic to us. In other words, the chief source of spiritual nourishment for any people must be its own past perpetually rediscovered and renewed. Past is not to be treated as drag but as a strong launching pad for the future.

But the saddening fact is that in spite of tremendous development in education since independence, we have not been able to eliminate fanaticism in the country. We have a set of educated people who denounce everything that is modern, romanticize the past and even disregard the developments in science and technology which have revolutionized the social and economic life of the country. On the other, there are also people who look to the past with contemptuous feelings and worship the present with great reverence. Both these attitudes do not help to either promote cultural heritage nor the scientific outlook. A society without the knowledge of the past which has made it would be lacking in depth and dignity. Similarly, a society without scientific discoveries and technological improvements will remain stagnant forever. The present which moves backwards and forwards, which is a summary of the past and a prophecy of the future, is, as pointed out by Radhakrishnan Commission, hallowed ground and we who tread on it, should face it with quality of reverence and the spirit of adventure.

Again education should not mean accumulation of facts. Since education is both a training of minds and a training of souls, it should give both knowledge and wisdom. Plato distinguishes between factual information and understanding. Radhakrishnan Commission points out that no amount of factual information would make ordinary men into educated or virtuous men unless something is awakened in them, an innate ability to live the life of the soul. This implies that Universities should train intellectuals who become the sanctuaries of the inner life of the nation. Sir Arthur Lewis, making a distinction between Education and Development pointed out, "Education was not invented in order to enable men to produce more goods and services. The purpose of education is to enable men to understand better the world in which they live, so that they may more fully experience their potential capacities .....". On the other hand, while discussing investment strategy in education, Lewis would also produce more educated people than can be absorbed as a part of the process of economic development. This shows that education as a strategy in developing countries can be used for economic development by increasing technical skill of educated men to bring about changes in economic parameter.

But what we see in Universities is outdated content and dubious quality of education. As stated by Deputy Director-General of UNESCO: "The learning techniques . . . remain the same: the rote method, the technique of cramming, and, once the examination menace is passed, of forgetting all these useless impediments. The examination system is not an evaluation of a student's personality and intellectual equipment, his powers of thinking for himself, reflection, and reasoning.... Looked at as a business enterprise, the school and college present deplorable spectacle. We find in education antediluvian technology which would not survive for an instant in any other economic sector. The teaching methods and learning techniques . . . are rusty, cranky and antiquated". In the words of T.S. Eliot,

> Where is the wisdom we have lost in knowledge?
> Where is the knowledge we have lost in information?

All this implies that accumulation of facts cannot increase knowledge or wisdom. What is more, the acquisition of college certificates and higher degrees may not necessarily be associated with the students' improved ability to undertake productive work. Higher education is supposed to provide society with competent men and women trained in agriculture, medicine, science and technology and various other professions, which can provide necessary technical know-how for bringing about economic change of the country. It may be noted here that growing influence of telecommunications and advances of information technology have significantly influenced human life and provided an opportunity to expand the range of services and create new ways of delivery of the essential product of the Universities, the Knowledge. The higher education system has to accept this changing environment and mould the economic and social system to overcome the traditional boundaries. The Indian tradition had the conceit to anoint someone, someone who knows everything. So it is not surprising that research to create new knowledge does not come naturally to the Indian establishment. Precious little has been done so far to undo this damaging tradition.

Attainment of scientific know-how is one important element of educational attainments. This will make educational system more relevant to meet the social needs of modern age. It may also be noted here that a degree is not the end of education, because examinations cannot end the trials of life. Arnold Toynbee has rightly said, "It is both absurd and unjust to classify a person once for all, as being first class or third class when he is only twenty two years old. There are slow growers who blossom late in life and conversely there are brilliant starters who fail to fulfil their early promise".

AGENTS OF CHANGE

What we mean is that the Colleges or Universities cannot be rated high or low only on the basis of number of professional graduates they produce. If these graduates, even with first class, do not develop any self-reliance and only search for cosy jobs for maintaining their livelihood or to improve their economic status, they fail to discharge their duties to solve the real needs of development. The Colleges and Universities are supposed to produce trained men and women who can function as agents of economic and social change. It has been said that human resources constitute the ultimate basis for the wealth of nations. Capital and natural resources are passive factors of production; human beings are the active agents who accumulate capital, utilize natural resources, build economic organizations and carry forward national development both in economic and social spheres.

If a University is unable to develop the skills and knowledge of its students and the latter fail to utilize them effectively for national reconstruction, education does not serve any purpose. On the other hand, education may encourage attitudes and aspirations which are inimical to national interests. It has been observed at different levels that some of the educated people have become so self-centred that they do not think they have any obligation to the society. They try to improve their private interest even sometimes at the cost of the society.

If education does not create attitudes and values which can create a good life in individuals and society, it does not serve any social purpose. Particularly in case of India, the 'social' cost of education (i.e., the opportunity cost to society as a whole resulting from the need to finance costly educational expansion at higher levels when these limited funds might be more productively used in other sectors of the economy) increases rapidly as students climb the educational ladder. And the private costs (those borne by the student himself) increase more slowly or indeed may decline. When the society incurs so much expenditure for providing training to the students of higher education, they should try to do something to improve social life. In fact, education is not worth a penny for the learners if it does not help them to serve the community.

In an assessment of higher education, Moonis Raza also points out that education can be efficient and equitable if the majority of people, the poorer having proportionately more opportunities, are able to benefit from it; it is both inefficient and inequitous if only the affluent minority succeeds in garnering all the benefits. Education at higher level, particularly in developing countries should aim at (a) changing social structures in response to the needs of time, (b) assisting in the process of economic development, particularly of rural areas where vast majority of people live in poverty and squalor, and (c) establishing close links with Indian cultural traditions.

All these three aspects have special relevance for India. Changing social structure will enable men to meet the challenges of fast-changing future. As Arnold Toynbee has said, civilization is not a harbor, but a voyage. In a voyage, we meet a number of impediments. An old society like ours is steeped in many undesirable elements like superstition, exclusiveness, casteism, regionalism, linguism, etc. Human values and aspirations cannot survive without a thorough change in cultural and social milieu of the society. Education should serve as a route to social mobility.

QUEST FOR QUALITY OF LIFE

Education at the technical level should see that our people are on the move for a life of prosperity and abundance. Poverty anywhere is a danger to peace everywhere. Since educated people have the privilege of knowledge and technique, they should utilize such resources to ameliorate the economic condition of poor people. Growth with equity is one of the major objectives of Indian Planning. Growth without equity increases structural disequilibrium, perpetuates poverty which is itself a constraint to growth. And Equity without growth is, as pointed out by Moonis Raza and others, a stagnant cesspool, wherein only misery, ignorance, obscurantism and superstition can be equitably distributed. Though the Government in a developing country has to play a dominant role in removing poverty and unemployment and accelerate the process of development, the educated and enlightened have to take active interest and participate in this social and economic change.

Gandhiji analyzing the concept of Antyodaya once gave the following Mantra:

> I will give you a talisman. Whenever you are in doubt or when the self-becomes too much with you, apply the following test:

Recall the face of the poorest and the weakest man whom you may have seen and ask yourself if the step you contemplate is going to be of any use to him, will he gain anything by it? Will it restore him to a control over his own life and destiny? In other words, will it lead to Swaraj for the hungry and spiritually starving millions?

And the most important aspect of education is that the Indian Universities should be integrated into Indian life. As pointed out by Prem Kirpal in his "Role of Universities as Agents of Change", the Indian intellectual remains a cultural displaced person, nostalgically treasuring his threads of communication with western countries. The intellectual community is still divorced from traditional culture as a result of which there is a complete alienation of these educated people with common people of villages. Pandit Jawaharlal Nehru addressing the convocation of Allahabad University in 1947 after independence where the writer had the privilege to be present as a student of the University pointed out, "A University stands for humanism, for tolerance, for reason, for the adventure of ideas and for the search of truth. It stands for the onward march of the human race towards even higher objectives. If the Universities discharge their duties adequately, then it is well with the nation and the people". All this implies that educated people should change their outlook and give a new sense of identity and quality of life to the people.

HOW CAN WE CHANGE EDUCATIONAL SYSTEM

How can we reorient the educational system so as to meet the real requirements and aspirations of the people? At present, higher education is often consigned to the citadels of elites' content with their narrow specialization and remaining aloof from the problems of larger society. Since educational systems largely reflect and reproduce, rather than alter, the economic and social structure of the societies in which they exist, any programme or set of policies designed to make education more relevant for development becomes a failure. In other words, it does not respond to the needs of changing social structure. On the other hand, the content of education reflects, as pointed out by Malcolm S. Adiseshiah, the values of the dominant class. He, therefore, asserts that we cannot have an educational system promoting knowledge, discipline, equity and truth unless we have a society embodying them. While education can be a pace setter for society, equally and even more, education, including the University, is also alas, a faithful mirror or society.

Though an improvement in the social system is an important problem and requires a number of revolutionary changes we cannot deal with such a problem in an essay on educational development. We will, therefore, confine our attention to changes in educational system which can serve the interests of common man. There are many areas where some reform can be initiated to change the outlook of educated men and make the educational programmes and processes related to the needs of the changing society.

(i) Reduce Class Distinction in Education

First we have to consider why there is heavy demand for higher education. Todaro in his "The Economics of Education" points out that most people in less developed countries do not demand education for its intrinsic benefits but simply because it is the only way to get highly paid employment. These derived benefits must in turn be weighed against the costs of education. There are two aspects here. One aspect is the difference in the wage or income differential between jobs in the modern sector and those outside it which is generally called traditional sector. The demand for higher education is positively related to the modern-traditional sector wage differential. If we can reduce such wage differentials, we can restrict the demand for higher education to a great extent. And the wage differentials can be reduced provided the productivity of the traditional sector can be increased substantially through greater investment in infrastructure and other aspects of development.

Again the demand for education is inversely related to direct private costs of education. The private cost of higher education is exceedingly low. And so long as higher education remains essentially privately free and modern sector jobs are relatively lucrative, the demand for higher education must be excessive. It is, therefore, imperative that (a) educational costs borne privately should be substantially increased, (b) the rate of educational subsidy at a higher level be reduced, and (c) the meritorious and deserving students should be given adequate assistance both by subsidy and loan so that they continue their studies without any difficulty. If these three measures are taken the demand for higher education can be curtailed to a great extent.

The educated people in modern jobs also acquire certain amount of social distinction particularly in developing countries like India. During the British period, the upper class Indian elite by supporting imperial rule enjoyed some crumbs of privilege and affluence. Even after independence and in spite of democratic set up, there was little change in cultural learning and the same alien notions continued in administration for which the employees in the modern sector, with a 'babu culture' enjoyed privileges of power and position which were denied to the people in the traditional sector. These distortions can be corrected if (a) degrees are de-linked with employment, (b) course contents are changed in conformity with national identity, and (c) class room learning is integrated with rural work apart from the fact that rural sector is developed along with the urban sector with higher investment.

(ii) Degrees should not Determine Employment Pattern

The University degrees now determine the employment pattern. That is the main reason why a large number of non-academic students take admission in colleges and Universities to secure degrees. Award of degrees necessarily leads to examinations which are, according to Malcolm, the single most generator of corruption, cheating, violence, to being an unscientific exercise. Examinations proliferate the production of profuse note books and coaching classes. Education, therefore, becomes a business. The University's objective of learning becomes distorted with cramming of points enumerated in note books. The students do not read original books, do not apply their imagination and nor get a chance to think or apply their minds for solving the problems of the country. And again, universities create a number of educational outcasts called failed candidates which is a colossal waste of manpower. While acknowledging the need to motivate the youth, the types of examination lead to demotivation and demoralization. The system results in severe mental stresses and strains amongst sensitive and growing youth. The system of examination cannot be oblivious to these trends and tendencies. If degrees and examinations are eliminated, not only the number of students in higher education will be less, the quality of education will considerably improve. The employing agencies instead of depending on degree holders will devise their own system of evaluation to select candidates for their institutions.

Another advantage which would accrue from the abolition of degrees and examinations is that there would be intimate contact between the students and teachers. Because of large number of students, there has been an increasing measure of mechanization and routinisation of teaching and evaluation. In the process the universities have, as pointed out by Suma Chitnis in his, 'Some Dilemmas in Higher Education' been transformed from small communities of teachers and students engaged in the quest for knowledge, to large organizations which conduct education in highly impersonal manner. The administration in the University becomes also bureaucratic in character with large number of non-academic staff in the office, in the senate, syndicate and academic council exercising tremendous influence in policy decisions of the University. Devoid of their influence in academic matters, the academic staff engages themselves in politics to secure certain privileges in the University. If the size of the University is reduced, the cultural atmosphere of the University will have a better chance to flourish.

(iii) Change in Course Programme

Another area which requires immediate attention is the change in course programme. The course programme does not respond to changes in society. In most of the cases, it is found that the content of educational programmes reflects the value of the dominant class. The training and skill imparted in the colleges and universities perpetuate the economic and social system instead of making any attempt to change the educational programme and make it more relevant for developmental needs. We cannot implant an educational system which is prevalent in developed countries. Each society must try to orient its own programme of educational activities to solve the basic problems of development. India's major problems are poverty, unemployment, illiteracy, squalor, etc. It is said that the University is a liberal and liberating agency for individual and social transformation. But if the educational programmes follow the traditional pattern which perpetuates the existing system of social rigidity and assists the rich to become more richer, the University loses its importance as an agent of change. It is, therefore, imperative that the course programmes should be in conformity with the real needs of a poor society. In other words, the course programme should provide the students the knowledge, skill and ideas which will enable them to function efficiently in rural environment.

Gandhiji analyzing the importance of national education and commenting on the existing mode, made a pertinent remark in 1921 which is even valid today. According to him, "the student is never taught to have any pride in his surroundings. The higher he goes (in the field of education) the farther he is removed from his home, so that at the end of his education, he becomes estranged from his surroundings. He feels no poetry about his home life. The village scenes are a sealed book to him. . . ." What is most unfortunate is that our educated youth suffer intellectually and emotionally and become alienated from their motherland, village, community and the nation. Greater the level of education higher is the alienation. In such an environment education cannot prepare people's minds to receive new ideas and accept new tools, new relationships and new forms of organization.

(iv) Participation of Intellectuals in Rural Work Programme

It follows from this that each student along with class room learning must take up some ameliorative activity in rural areas. This should be a part and parcel of course programme and both the teachers and students must be involved in the process of rural work. No educational system can, as pointed out by Todaro, make an effective contribution to the nation-building activity if the economic and social structures in which the intelligensia operate are inimical to the maximum participation of all people in both the work and the rewards of nation-building. The alienation of the intellectual from the masses of people have not only divided the Indian society, but weakened the identity of the nation and distorted the methods and goals of Indian development. If we can establish a link between class room learning with rural work programme, it would help to reduce the growing gap between the poor and rich and help the University contribute its knowledge and technology to improved living conditions of the poor. What we have seen in India that investment in education (human capital) between 1950-70 produced some increase in life expectancy and little change in fertility, population growth or productivity. Therefore, even today, the return to higher education in India remains high enough to justify additional investment (Ram and Schutz—1979).

(v) Need for Additional Investment

It is unfortunate that our investment in education is not adequate. The Kothari Commission in 1966 recommended for an investment of 6 per cent of GDP in education. Even after 44/45 years, the investment comes to only 3.5 per cent. Of course, there is now an attempt to step up investment in education. In the 10th plan, the total allocation for education was only Rs. 9000 crore. In the 11th plan, the allocation has increased to Rs. 84,000 crore. A time has come when probably there is greater necessity to increase student contribution to higher education. When the Universities are facing great difficulty in meeting required resources in meeting the demands of different areas of development and facing deficit almost every year and the Government has to meet the enormous cost of Right to Education and Food Security, a part of Higher Education has to be met by students who can easily afford to pay such expenses. Those who cannot afford to pay, they may be given loan by the Government at a concessional rate with the condition that they will be required to begin paying back the costs paid as soon their incomes are above a threshold as recommended by a Statutory authority. Since the graduates of higher education with improved skill have great opportunity to secure good jobs in some of the private companies which are being opened in recent years or in expanding government avenues of employment, they ought to make a contribution to meet the cost of their education.

Lord Browne report in England notes that as a consequence of compelling evidence in favour of substantial private gains from higher education, "it is not surprising that the argument for a private contribution in higher education has been made—and won—in countries with wide range of political values such as Australia, New Zealand, the United States, Canada, Japan and Korea". It also states, "throughout the range of submission that we have received, there is broad agreement among groups with an interest in higher education that those who benefit directly from higher education as graduates ought to make a contribution to the costs. Take the case of England. Until 1997, college and university students paid no tuition fees whatsoever. With public expenditure on higher education stagnating, on the recommendation of the Lord Dearing Committee, which reported in 1997, a fee of 1000 pound was introduced. But since it proved inadequate, The Higher Education Act, 2004 which came into effect in 2006, raised tuition fees further, but placing a cap on it at 3000 pound. This shows there is a sea change in the attitude of advocates of welfare economists who supported free university education earlier.

CONCLUDING REMARKS

Our analysis implies a few important changes in higher education. The main purpose of education should not be conceived only from the point of view of economic development. It is a part of broad feature of educational development. The Universities would seek and cultivate new knowledge, understand better the world in which they live and at the same time make the educational system more relevant to meet the social and economic needs of modern age. Both aspects of educational needs should be combined together so that none is emphasized more than the other. First, we have to try to improve the quality of education. In the context of economic and social change, there is need to alter the course programme which can have some relevance to the social and economic structure of the country. Educational system should not perpetuate inequality or social rigidity. It should try to modernize the economy and also the society by active participation in developmental programmes of the country. Educated people have privileges which are denied to others. These privileges must be used for social interest. Higher education has become very costly. Though the Government can subsidize higher education for poor and deserving students, the rich ones must bear a large part of expenditure so as to provide adequate facilities for improving training programme. And instead of awarding degrees, the Universities should try to increase the process of learning of the students which can improve their creative potential to meet the challenges of modern society.

We may further add that the University is not only an academic institution, it is also a social organization. The University has, therefore, to promote new ideas, provide skilled manpower and render service for the furtherance of human equality, human dignity and human development. The system of education should be such that it should create an element of creativity, promote original thinking, sharpen human intellect and harness the great human potential which is our biggest asset to achieve overall development of the society.

We can follow the five-point strategy of education as enunciated by Mashelkar in his address to the Indian Science Congress Session, held in Pune in January 2000:

(i) Women Centred Family
(ii) Youth Centred Education

(iii) Human Centred Development
(iv) Community Centred Society
(v) Innovation Centred India

In point (ii) we have used youth in place of child. We can further add that higher education should be youth-centric instead of being exam-centric. We guess this approach will improve an indigenous system, rooted in Indian culture, but at the same time committed to progress on par with other developed countries, based on science and technology.

References

Adiseshiah, Malcolm S., Role of Universities as Agents of Change in Higher Education in the Eighties, Opportunities and Objectives, edited by J. Vera Raghavan, Lancer International, New Delhi, 1985.

Chitnis, Suma, Some Dilemmas in Higher Education in 'Higher Education in the Eighties'.

Kirpal Prem, Role of Universities as Agents of Change, in 'Higher Education in the Eighties'.

Kothari Commission Report, 1964-65.

Lewis W. Arthur, Education and Economic Development, *International Science Journal*, 14(4), 1962, pp. 685-99.

Panagariya, Arvind, Raising Investment in Higher Education, *Economic Times*, 27.10.2010.

Jadhav, Narendra, Member, Planning Commission—'Education System has a long way to go', *Statesman*, 12.6.2010.

Radhakrishnan Commission Report, 1948-49.

Ram, Rati and Theodore, W. Schultz, "Life Span, Health, Savings and Productivity", *Economic Development and Cultural Change*, Vol. 27, 1979, pp. 399-421.

Raza, Moonis, Aggarwal, Y.P., Hasan Mahbub, Higher Education in India—An Assessment, in "Higher Education in the Eighties".

Saiyadain, K.G. and Others, The Educational System, Oxford University Press, 1945.

Todaro, Michael P., Economics for a Developing World, Longman, 1977.

CHAPTER

12

Problems and Prospects of University Administration

It may be mentioned here that educational administration is not the same thing as public administration. There are at least two reasons for this. First, teachers, research scholars and students are not subordinates to the administrator. They are all partners to improve the quality of educational standard, those standards of thought and action which make an individual and a nation. As the Prime Minister Jawaharlal Nehru (1947) addressing the Convocation of Allahabad University (of which the author was a student of the University at that time), eloquently stated, "A University stands for humanism, for tolerance, for reason, for progress, for the adventure of ideas and for the search of truth. It stands for the onward march of the human race towards even higher objectives". Education, in fact, is the process that enables you to have knowledge. Education allows us to access the collected wisdom, learning and conclusion of the human race since methods of knowledge transmission began. Gilbert, K. Chesterton therefore says,

'Education is simply the soul of a society as it passes from one generation to another'.

Second, the Universities must bring the academic talents of their faculties and idealism of their youthful students to bear on the problems of the common people of the land. As the University Grants Commission, 1987 affirms, "All Universities and Colleges should develop close relationships, of mutual services and support, with their local communities, and all students and teachers must be involved in such programmes as an integral part of their education".

Even though the nature of public administration in recent years has changed, it is still more concerned with maintenance of law and order which in most cases alienates the administrators from the common man. Even when the public administrators are entrusted with development work, the officers hardly maintain any productive relationship with the multitude of common men who are deprived of the minimum privileges of a dignified life. Public administration, by and large, is a bureaucratic organisation without having any conducive environment for meaningful and fruitful co-operation among different levels of administration (which is hierarchical in character) and with common men who are desperately trying to meet the challenges of life. Educational administration therefore implies a different connotation in comparison to public administration.

ROLE OF THE VICE-CHANCELLOR

First we have to examine the role of the Vice-Chancellor who is the Chief Executive of the University. Effective managerial performance depends upon the successful interplay of a number of factors including the personal competence (in terms of skills, knowledge and aptitude) of the Chief Executive and his senior colleagues, and the existence of a stable institutional framework in the form of policies, rules, guidelines, conventions and information. The Chief Executive has to be not only a leader, but also a motivator, co-ordinator and facilitator. He has to have the skill for guiding actions and controlling situations in a manner that yields results that best meet the objectives of the University (Power).

This means the Chief Executive must have : (a) a clear perception about the goals and objectives of the University, (b) an understanding of strengths and weaknesses of the institution, (c) a full knowledge of the functioning of all divisions and units in the institution, (d) the ability to take timely (and sometimes unpleasant) decisions, and (e) an appreciation of the need to change and with it the willingness to adopt new and innovative strategies for improving the quality of the institution.

As Goleman (1998) and Watson (2000) point out, a successful administrator must have the following attributes in order to succeed in his endeavour :

(1) Self-awareness, i.e. an understanding of one's administrative style and behavioural pattern and its impact on others. This requires a capacity to correctly judge the mood of different stakeholders and take decisions which are fair and reasonable.

(2) Self-control, i.e. the ability to control one's disruptive impulses and moods and to think before acting. This implies that he should not take any decision in haste, examine things calmly and methodically and take actions after judicious exercise of judgement.

(3) Motivation, i.e. the ability to pursue goals and work with commitment without thought of personal benefit. If decisions are actuated by personal benefit, the Chief Executive cannot inspire confidence among his colleagues, students or other officers who are working with him.

(4) Empathy, i.e. the ability to understand and appreciate the feelings and emotions of other stakeholders of the University. In other words, there should be equanimity coupled with a sensitivity to the feelings of co-workers.

(5) Social skills, i.e. proficiency in managing relationships, finding common ground and building bridges. In other words, he takes into confidence his colleagues and other partners and shares with them regarding the programmes of actions that should be

pursued to improve the academic standard of the University. Nothing should be done in secrecy.

It is of course difficult to find people with all these attributes. However, the Chief Executive has to make strenuous effort to discharge the heavy responsibility that is bestowed on him. When one occupies a higher position, it is expected that he would rise to the occasion and demonstrate a reasonable level of administrative efficiency to achieve the prescribed goals of the University.

MAINTENANCE OF AUTONOMY

Another area which is important in University administration is autonomy. We emphasize autonomy because over the years there has been a continued erosion of the freedom, rights and privileges of the Universities. As Tight (1988) points out, "academic freedom refers to the freedom of individual academics to study, teach, research and publish without being subject to or causing undue interference". Now there is an attempt to prevent not only to change the courses of studies but also to appoint even senior staff members by political authorities. Even in many cases the Vice-Chancellor is appointed on political affiliation. Further, since many of the students in colleges and Universities have been given the right to vote, political parties try to utilize the students and some times staff members which destroy the academic ethos of the Universities.

Another reason why political interference becomes easy is that many of the functionaries of the University do not discharge their responsibilities, the Vice-Chancellor does not attend his office, shows favour to some who are loyal to him even though they do not have necessary academic excellence, some of the teachers neglect their teaching or research assignments, there are financial irregularities and many such other causes which give a chance to the Government to interfere. It is true that an academic institution is not an ivory tower. As Iqbal Narain notes, "educational administration, in general, and particularly University administration, cannot be studied in isolation from the dynamics—in fact, the pulls and pressures—of polity, economy and society in the country".

Particularly when the educational institutions depend on financial support of the Government M.S. Gore, the Vice-Chancellor of Bombay University (1986) while discussing inadequate funds provided by the Government and their repercussions, said that the Vice-Chancellor has to function on the basis of a fast dwindling prestige, since he is constantly at the doorstep of government officials for money to keep the University going and, on the other hand, he has to compromise at every step to get his way in bodies whose members are not accountable for the impact of their decisions on the working of the University.

Iqbal Narain further adds, "This is even more true when Universities have to turn to the government almost everyday for the maintenance of law and order on the campus, on the one hand, and for finances, for survival, leave alone development, on the other". Again, 'whatever still remains of University autonomy is doomed when teachers, instead of setting their own house in order, run to the government frequently to inform them that the University administration is being mismanaged and they should come to its rescue'. This implies that the Vice-Chancellor and University bodies have, on occasions, given the government a reason to intervene by taking actions that placed a liability on the government.

Though it is admitted that the government has a right to intervene whenever there is a dislocation in normal functioning of the University, such intervention should not be to control the University authorities, but to help them to discharge their responsibilities with greater efficiency. The Gajendra Gadkar Committee Report (UGC, 1971, pp. 9-10) states, "The concept of University autonomy is often misunderstood. It is not a legal concept", not even a 'constitutional concept'. It is an ethical concept and an academic concept. The concept does not question that, in a democratic society like ours, legislatures are ultimately sovereign, and have a right to discuss and determine the question of policy relating to education, including higher education. . . . The concept of University autonomy, however, means that it would be appropriate on the part of democratic legislatures not to interfere with the administration of

University life, both academic and non-academic. The claim for autonomy is made by the Universities not as a matter of privilege, but on the ground that such an autonomy is a condition precedent if the Universities are to discharge their duties and obligations effectively and efficiently:

This emphasizes that if the autonomy of the Universities is jeopardized they will not be able to deliver education of required quality and relevance. However, it has to be emphasized that the autonomy will have to be complemented by accountability. The accountability of a University can be discussed with respect to its administrative, academic and finance-related actions.

Administrative accountability relates to the managerial functions that are necessary for the smooth functioning of the University. The Chief Executive may not be able to take quick decisions and implement them effectively, if the organizational structure is heavily bureaucratized and requires confirmation by several bodies. To prevent such bureaucratization, it is desirable to have decentralization of authority with specific powers and responsibilities assigned to appropriate agencies. However, along with decentralization, the Chief Executive should coordinate activities of different units through frequent meetings and interactions, monitor the progress of work from time to time and assess performance periodically, through recognized performance indicators.

Academic accountability is concerned with the implementation of academic programmes to ensure minimum standards of education. Two or three problems most of the time create dissensions in the academic field. Courses are not covered in time. Some of the students often demand postponement of examinations. Even when examinations are held, there is delay in publication of results. It is the responsibility of the Vice-Chancellor to take personal initiative in tackling these problems by involving teachers, students and officers who are entrusted with the conduct of examinations and publication of results. An efficient information system along with good inter-personal relationship may solve some of these problems without much difficulty.

Financial accountability deals with not only procurement of funds, but also efficient utilization of resources. When funds are plenty there is proliferation of programmes and activities. When funds are scarce, there is an all-round cut in expenditure. This is not a healthy feature of financial management. Since in most cases, resources are limited, two things should be done for efficient utilization of funds. The budget should be divided in two parts, one is core and the other is peripheral or additional. The core budget should take care of essential requirements of the institute and peripheral budget to meet the optimum needs of the programme. And second, there should be constant monitoring of expenditure so that there is no misutilisation of funds.

RESTRUCTURING UNIVERSITY EDUCATION

Today it is recognized that University education is not only an important element in improving high intellectual standard, but also to provide right kind of leadership for social and economic improvement and strive to promote equality and social justice by reducing social and cultural differences through diffusion of education. The National Policy on Education, 1986 (Government of India) also visualized that education is to be:

(a) A process of empowerment which is to be promoted through the development of knowledge, skills and values (Education for Development), and
(b) An instrument of social change that provides means for upward economic and social mobility through enhancement of qualification (Education for Equality).

The major question which needs a critical analysis is how far higher education in India has been an instrument for the nation's progress, security and welfare and what kind of changes should be introduced so that they can meet the challenges of the 21st century.

(1) Partnership between World of Knowledge and World of Work

It will not be an exaggeration to say that most of the

Universities in India have an 'ivory tower existence', sharply differentiated between theory and practice and placed a premium on aloofness. The traditional value system has made them more or less elitist in character and divorced from realities of life. A time has come when the Universities will have to function under the all pervading influence of the electronic communication revolution which has underwritten world economy on the basis of globalised knowledge, accelerated innovation and facilitated individual access to information and skills (Lucas, 1998a). The Director General of UNESCO (Mayer, 1991) also pointed out, "I should like to see the University cultivate closer relations with the worlds of business, commerce, industry, agriculture, journalism and administration . . .". This means the Universities in the coming years should build partnerships with the various sectors of the society. The growing relationship between the 'World of Knowledge' and 'World of Work' would facilitate employment opportunities for all those who get the privilege of studying in Universities.

(2) Access

Since higher education investments are important for economic growth, increase in individuals' productivity and incomes also having significant external benefits, it is necessary that access to higher education should significantly increase to utilize the benefits of knowledge society. In fact a highly competitive knowledge society will make unprecedented demands on Universities in the areas of higher education. Though there has been some improvement in the number of students, yet the stark reality is that only 11 to 12% of India's population in the relevant age group of 17 to 23 is generally getting the benefit of higher education compared to over 50% in OECD countries and 21% in middle income countries. Though India has reached the stage of middle income countries, the level of higher education is not more than that of low income countries. Every effort has therefore to be made to increase the level of higher education at least up to 20% during the second decade of twenty first century.

(3) Relevance and Quality

The type of education imparted in most of the Universities is not relevant to the needs of the society. There is a mismatch between what is taught in our academic institutions and requirements of the industry, business, administration, the professions and 'society at large'. According to World Declaration on Higher Education, 'Relevance in higher education should be assessed in terms of the fit between what society expects of institutions and what they do'. Relevance is a dynamic concept, it goes on changing from time to time according to social and economic change. Kothari Commission Report therefore emphasized that there has to be : (a) a radical improvement in the quality and standard of higher education to make it an instrument for the nation's progress, security and welfare, and (b) an expansion of higher education to meet manpower requirement of the nation and rising social ambitions and expectations of the people.

This implies that since there is explosion of knowledge and new areas of innovation in the technique of production, students should have the capacity to adapt themselves to the constantly changing needs of a knowledge-based society. Therefore, University courses of higher education should change from time to time in order to enable the students to convert information into knowledge. There should not be a rigid course programme. As has been done in most of the developed countries, there should be a flexible structure of course programme, a 'cafeteria type' approach which will allow the students to select courses from a wide ranges of options. A time has come when teaching has to shift from teacher-oriented to student-oriented courses.

However to improve the quality of higher education, we have to make huge investment in infrastructure so as to provide basic facilities for introduction of knowledge-based course programme. We have now a few 'islands of excellence in a sea of mediocrity'. There cannot be any worthwhile change with only a few 'showpieces of excellence'. There are Universities where you do not have adequate class rooms, the class rooms that are available are not properly cleaned, latrines adjacent to class rooms give stinking smell, libraries do not get up-to-date journals or recent books, some of the teachers hardly take their classes and even if they take, they never come prepared. In view of this, it can be safely said that such Universities will fail in their ability to keep pace with the demands of technology or social needs.

(4) Need for Change in Examination System

Examinations have been be-all and end-all of University administration in India. In some cases examinations continue throughout the year. One of the criteria to evaluate the success of the Vice-Chancellor whether he can hold the examination and publish its results in time. Very often there are strikes by some of the students to postpone the examination and the administration has to submit to their demands to avoid troubles. The examination results do not really judge the merit of students. Many examiners evaluate the examination papers only by counting points. Students therefore prepare for the examinations on the basis of rote learning and memorizing. There is no scope for original thinking.

Some drastic changes should be taken to enable the students to acquire knowledge instead of only trying to get degrees by hook or crook. There will be no harm if degrees are abolished. Because different institutions in the job market are now making their separate evaluation to select candidates for jobs. Second, instead of having University examination at a centralized level which sometime leads to leakage of papers, fraud and indiscipline, the teacher concerned may evaluate their students in class rooms on the basis of internal assessment, class discussion and by giving assignment for presentation of papers in class rooms. A continuous process of evaluation will reduce the burden of the University, avoid malpractice and indiscipline and enable the students to acquire some knowledge instead of memorizing only points which they forget just after the examination.

(5) Financing Higher Education

Finally, we may just indicate whether the state should have some responsibility in financing higher education. It is wrong to think that the state should not bother about higher education. The quality of higher education not only improves the status of the country but also provides plenty of scope for intellectual advancement. But this does not mean that the private agencies should not participate in providing financial support for higher education. Even in some of the capitalist states, there are State Universities, where the state plays important role in providing adequate funds. However, in view of the importance of primary and secondary education for which the state has a major responsibility of providing finance in India and there are resource constraints, an effective cooperation between the state and private agencies will go a long way in promoting the quality of higher education. Development of higher education is not only the responsibility of one agency, it is a societal responsibility for which all the beneficiaries should make effective contribution.

References

Gore, M.S. (1986), Universities and the Government, *University News*, Vol. 34, Jan.

Government of India (1966), Report of the Education Commission (1964-66), Education and National Development, GOI, New Delhi.

Government of India (1985), Challenge of Education: A Policy Perspective, GOI, New Delhi.

Government of India (1986), National Policy on Education, 1986, GOI, New Delhi.

Narain, Iqbal (1987), Administration of Higher Education in India published in 'Education and the Process of Change', edited by Ratna Ghosh and Mathew Zachariah, Sage Publications, 1987, New Delhi.

Power, K.B. (2002), 'Indian Higher Education', A Conglomerate of Concepts, Facts and Practices, Concept Publishing Company, 2002, New Delhi.

CHAPTER

13

Financing of Higher Education in India

"Human History becomes more and more a race between Education and Catastrophe".

—H.G. Wells

Though in the last six decades there has been impressive growth in higher education, with a large increase in Universities and Deemed Universities (from 30 to 500), Colleges from (750 to about 24,000) and students (from 0.2 million to about 20 million), the spread of higher education has still been confined to 11 to 12 per cent in India with a population of more than 1.20 billion. Russia with a population of 145 million has the same number. The US with a population 300 million has three times as many people with tertiary education. The importance of higher education can be seen from the fact that in most developed countries, four-fifths of the total income is return to human capital and four-fifths of the annual rate of growth is attributed to the growth in the productivity of human beings. The lesson for India is apparent.

We must invest more in education and human resource development, especially at the tertiary level. India has one advantage of 'demographic dividend' in the sense that the size of the working-age population is expected to grow until the year 2040. If we have to avail this dividend, we have to expand the opportunities for higher education, so that the young people should have skills to compete in the job market (Chidambaram).

But the unfortunate part is, inspite of considerable increase in institutions of higher education, the enrolment of students in higher educational institutions has not made much progress. The Union Commerce Ministry in 'A Consultation Paper on Higher Education in India and GATs : An Opportunity' published recently indicates the enrolment in higher education institutes is 10.5 million, which is just 11 per cent of the total relevant age group (17-23 years) in the population. On this count, India fares poorly compared to most South-East Asian countries like Philippines (31 per cent), Thailand (19 per cent), Malaysia (27 per cent) and China (22 per cent). What is more disturbing is that there is a significant slide in the growth of higher education enrolments locally during 2000-05 compared to the last two decades. While student enrolments had grown by some 20 per cent between 2000-05, they grew nearly 100 per cent in 1990-2000 and 57 per cent between 1980-90.

If we take the case of number of higher institutions, they have touched 57 per cent between 2000-05 against 92 per cent in 1990-2000 and 22 per cent between 1980-90. In absolute terms, India has the third largest number of higher education enrolment after China and the US. And India tops global charts with about 18000 institution. This means the average number of students per educational institutions here is lower than in the US and China. Raising seats in institutions of higher learning by about 50 per cent would require an investment of Rs. 20,000 to Rs. 25,000 crore. Regarding public expenditure on higher education, the paper says India is among the lowest in the world, with public expenditure per student at $ 406, compared to China ($ 2728), Brazil ($ 3986), Indonesia ($ 666) and Malaysia ($ 625).

The National Policy on Education (NPE), 1986 as modified in 1992 had set a goal of expenditure on education of 6 per cent of the GDP (as recommended by Kothari Commission). As against this target, the combined total expenditure on education by Central and State Governments was 3.49 per cent of GDP in 2004-05 (BE) which was lower than the average of 3.8 per cent of GDP for the developing countries. And the expenditure on higher education is lower, at 0.1 per cent of GDP and for science and technology education, it is 0.05 per cent of GDP (Anil D. Ambani). Ambani's calculation also shows India spends barely $ 3 billion on research which is less than 1 per cent of GDP whereas the US spends US $208 billion on research annually which is about 2.6 per cent of its GDP. One calculation of Economic Times (Editorial 12.12.06) shows that India spends $ 6 billion on R&D in a year whereas General Motor's R&D budget comes to about $ 10 billion.

In the Tenth Plan Document, it is specifically mentioned that the quality of higher education needs improvement through modernisation of syllabi, examination reforms and greater attention to issues of governance. It is also admitted that the part of the problem facing Universities is the inadequate provision of budgetary resources from the Government. But at the same time there is a categorical statement that since budget resources are limited, and such resources as are available, need to be allocated to expanding primary education, it is important to recognise that the Universities must make greater efforts to supplement resources from other sources (Tenth Plan, Vol. 1, p. 17).

All this arises because when the Finance Ministry considered the question of reducing financial subsidy published a discussion paper in which it was stated that subsidies should be given to only merit services and not to non-merit services. And in respect of education, the Discussion Paper stated that primary education is a 'merit service' because its benefits "spread well beyond the immediate recipients" while higher education is a 'non-merit' service because "most subsidies to higher education accrue predominantly to the better-off sections of society as they have an overwhelming advantage in competing out prospective candidates from the other sections in getting admission to courses that are characterized by scarcity of seats". In a more specific statement, the Paper says, "A significant portion of subsidies in higher education is appropriated by the middle to high income groups, because shortages of seats in this sector are cleared by quality based clearing in the shape of entrance examination, interview, group discussion, etc. where the proper sections of society are easily competed out".

The World Bank document, "Higher Education : The Lessons of Experience" (1994) also states, "Indeed it is arguable that higher education should not have the highest priority claim on incremental public resources available for education in many developing countries especially those that have not yet achieved adequate access, equity and quality at the primary and secondary levels. This is because the social rates of return on investment in primary and secondary education usually exceed the returns on higher education. . . ." (World Bank, 1994, p. 3).

Tunnermann in a reply to the World Bank observations points out "A core problem is that conventional estimations on the return rates do not equate the social benefits of education at any of the levels—the existence of those benefits in higher education, in functions covering not only teaching activities, but also research and strengthening of national identity (nation building). The social return rates do not take into consideration the non-private benefits of education emerging from 'positive external factors'. The latter are higher in the case of higher education than for other educational levels, which might put in doubt the legitimacy of a redistribution of the public expenditure allocation in education to the detriment of higher education.

If we consider the implication of the Discussion Paper which considered the reduction of subsidy in higher education we find that it has made a number of assumptions. The assumptions are: (1) The benefits of higher education accrue primarily to recipients (and that society at large does not benefit substantially), (2) A reduction in the number of recipients would not be harmful to the nation's interests, (3) A substantial increase in user prices is possible, (4) The beneficiaries of higher education are predominantly from the middle and higher classes, and (5) The middle class, including the higher salaried class, will be able to afford unsubsidized or nominally subsidised professional education (*University News*).

The assumptions made in the Discussion Paper do not fully realise the benefits of higher education. It is not correct to think that the benefits of higher education accrue primarily to the recipients, higher education plays a dominant role in national development. It provides the competencies that are required in different spheres of human activity ranging from administration to agriculture, business, industry, health, communication and extending to the arts and culture. The World Bank document referred to above also states, "Higher education is of paramount importance for economic and social development. Institutions of higher education have the main responsibility for equipping individuals with advanced knowledge and skill required for positions of responsibility in government, business and to professions.... Estimated social rates of return of 10 per cent or more in many developing countries also indicate that investments in higher education contribute to increase in labour productivity and to higher long-term economic growth, which are essential for poverty alleviation". UNESCO in a policy paper, Document of Policies for the Change and Development of Higher Education (1995) maintains that there is a well established correlation between investment in higher education and the level of social, economic and cultural development of a country. It further maintains, 'State and society must perceive higher education not as a burden on federal budgets but as a long-term domestic investment, in order to increase economic competitiveness, cultural development and social cohesion. . . . Public support to higher education is still essential in order to ensure its educational, social and institutional mission'.

The second assumption that the number of reduction of recipients would not be harmful to the nation's interests does not comprehend the educational development of India. Only about 11 to 12 per cent of Indian people in the age group of 18-23 years receive higher education in India. In the OECD countries, the number is almost 51 per cent and in the middle income groups, it is about 21 per cent. Any curtailment of higher education will have disastrous consequences. As the

UNESCO document points out "Access to higher education and the broad range of services it can render to society, is part and parcel of any sustainable development programme in which high level human expertise and professional skills required".

Regarding the question of increase in user fees, certainly there is some scope for increasing user fees. But the question is how much? It is true that tuition fees in higher education establishments are extremely low. But we cannot possibly shift the entire burden of higher education to the students. Higher education, particularly professional ones are highly expensive and it is not possible on the part of even middle income groups to meet all such expenditures. Since there is a great deal of heterogeneity in higher education, we can classify courses into tradeable (market-oriented) and societal (non-tradeable) courses. The former include degrees in engineering, medicine, accountancy, etc. The latter cover degrees in sociology, economics, anthropology and so on. The financial responsibility may be shared among the students, government and industry. K.R. Shah has given the following suggestions regarding sharing of financial responsibility:

	Student	*Government*	*Industry*
Marketable courses (Vocational and Professional Education)	30%	20%	50%
Non-Marketable Courses (General)	20%	60%	20%

All this means that all those who benefit from higher education should contribute a part of the expenditure so that the entire burden does not fall on one section of the community. The government resources are limited and there are many competing agencies which require financial support. The industries also derive substantial benefit from higher education and as such they should participate in the sharing of financial responsibility.

The fourth assumption made in the discussion paper is that the beneficiaries in higher education are predominantly students from the middle and upper classes. May be in case of professional courses like medicine, engineering or management, but not for higher education as a whole. Further, there is no reason why we should deny such professional education to poor students who deserve such courses on the basis of their merit. And what about general education? If the entire cost is imposed on the students, large number of students would never have an opportunity to enter the portals of a University. In this context, it may be necessary to point out the vision of 'National Policy of Education', 1986 (Government of India) which enshrines:

(a) A process of empowerment through development knowledge, skills and values (Education for Development), and
(b) An instrument of social change for upward economic and social mobility, through enhancement of qualifications (Education for Equality).

This implies that education should be broad-based in order to provide opportunity for all those who are able and willing to join the educational stream for over-all economic and social changes.

It is worthwhile to mention here that though there is a logical sequence from primary to secondary to higher education, we cannot wait till the first stage is fully in place before we start to build the second or the third stage. Most people would agree that though primary and secondary education should be universal and provided to all those who are eligible, higher education should not be judged only on the basis of private return rates. As I.G. Patel points out, 'education and higher education in particular, is a part and parcel of the human endeavour for a more civilized existence, an end in itself, even as it is a means to other ends. There is, therefore, a fundamental democratic or humanitarian sense in which education of every kind and level, should be made available to every one at all ages and places to the extent that he or she is capable of absorbing it, not just to those who are able to put it to the best use whatever it may mean, but to everyone who can put it to some use. Not to each according to his ability only, but to each according to his needs as well. Quality and quantity are thus both important and have to be reconciled as best as one can".

All this implies that if we take into account the non-private benefit of higher education emerging from 'positive external factors', this questions the legitimacy of a redistribution of the public expenditure allocation to the detriment of higher education. Further, it is also stated that the aspect relating to the strengthening of cultural identity developed at the Universities are not easily quantifiable. Therefore, higher education should not be considered as private goods, they should be treated as public goods.

References

Ambani, Anil D., Knowledge is Growth (2000), An Address delivered at the India Economic Summit, 2000.

Chidambaram, P., Convocation Address on December 2, 2006 at Symbiosis International University, Pune.

National Policy on Education (1986), Government of India.

Patel, I.G., Financing of Higher Education : The Emerging Scenario Quoted from Indian Higher Education (*op. cit.*)

Power, K.B., India's Higher Education (2002), Concept Publishing House, New Delhi.

Tenth Five Year Plan, Vol. 1, Government of India.

Tilak, Jandhyala, B.G. (Ed.), A.P. Publishing Corporation, New Delhi.

Tunnermann, C. (1966), A New Vision of Higher Education, Higher Education Policy, quoted from Power, K.B.

University News, 150 years of Indian Higher Education—Special Issue (November 27, December 3, 2006).

CHAPTER

14

Agricultural Education and Value Addition

NEED FOR AGRICULTURAL EDUCATION

Agricultural education is different from that of general education. The former has to meet the challenges of agriculture and add value to the agricultural economy. As Radhakrishnan Commission discussing about education points out, 'Universities which promote general education are houses of intellectual adventure. This implies that the products which come out from these Universities would seek and cultivate new knowledge, engage vigorously and fearlessly in the pursuit of truth and interpret old knowledge and beliefs in the light of new needs and discoveries'. Not that these are not necessary in agricultural education. In additon to these, agricultural education will have to have some specific objectives to improve the productivity of land and labour who are engaged in agriculture, train the farmers to improve their capability to acquire new knowledge and adapt them effectively. Further, it should help in promoting economic development, opening new opportunities for employment, facilitating social change and democratic growth which the nation has decided as its basic goal.

CHALLENGES OF AGRICULTURE

We are now facing tremendous crisis in the agricultural front. As the 21st century begins with a momentum of development, agricultural development faces some unprecedented challenges. Even though agricultural production has increased, even now about 260 million people in India do not get adequate food. According to Dr. P.V. Sukhatme, a quarter of the total population of India suffers from malnutrition and half has more or less enough food in quantity though the diet is unbalanced. Secondly, the new technology which has been evolved to increase production is losing its attractiveness and meeting with resistance. The country has reached a plateau in technology. In other words, the rising phase of production surface has already been obtained. A poor country like India where there are large number of small and marginal farmers cannot afford to have such a high cost agriculture in a farm-based economy.

In spite of high yielding variety, the share of agriculture in GDP is gradually decreasing from about 41 per cent in the year 1972-73 to about 15.7 per cent in 2009-10 with 52 per cent work force engaged in agriculture. Another distributing feature of the new technology is ecological imbalance. Increased use of chemical fertiliser and water along with pesticides for increasing agricultural yield has brought about a steady depletion of micro nutrients from the soils, lower the water table, sometimes to a depth of 300 ft., erosion of top soil, spread of salinity and water logging, etc. All these imply that agricultural education must address issues and concerns of the new millennium that of providing nutritional and food security, maintaining sustainability of farming system, protecting environment, optimising farm inputs especially water, fertilizer and chemicals (R.S. Paroda).

ROLE OF AGRICULTURE UNIVERSITIES

(i) Adoption of New Technology

The main purpose of Agriculture Universities is to produce human resources for the development of agriculture and allied sectors. Food, nutrition and education are important elements for sustainable human growth and development. The human resources developed so far by National Agricultural System have no doubt played a significant role in agricultural transformation ushering in green, blue, yellow and white revolution. However, in view of the rapid technological change taking place globally, we have to accept them to meet the growing demands for foodgrains, remove the deficiencies of existing technology and improve ecological balance. Knowledge is growing at the rate of 300 words per minute and the gap between developed and developing countries is widening. We have to keep pace with these new developments so as to successfully compete with the developed countries.

We can now introduce new knowledge, skills and attitudes necessary for raising productivity and improving the quality of life. For example, biotechnologies and information technologies as well as indigenous technologies and knowledge are viewed as tools for achieving incremental advances in yields and maintaining the yields in a sustainable basis (N.H. Rao). We are now living in a technology driven world. The World Bank estimates that bio-technology can help to increase crop yields in rice by 10 to 20 per cent in the next ten years. It is necessary to adopt the new technology to provide economical benefits to farmers through value addition. Paroda suggests that the new technologies need to be developed, refined, assessed and transferred to farmers without loss of time. New partnership with new different stakeholders would lead synergies.

(ii) Course and Teaching Programme

As we have already indicated Agricultural Universities have been established to meet human resource requirement. Therefore, though scientific courses pertaining to new knowledge have to be included in the course programme, there should be some rural-oriented courses to enable the faculty members to understand the problems of rural areas. It has been suggested by some agricultural scientists that 70 per cent of courses should be of fundamental type and 30 per cent to take care of local and regional requirements. What is most important in agricultural education is that teaching, research and extension should be integrated since these three are the main organs of agricultural production system. The integration has some definite objectives. The purpose of teaching is not only to confer degrees but to enable the students to follow agricultural pursuits as and when necessary and try to solve problems which can assist agricultural development. The aim of research is to undertake, aid, promote and coordinate research with a view to solving some of the major problems of farmers and suggest new areas of development for agricultural transformation. And extension work is organised to transfer the results of research to farmers. By and large the Universities have made substantial progress in these three areas. However, we have still to go a long way in raising the productivity, profitability and sustainability of major farming systems which will be the most effective safety net against hunger and poverty in India. This is where the scientists and alumni of the Agricultural Universities can play a catalytic role. Faculty competence is therefore critical to discharge such arduous responsibilities. They should first of all keep abreast with the new development of science and technology. Without such knowledge, it is hardly possible to impart the necessary skill to the graduates. And further they must understand and appreciate the problems of the farmers and have necessary inclination to go to the villages and suggest relevant methods to improve their economic viability.

(iii) Farmers' Training

The Government of India has established a number of Krishi Vigyan Kendras which are integrated teaching centres where the method of teaching is learning by doing. These Kendras serve a number of purposes in promoting agricultural education. First, these are need-based training centres designed to help practising farmers and in-service personnel to improve their skill in farming. These Kendras help in carrying the latest advances in science and technology to the field through the provision of appropriate training. Most of these Kendras form an integral part of Agricultural Universities. Second, the candidates selected for training are regular farmers and are supposed to go back to farming after training. The Kendras do not provide jobs for the trainees. Third, the content of the training programmes relates mostly to the specific problems faced by the trainee in his/her own area with some universal principles of development. The Krishi Vigyan Kendra also serves as a focal point in providing training to women folk through the help of mobile training teams. Finally, the Kendra also maintains continuing links with the trainees through visit, and demonstrations until he or she becomes fully self-reliant. Links are also maintained with input agencies for the benefit of the trainees. This new venture is expected to bring about a substantial change in the rural economy through modernisation of agricultural and allied sectors.

BROAD CONTOUR OF AGRICULTURAL EDUCATION

There are atleast three areas which agricultural education should emphasise to change the contour of rural life. One such area is improvement of agro-based industries. Agriculture alone cannot provide adequate employment to the rural people. There is already a heavy pressure on land. It is so much so that about 80 per cent of farmers in India possess only 0.5 hectare of land. With such tiny plots there can hardly be any modernisation in agriculture and creation of additional employment opportunities. If along with agriculture, a large number of agro-industries are developed, such industries will not only reduce pressure on agriculture by providing additional employment opportunities but also assist in technological improvement. The Government and Universities can collaborate with each other to promote such industries, the Government providing necessary infrastructure and Universities imparting vocational education. Krishi Vigyan Kendras may enlarge their operation to provide necessary vocational training for successful management of such agro-based industries.

Another area which is equally important to improve the economic profile of rural India is attitudinal change. It is admitted on all hands that attitudinal change depends on social change and social change is possible through education. Agricultural education will train people about the meaning and significance of rural development programmes and creating opportunities for them to practise and enhance relevant skills and attitudes. As the Planning Commission writes, "Provision of adequate facilities for education at all stages, especially in rural areas where ignorance and illiteracy are rampant—is therefore one of the objectives of planning". Prof. H.W. Singer has broadened the concept and has said that social change is a pre-requisite to development and should be the primary target of any planning policy. According to him, "In providing the initial resources for better health, better education, better nutrition, better housing, greater social security, etc. which are keys to growth, we must make people aware of the possibilities of improving the quality of life. The raising of the level of the people's life is both the objective of development, and also instrument". This is a field where close collaboration is necessary between the Government and Agricultural Universities. While the Government would make additional investment in social sector as a whole, the Agriculture Universities will try to develop human resources in rural areas by improving the knowledge, skill and attitude necessary for raising productivity levels.

It would also be worthwhile to analyse and discuss in depth the constraints and difficulties faced by the farming community in working towards the goal of self-reliance and sustainable agriculture. Jules, N. Pretty points out that the basic challenge for sustainable agriculture is to make better use of available physical and human resources. This can be done by minimising the use of external inputs, by regenerating internal resources more effectively or by combination of both. This ensures the efficient and effective use of what is available, and ensure that any changes that persist as dependencies on external systems are kept to a reasonable minimum. He has suggested three steps of sustainability:

(i) Modifying conventional systems in order to reduce consumption of inputs, so that wastes and adverse environmental inputs are substantially reduced.
(ii) Regenerative technologies are introduced to make best use of all localy available biological and human resources. Some technologies are dropped (e.g., pesticides) and new components added. There is more reliance on management, skills and knowledge, requiring shifts in attitude and values among farmers.
(iii) Redesign with communities. This comprises resource conserving technologies that are fitted to time and place, and varied adaptively by farmers. Agriculture is seen as an area-based activity and local groups and institutions are strengthened in order to undertake natural resource management and financial resource management.

The above analysis clearly shows that sustainability can be attained to a great extent by improving the quality of agricultural education and by developing human resources by taking advantage of the new technology generated in frontier areas of science including biotechnology.

CONCLUSION

As we stand on the threshold of a new millennium, we are witnessing the remarkable transition from knowledge as a factor in development to knowledge as the key to development (Khan). As Swaminathan points out, knowledge creation and dissemination will sustain the dramatic advances in the agricultural sector: the gene revolution, the information and communication revolution and the eco-technology revolution. In the knowledge society, the Agriculture Universities will have the responsibility of generating new knowledge through extension and train the farmers for intelligent utilisation of knowledge. This is the most important contribution of agricultural education to increase the value system of agriculture among rural communities.

References

Etienne, Gilbert (1968), Studies in Indian Agriculture—The Art of the Possible. University of California Press and Oxford University Press, Bombay.

ICAR (1999), International Symposium on Agricultural Education in the Next Century—Lesson Learnt and Prospects.

Jakhar, Bal Ram (1993), New Horizons in Agriculture in India. *The Coop Times*, New Delhi.

Naik, K.C. (1961), Agricultural Education in India, ICAR, New Delhi.

Naik, N.H. (2004), Sustainable Agriculture: Critical Challenges facing the Structure and Function of Agricultural Research and Education in India, *University News*.

Roling, N.C. and Wagemakers, G.A.E. (1998), Facilitating Sustainable Agriculture, Cambridge University Press, U.K.

Singh, U.K. and Nayak, A.K. (1997), Agricultural Education, Commonwealth Press, New Delhi.

CHAPTER

15

The Strategic Value of Information and Communication Technologies

Information and Communication Technologies have changed the entire social, political and economic framework of most of the countries of the world. In the nineteenth and early twentieth centuries, the Knowledge of English and harnessing the steam were crucial for transformation of the social structure: it is now the Information and Communication Technologies that have brought about a revolutionary change in each and every sphere of social life. The compass of change is so vast that it is difficult to comprehend all the aspects with the limited knowledge that we possess, and particularly when there are long waves of dynamic change. We propose to consider only a few important aspects that are often discussed by most of the non-technical scholars. These are: (a) Technological innovation in the process of growth, (b) Effect upon employment, (c) Political and Social repercussions and finally, (d) Policy guidelines. The universities will have to play an important role in policy formulation and implementation in such cases. We start with the Prospects of Economic Growth due to ITC.

TECHNOLOGICAL INNOVATION AND ECONOMIC GROWTH

The IT sector is defined for the study covering computer hardware, software and services. Telecommunications, semiconductors, and other electronics industries are also a part of the IT infrastructure—supporting and complementing the production and use of computer products and services (Kraemer and Dedrick). It is now acknowledged by most of the people that investments in technology and particularly by ICTs (Information and Communication Technologies) stimulate economic growth and productivity. Investment in IT increases labour productivity in several ways. First, IT increases labour productivity directly by substituting labour. Many of the TNCs have increased production by downsizing labour. For example, in the USA IBM alone laid-off 85,000 workers in 1992 and 50,000 in 2002, yet there was no adverse effect on production. And this is a continuous process. Between the mid-eighties and mid-nineties in the U.S. alone, some three million manufacturing jobs disappeared. During this period the high tech industry created only one million jobs. Between 1979 and 1992 productivity increased by 35 per cent in America but the jobs declined by 15 per cent (Anil Rajimwale). The same process was also shown in some of the Indian industries. Tata industries for example reduced their employees from 70,000 to 50,000 in nineties without reducing production.

This is possible because when computers are installed, they perform many routine data processing functions enabling labourers to engage themselves in different types of productive work. The computers also provide the workers with timely information and tools for planning and carrying out their work. Secondly, IT also improves capital productivity by complementing other investments. For example, there is improvement in the efficiency of plants and equipment through the use of computer system which allows automation processes and greater flexibility. This helps the productivity of capital. In fact, the computer system improves the entire production system through proper planning and coordination of activities. And increased productivity of capital also increases the productivity of labour since the workers are now in a position to work with efficient tools and equipment.

Thus, there is a dynamic relationship between IT investment between GDP growth and productivity growth. Table 1 shows the correlation of growth in IT use with growth in GDP and productivity.

TABLE 1

Person Correlation of Growth in IT use with Growth in GDP and Productivity

Variable	*Average annual growth in IT investment : 1984-90*
Average annual GDP growth : 1984-90	0.76**
Average annual productivity growth : 1984-90	0.61*

* Significance Level = 0.05
** Significance level = 0.01
Source : Kenneth L. Kraemer and Jason Dedrick.

IT investment is related to wealth. Therefore, developed countries make more investment in IT followed by newly industrial economies (NIEs) and then the developing countries. Return on IT investment itself is much higher than other investments. For example, a study of MIT's Sloan School in respect of 380 of the 500 largest U.S. companies from 1987 to 1991, representing over $ 2 million in output (which is about one-third of US GDP) showed that there was a return of 54.2 per cent for computer investment compared to 4.1 per cent for all other investments. This shows that IT investment has great importance in increasing return from investment.

Many countries have therefore, started making investment in ICT. Another great advantage of ICT investment is that emergence of industry standard products (based on ICT) creates markets which bring users lower-cost products, a wider choice of suppliers and some degree of confidence that a product will not become obsolete (Swan, 1990). These have increased interest in IT education and investment in some NIE and developing countries as shown in Table 2.

TABLE 2
IT Investment in NIE and Developing Countries

Developing Countries	*IT Investment as % of GDP 1990*	*IT Investment as % of total investment 1990*	*Average growth in IT investment 1984-90*
Singapore	1.84	3.89	18.06
Hongkong	1.19	5.18	15.22
South Korea	0.91	2.19	24.49
Taiwan	0.83	3.60	21.64
India	0.37	1.36	22.21
Thailand	0.36	0.83	25.00

Source : Database at CRITO, University of California, Irvine.

The difference in the rate of return in proportion to investment depends to a great extent on environmental factors. However, all that we emphasize is that investment in ICT has become a common feature in many countries since it facilitates GDP growth through productivity increase.

ICT AND EMPLOYMENT

It has been observed by many that technological change creates unemployment. As we have seen already many of the MNCs have downsized labour force in order to increase production and productivity. David Ricardo, an outstanding economist of the 19th century (who is also considered as a pioneer of classical economy) pointed out in 1821 that introduction of technology is detrimental to the creation of employment. As he states:

> 'The opinion entertained by the labouring class that the introduction of machinery is frequently detrimental to their interests is not founded on prejudice or error but conforms to the correct principles of Political economy'.

Particularly when unemployment is more or less a common feature in many countries, developed and developing, Ricardo's analysis is considered to be more or less correct. That is why many economists have suggested for the establishment of labour-intensive industries to create additional employment opportunities. E.F. Schumacher's 'Small is Beautiful' is a concrete illustration of this phenomenon. He of course has considered many other human problems in addition to employment. According to him 'Small is Beautiful' is 'A Study of Economics as if People Mattered'.

It is true that when some new technology is introduced in a particular firm or industry, there is bound to be some loss of employment. This structural maladjustment may be prolonged for a long time with a lot of hardship to the labourers who are thrown out from the industry. The new jobs that would be created may not suit the old ones either in skills or location. But it has been seen that job creation effects of technological change subsequently lead to the job destruction impacts in the long-run, albeit accompanied by a steady reduction in working hours throughout the nineteenth and twentieth centuries (Christopher Freeman). However, Schumpeter has given a new twist to the debate of technological change and its impact on employment or unemployment by his conception of 'long waves' of successive industrial revolution. In each cycle, new technologies could give rise to major waves of new investment and employment in new industries and services. His theory of 'Creative Destruction' approach shows how job destruction and job creation in the long wave cycles produce new type of jobs in place of old ones.

According to Schumpeter, a revolutionary new technology can create the basis for a virtuous circle of growth in which investment is high, labour productivity grows fast – and output even faster. The result is a net growth of employment. Whether this virtuous circle can be sustainable depends on macroeconomic employment and trade policies as well as on the new technologies. Prolonged periods of full employment are possible if there is a good match between technologies, policies and institutions (Freeman). As a matter of fact there was sustainable growth along with employment in Europe, Japan and North America in fifties and sixties due to cheap oil, great increase in the production of automobiles and other consumer durables.

However, there was a change in the pattern of job creation. More jobs were created in high-skills due to improvement in sophisticated technology. It is also observed that the creation of new jobs has not been able to offset the loss of jobs in the lower skill and lower-tech sectors. The new type of jobs which requires a great deal of skills include the manufacture of computers, software, microelectronics, televisions, video-cassette recorders and so on. One important change that has been noticed because of ICT is that services are becoming the main sources of jobs in advanced industrial countries. Within the overall expansion of employment in the service sector, business services, financial services, software activities and telecommunication activities became more important. These developments were not only confined to highly industrialised countries but also Asian Tigers and other newly industrial countries. We can give just one example to illustrate the points. In Taiwan for example business services employment alone increased from 79,000 in 1983 to 205,000 in 1993. The same thing also happened in Hong Kong, Thailand, Malaysia, China and the other NICs. Another change that is noticed in new technology is that prospects of lifetime employment are vanishing. The present trend is towards part-time and contractual employment.

The question is what should be done for the creation of lower skill jobs. Several measures can be taken to absorb these people in different kinds of jobs. If there is improvement in infrastructure, many small industries can be established and if they are tagged to mega industries, impetus of technological change can percolate to these industries making them more viable. Second job creation can be added by satisfying the growing demand for more personal and community services like education, health, sanitation, tourism, entertainment, etc. These are all by-products of economic growth. In fact, the Asian Tigers have been able to improve employment opportunities by creating a large number of non-traded personal services. Only provision for proper training has to be imparted by educational institutions to enable these low-skilled employees to acquire necessary skill to handle these jobs. In over populated countries, in addition to training and improvement of infrastructure, effective steps should be taken to control population to reduce labour force which competes in the market for jobs.

POLITICAL AND SOCIAL CHANGES

Improvement in ICTs is the heart of the process of Information Society which brings about radical changes both in the character of the government and social behaviour. ICTs go a long way in realising the vision of good governance. Now e-governance has become a buzzword. It means taking the government to the doorstep of people through networking. The citizens can get online immediate access to information, which may be otherwise time consuming. It makes the governmental functioning transparent that could also help in checking corruption (Gujral).

Democracy has been defined as a government of the people, by the people and for the people. But it seems in many developing countries where democratic form of government has been introduced after the Second World War, the political system has been distorted due to money and muscle power. N.A. Palkhivala has gone to the extent of saying that

> 'the quality of our public life has reached the nadir. Politics has become tattered and tainted with crime. The moral standards of our politicians, policemen and criminals are indistinguishable from one another'.

But since no other type of government is better than democracy, we have to sustain and promote democracy by enabling the citizens to know the nature of the work done by the government, allowing them to communicate with the government, participate in the government's policy-making and to communicate with each other. E-governance is a tool through which the citizens participate not only in the government decision-making process, but reflect their true needs and exercise some control over the government to implement some of the welfare programmes for the interest of the community.

For example, in case of India though huge investments have been made in different plans to improve the living standards of the people, the overall development in most of the sectors has been much below the desired. Even when the policy of distributing resources to the poor and destitutes was accepted at the national level, it could not be properly implemented at the local level due to heavy leakages. Both the quality of political Elite and the nature of bureaucratic administrative set-up perverted the entire planning process and manipulated it to enrich the privileged few. The political process undermines the role and authority of basic institutions which Rajni Kothari labels as 'institutional decay'. This has converted politics as 'power politics' and the politician, the 'power politician' indulging manipulative politics. Later on politics became a lucrative business. Instead of a culture-oriented politics, we developed a politics-oriented culture which resulted in wide-spread incidence of corruption.

And different layers of civil service having extensive control over administration, increased the level of regulation and impersonal way of operation (due to complete aloofness with general public) and rigidity in adhering to formal rules and regulations resulted in a downward spiral in the effectiveness with which the civil service could carry out the tasks. What is worse, as Bhambhri in his 'Bureaucracy in India' argues, senior administrators forged an alliance with politicians not only to brighten their own career prospects but also to articulate political views and gain a greater share of social resources. It is needless to say that we have to change the nature of development administration to improve the quality of life of people by reducing poverty, increasing employment opportunities, reducing income inequalities, improving the quality of education, health, social security and so on. Though work can be done in many areas for changing the economic system to make it more responsive to the people's needs, ICT can play an effective role to achieve some of the important goals of planning.

ICT provides freedom to every citizen to secure access to information in order to promote openness, transparency and accountability. This enables people to fight injustice, secure benefit from the government which they deserve and shape their own destiny under an environment of friendly climate. Access to information technology will not only empower people, it will also provide great benefit for the common man in e-governance. This refers to the use of IT networks for various types of interaction between the government and the citizen. Anyone who needs some government permission or certificate like a ration card, a driving license or a certificate relating to land ownership has to go through a procedure which is not only cumbersome but also dilatory. These cumbersome procedures also encourage petty corruption, which has become the bane of everyone's life. These problems can be greatly reduced if citizens could undertake these transactions through an IT network which can be assessed at any time of the day from the nearest STD booth. This will also help downsizing administration which has great importance for bringing about better governance, of optimum utilization of resources of manpower and funds, providing more services to the people and of improving productivity in the offices (Montek Singh Ahluwalia).

SOCIAL CHANGES

There are also many social changes due to ICT. To use the expression of Arthur C. Clarke, there is something magical about it, people little knowing what goes on inside a computer and the electronic gadgets. ICT brings about many changes upon work, upon economic life and upon society as a whole. We can make a distinction between formal economy and informal economy. Due to ICT we notice the following important differences between Formal Economy and Informal Economy.

(a) In formal economy there is closer linkage between production and remote markets and head quarters. This means ICTs remove the constraints of distance, time and location. This leads to greater competition in the field of economic activity which requires enterprise and a spirit of adventure. In informal economy, mostly traditional jobs continue to produce goods and services to meet the requirements of local people. In informal economy, there are no economies of scale and goods and services produced are of simple nature.

(b) Another difference which is significant between the two is that while in formal economy services are more important, in informal economy, primary sector is the dominant feature. Changes in formal economy is not just a matter of individual work experience. There are important changes in the structure of and interrelationship between organisations.

(c) One important change that characterises the sophisticated economy is that the society must invest new learning skills in their people. A super advanced economy will work only if it is super-creative with the ability to market and sell its creations rapidly. This implies that there shall be substantial improvement in technical education in a sophisticated formal economy which may gradually produce its impact on other spheres of social behaviour. The Universities will have the responsibility to impart such training.

POLICY GUIDELINES

As we have seen the new technologies have made so many qualitative changes that the existing disciplines or theories are unable to cope with them. But what is most important is that these must be used for the interest of human beings. There is a danger that the insatiable greed of man may sabotage the benefits and turn them to nightmares. Instead of eradicating poverty, unemployment, illiteracy and improving the quality of life, these technologies may be harnessed to poison springs of life and contrive engines of mass destruction (S.S. Gill). Efforts therefore have to be made to guard against the misuse of ICTs and use these to achieve their development goals. According to UNDP,

> "Information and Communication Technologies are not only a significant factor on the performance and growth of economics—the importance of which is continuously

growing, these are also an effective tool to advance sustainable human development".

Particularly in case of developing countries where the challenges of growth are formidable, ITCs should be effectively used to strengthen the economy and enrich the life of the people. In case of India ITCs have already made some progress. It has emerged as the fourth largest spender on IT. It is further understood that about 20 States and Union Territories have initiated IT policy to change their economy and social life. Karnataka has made several improvements in administrative set-up through IT. Inspite of our limited resources, the International Telecommunication Union (2003) places India in the category of middle access economies. And the Global International Technology Report (2003-04) ranks India at numbers 37. Even though it has ranked India above China, we still find great difference between China in respect of poverty, illiteracy, unemployment, rate of growth and so on. Particularly our rural areas are deprived of many basic facilities of life.

We therefore suggest that the disparity between urban and rural areas should be bridged through the ITC. First, there should be improvement in both physical and social infrastructure. This will help economic growth and the quality of life. If economic growth reduces poverty and improves the quality of life of the rural people, poverty will not be exported to urban areas to increase the number of slums. Second, information centres should be started in all the States and Union Territories of India to improve the quality of e-governance. Unless there is significant change in transparency and accountability, much of the expenditure incurred by the government would not reach the people who deserve it. Third, it is utilised mostly for increasing exports. There is no doubt that export potentials are vast. But what is more important is to improve human capability both in rural and urban areas by providing access to education, health care, technology and market facility. This can be done only by educational institutions by changing their course programmes and teaching methods and spreading their network throughout the length and breadth of the country.

References

Dutton, William H., ed. Information and Communication Technologies, Vision and Realities, Oxford University Press INC, New York, 1996.

Gill, S.S., The Information Revolution, Rupa and Co., New Delhi, 2004.

Gujral, I.K., Thinking for the Future, *Mainstream*, August 14, 2004.

Misra, Baidyanath, Emerging Concerns in Development Administration, *IASSI Quarterly*, Vol. 18, No. 2, 1999.

Rajimwale, Anil, IT Revolution: Beyond to Old Mindset, *Mainstream*, August 14, 2004.

CHAPTER

16

Financial Relation between the Centre and States and the 13th Finance Commission

India has a federal constitution. In a federation, there is likelihood of imbalance between different regions. On the one side, it is unlikely that the duties and financial powers would be in harmony at different levels of government. The discrepancy between the resources available to the centre and the states increases due to the fact that on account of efficiency, economy and many other criteria, the centre gets those resources which are elastic in nature while the states are mostly saddled with inelastic revenues. On the other, the pace of expansion varies substantially between different regions. Economic development is not an even process. Even in developed countries, there are significant differences in income and employment between different regions. But the regional imbalance is of greater significance in poor countries. As Gunnar Myrdal has said, 'the higher the level of economic development that a country has already attained, the stronger the spread effect will usually be. In contrast, the spread effect is weaker in poor countries. It follows from this that deliberate steps should be taken to bring about regional balance in a developing country like India'.

DIVISION OF POWERS BETWEEN THE CENTRE AND STATES

Once it is admitted that regional balance is necessary, it may be examined how this can be done in a Federal State like India where functions and financial powers are divided between the centre and states on the basis of certain norms. The centre generally assumes responsibilities which concern the whole nation whereas the states tend to take up activities which are of regional or local importance. Take the case of defence. It is not only a public good, but it has got a great deal of externalities. For the interest of the country as a whole this has to be assigned to the centre. Similarly, the centre will assume responsibility in case of services which cover more than one state like inter-state transportation, communication, trade and commerce since in such cases costs and benefits spill over the boundaries of a state. On the other hand, there are services like sanitation, medical aid, etc. which are local in character and should be conveniently managed by the state governments from the point of view of administrative efficiency.

There are certain areas which can be handled efficiently by both the centre and states. Education is such an element which is allotted to concurrent list. In education both the layers of the government can make laws and to avoid conflict of jurisdiction, the centre has been given overriding power to maintain uniformity if considered necessary.

DIVISION OF FINANCIAL POWERS

Along with the division of powers, there is need for the division of financial powers. This is necessary firstly for maintaining financial responsibility. If a particular state government is allowed to perform certain functions without raising the necessary resources either it may over spend which may lead to inefficiency or wastage, or it may not be able to get the required funds to discharge the assigned functions. Resources obtained without any legitimate control or discipline ultimately lead to financial irresponsibility. Secondly, if both the layers of government are allowed to raise taxes from the same head, there may be double taxation causing economic injury to the society. Similarly, in respect of certain taxes, there might be competition among certain states. One state may impose lower sales tax to attract outside capital whereas another may not. Such competitive rates may hamper inter-state trade and commerce. All these imply that resources should be divided between the centre and states on certain guiding principles.

The guiding principles which should be followed in dividing financial powers between the centre and states may be considered from the point of view of efficiency, economy, fiscal discipline and adequacy. From the point of view of efficiency, sources of revenue which are of national character like Income Tax and Corporation Tax should be allotted to the Centre. If each state is allowed to levy such taxes, (a) each state may impose such taxes with different rates or exemptions leading to imbalance in the economy, (b) further in such taxes, it is difficult to demarcate the jurisdiction of various states in a definite manner. An individual (or firm) may get his (or its income) from more than one state. If different states impose income tax or corporation tax, there may not be proper assessment of the tax yield, (c) similarly, if the income originates in one state while the individual (or firm) may be a resident of another, what will be the basis of tax assessment? (d) a still more complicated case may arise when the origin of income cannot be identified. In such cases, tax evasion becomes easy.

We may therefore, note where the tax base is multiple (like income tax, corporation tax, customs duty, wealth tax, gift tax, excise duty, etc.) the federal government should have the exclusive power to impose tax. That is why in Indian Federation, the Central Government has been assigned the financial power to impose such taxes. On the other hand, state governments are assigned to impose taxes of local origin like land tax, irrigation tax, electricity duty, entertainment tax, etc. for efficient scheduling and collection.

BASIC PRINCIPLE OF DIVISION OF FINANCIAL POWER

The principle of economy implies that taxes should be so divided that they can be collected without much cost and there is not much scope for fraud, evasion and administrative delay. A sales tax, for example, can be easily collected by the state rather by the Centre (that is why sales tax is assigned to states). Since no economy is rich enough to waste its resources, the canon of economy has to assume importance in the allocation of resources. As Seligman has said in his 'Essays in Taxation', 'no matter how well intentioned a scheme may be, or how completely it may harmonise with the abstract principles of justice, if the tax does not work administratively it is doomed to failure'.

What is meant by fiscal discipline is that taxes are not only imposed to raise revenue, but also to achieve certain economic objectives like : (a) control of inflation or deflation to maintain economic stability, (b) prevent the imbalance in balance of payments, or (c) to regulate the industrial policy of the country. Taxes like income tax and corporation tax mostly achieve the first objective, customs duty the second objective and excise duty the third objective. The Federal authority can take an overall view of the economy and take appropriate measures in the direction. And so these taxes are assigned to the Central Government. On the other hand, states are provided with local taxes, as mentioned above to discharge their fiscal functions without much dependence on the centre.

It is generally agreed that taxes allotted to the centre and states in such a manner that they are adequate to meet their respective needs. If the centre depends on the states for discharging its functions, it cannot maintain fiscal discipline or take an overall view of the growth of the economy. On the other hand, if the state depends too much on the centre, there will always be pulls and pressures by them to get as much aid as possible from the centre. No economic principle may be observed in determining the quantum of aid or assistance. It is therefore, desirable that as far as possible, adequate resources should be assigned to different units to discharge their allotted functions. Further, along with the principle of adequacy, the revenue powers should be sufficiently elastic so that each unit can meet not only the present needs, but also make plans for any possible future expenditure.

But whatever principle of distribution is accepted, there will always be some gap, some imbalance between needs and resources of different units. Further, since the resources assigned to the centre are more elastic than the resources of the states, and the states have been given mostly developmental activities which increase along with time due to increase in population and explosion of knowledge and aspirations, the states cannot fulfil their obligations with the assigned resources. The centre therefore, comes to the assistance of the states to meet their fiscal needs. Further, in the process of developmental expenditures and other calamities associated with different natural or accidental factors, there might be regional imbalance among different states. In such a prospective the centre's financial assistance assumes the nature of a balancing factor for meeting fiscal needs and removing regional imbalance.

NEED FOR FINANCIAL ADJUSTMENT

Since in the process of economic development the central authority assumes more power and at the same time receives more elastic sources of revenue, the states find great difficulty in discharging their obligations. Further, it is also noticed that the imbalance in some states is much greater than that of others. Trends in central and state finances show that the total revenue receipts of the centre are much more than that of the states. Table 1 shows major taxes of the centre since 2003-04. It can be seen from the table that there has been higher growth of tax revenues, particularly from 2004-05. This has been possible due to higher growth coupled with better tax administration and introduction of new taxes such as 'the fringe benefit tax'. The high buoyancy of direct tax revenues may be attributed substantially to improvement in tax compliance following the institution of the Tax Information Network (TIN) and its implementation by the National Securities Depository Ltd.

(NSDL). According to the Report of C&AG of India, in 2002-03 almost 80 per cent of assessees for tax deduction at source did not file returns. With the setting up of the TIN in January 2004, tax compliance has gone up significantly. Table 1 also shows that the gross tax-GDP ratio went up by over 3 percentage points in a span of four years from 9.3 per cent in 2003-04 to 12.56 per cent in 2007-08. Another redeemining feature in tax structure of the Central Government is that direct taxes have overtaken indirect tax collections. From less than 20 per cent share in total tax revenue in 1990-91, the share of direct taxes has increased to over 55 per cent in 2008-09.

As we can see from Table 1 Corporation tax has become much more elastic than Income tax. However, during 2007-08, there has been some increase in Income tax, but it has come down in 2009-10 due to an over-all recession. Both Customs duty and Union excise duty have also come down in the year 2009-10 due to recession. As the table shows Direct taxes have yielded more revenue than Indirect taxes since 2007-08. This is a redeeming feature of tax structure of the country. Total central gross revenue which was in the range of 9 to 10 has increased to more than 11 approaching 12.56 in the year 2007-08. Had there been no recession, gross tax revenue of the Centre might have increased further.

Table 2 shows the trends in Aggregate State Revenue Receipts. As we can see from the figures, there was improvement in all the components of revenue receipts of states between 2004-05 and 2007-08. Own tax revenues as a proportion of GDP improved from 5.78 per cent in 2004 to 6.07 per cent in 2007-08. Non-tax revenues improved, albeit sluggishly from 1.47 per cent to 1.63 per cent in the same period. There was also improvement in share in Central taxes and Plan grants and non-plan grants between 2004-05 and 2006-07. There was a slight decrease in the year 2007-08. There was also increase in Total Revenue of the states as a percentage of GDP—which increased from 11.49 per cent to 13.20 per cent between 2004-05 and 2007-08. An area of concern for states in the sharing of net central tax revenue is the sharp increase in the proportion of cesses and surcharges in the gross tax revenue of the Centre from 3.51 in 2001-02 to 13.63 per cent in

TABLE 1

Major Taxes of the Centre : Performance since 2003-04

Percent of GDP

Year	Corporation Tax	Income Tax	Total direct taxes	Customs duties	Union excise duties	Service tax	Total individual taxes	Total central tax revenues gross
(1)	(2)	(3)	(4)	(5)	(6)	(7)	(8)	(9)
2003-04	2.31	1.50	3.81	1.77	3.30	0.29	5.42	9.23
2004-05	2.63	1.56	4.22	1.83	3.15	0.48	5.47	9.68
2005-06	2.82	1.56	4.61	1.81	3.10	0.64	5.60	10.21
2006-07	3.50	1.82	5.57	2.09	2.85	0.91	5.89	11.47
2007-08	4.08	2.17	6.61	2.20	2.62	1.09	5.95	12.56
2008-09	(RE) 4.17	2.03	6.55	2.03	2.04	1.22	5.25	11.80
2009-10	(BE) 4.38	1.82	6.32	1.67	1.82	1.11	4.63	10.95

(Contd.)

Percent of Centre's Gross Tax Revenue

Year	*Corporation Tax*	*Income Tax*	*Total direct taxes*	*Customs duties*	*Union excise duties*	*Service tax*	*Total individual taxes*
(1)	*(2)*	*(3)*	*(4)*	*(5)*	*(6)*	*(7)*	*(8)*
2003-04	24.99	16.27	41.31	19.12	35.69	3.10	58.69
2004-05	27.11	16.15	43.53	18.89	32.50	4.66	56.47
2005-06	27.66	15.29	45.12	17.77	30.38	6.30	54.88
2006-07	30.48	15.86	48.61	18.23	24.84	7.94	51.39
2007-08	32.52	17.30	52.63	17.55	20.84	8.65	47.37
2008-09	(RE) 35.35	17.20	55.48	17.20	17.26	10.35	44.52
2009-10	(BE) 40.05	16.66	57.72	15.29	16.61	10.14	42.28

Source : 13th Finance Commission, Table 4.4, p. 45.

Table 2
Trends in Aggregate State Revenue Receipts

Percent of GDP

Year	*Own Tax Revenues*	*Own Non-Tax Revenues*	*Share in Central Taxes*	*Plan Grants*	*Non-Plan Grants*	*Total Revenue*
(1)	*(2)*	*(3)*	*(4)*	*(5)*	*(6)*	*(7)*
2004-05	5.78	1.47	2.49	1.31	0.44	11.49
2005-06	5.91	1.33	2.65	1.21	0.89	11.99
2006-07	6.11	1.62	2.92	1.44	0.82	12.92
2007-08	6.07	1.63	3.22	1.57	0.72	13.20

Source : 13th Finance Commission, Table 4.9, p. 51.

2009-10 (BE). This has considerably reduced the proportion in gross tax revenue of the Centre of net tax revenue shareable with states.

After analysing the trends of revenues of both the Centre and states, we can consider the pattern of expenditure of both the Centre and states. Table 3 shows the trends in central government expenditure. It is found from the figures that total expenditure of the Centre has increased as a percentage of GDP from 15.82 in the year 2004-05 to 17.43 in the year 2009-10 (BE). Total non-plan expenditure seems to be much more than plan expenditure. Expenditure on interest payments, defence, pay and allowances and subsidies are the main components of the Centre's revenue expenditure, accounting for about 63 per cent of the total.

Interest payments have become much more than other items of expenditure because of fiscal and revenue deficits. Persistent with fiscal problems, the Central Government enacted the FRBM in 2003 which came into force from 5 July 2004. According to FRBM, Revenue Deficit would be eliminated by 2008-09 and Fiscal Deficit to be reduced to 3 per cent of GDP at the end of 2008-09. There was some attempt to reduce both but because of recession there was again an increase in both items. Increase in subsidies was also another cause which aggravated the deficit. The following table shows explicit subsidies relative to the Centre's Revenue Deficits.

However, in order to analyse the financial relation between the Centre and States, we may consider the expenditure pattern of the states.

If we compare Table 2 where we have mentioned aggregate state revenue receipts with Table 5, we find that non-plan revenue expenditure of the states is much more than own tax revenue and own non-tax revenue of the states. The states therefore, depend on central assistance to meet their deficit. This is also a constitutional provision on the part of the Central Government to provide assistance to the states to meet their both plan and non-plan revenue expenditure. Generally there are three methods by which assistance is given to the states. These are tax sharing, loans and grants.

TABLE 3
Trends in Central Government Expenditure

(Percent of GDP)

Year	*Revenue Expenditure*	*Interest payments*	*Defence*	*Pay and Allowances*	*Pension*	*Subsidies*	*Capital expenditure*	*Total expenditure*
(1)	*(2)*	*(3)*	*(4)*	*(5)*	*(6)*	*(7)*	*(8)*	*(9)*
2003-04	13.14	4.50	2.18	1.21	0.58	1.61	3.96	17.11
2004-05	12.20	4.03	2.41	1.16	0.58	1.46	3.62	15.82
2005-06	12.25	3.70	2.25	1.08	0.56	1.32	1.85	14.10
2006-07	12.46	3.64	2.07	1.00	0.54	1.38	1.67	14.09
2007-08	12.58	3.62	1.94	0.97	0.51	1.50	2.50	15.09
2008-09 (RE)	15.10	3.62	2.15	1.33	0.61	2.43	1.83	16.93
2009-10 (BE	15.32	3.85	2.42	1.50	0.60	1.90	2.11	17.43

Source : 13th Finance Commission, Table 4.5.

TABLE 4
Explicit Subsidies Relative to the Centre's Revenue Receipts

(Percent)

Year	*Food*	*Fertiliser*	*Others*	*Total*
2003-04	9.55	4.49	2.77	16.80
2004-05	8.43	5.19	1.40	15.02
2005-06	6.67	5.34	1.73	13.74
2006-07	5.53	6.04	1.59	13.15
2007-08	5.78	6.00	1.31	13.09
2008-09 (RE)	7.76	13.49	1.74	22.99
2009-10 (BE	8.54	8.13	1.43	18.11

Source : 13th Finance Commission Report, Table 4.6, p. 47.

TABLE 5
Aggregate State Finances : Expenditure Indicators

(Percent of GDP)

Year	*Total Revenue Expen-diture*	*Interest payments*	*Pensions*	*Plan Revenue Expen-diture*	*Non-plan Revenue Expen-diture*	*Capital Expen-diture*
2004-05	12.74	2.75	1.18	1.89	10.85	1.88
2005-06	12.18	2.36	1.14	1.94	10.24	2.14
2006-07	12.21	2.29	1.13	2.17	10.04	2.32
2007-08	12.26	2.12	1.19	2.39	9.88	2.47

Source : 13th Finance Commission Report, Table 4.10, p. 52.

MECHANISM OF FINANCIAL ADJUSTMENT

In accordance with article 280(3)(a) of the Constitution, the Finance Commission is required to make recommendations as to the distribution between the Union and the States of the net proceeds of taxes which are to be or may be divided between them. The Indian Constitution does not prescribe any permanent formula for determining financial adjustment. The Finance Commission, a non-political expert body, is provided to review once in five years, federal state financial relationship and determine the principle of tax sharing and also the amount of grants according to changing economic and social conditions. This has provided elasticity in the allocation of resources and avoided friction in inter-state and federal state relations.

Further, due to some change in constitutional provisions, the scope and responsibility of the Finance Commissions also have changed. For example, article 270 provided for the compulsory sharing of the net proceeds of the income tax (excluding corporation tax) and article 272 permitted for sharing of the net proceeds of Union duties of excise (excluding duties of excise on medicinal and toilet preparations) if Parliament by law so provided. Consequently the principles adopted for revenue sharing differed between the two taxes significantly.

The eightieth amendment of the Constitution (2000) altered the pattern of sharing of Union taxes in a fundamental way. Under the amendment, article 272 was dropped and article 270 was substantially changed. The new article 270 provides for sharing of all the taxes and duties referred to in the Union List except the taxes and duties referred to in articles 268 and 269 respectively, surcharges on taxes and duties referred to in article 271 and any cess levied for specific purposes. Eleventh Finance Commission was the first to take these changes into account while recommending the share of the states in the divisible pool.

MANDATE OF THE THIRTEENTH FINANCE COMMISSION

The basic mandate of the Commission was to recommend a fair distribution of resources between the Centre and States and among the states *inter-se*. Therefore, the 13th Finance Commission was asked to suggest measures for containing a stable and sustainable fiscal environment consistent with equitable growth. For this purpose, the Commission has to take into account of : (i) the need to balance the receipt and expenditure on revenue account of all states and the Union and generating surpluses for capital investment, (ii) the need to improve the quality of public expenditure, (iii) the need to manage ecology, environment and climate change consistent with sustainable development, (iv) the need to ensure commercial viability of public sector and departmental undertakings, as also of irrigation and power projects, (v) the impact of the proposed implementation of the Goods and Service Tax (GST) from 1 April 2010, including its impact on the country's foreign trade, and (vi) the taxation efforts of the Central Government and each State Government and the potential for additional resource mobilisation to improve the tax Gross State Domestic Product/Gross Domestic Product ratio.

On the basis of these references, the Commission made a detailed study of the finances of both the Centre and each state and made necessary recommendations on different issues as specified above. We may first highlight a few important recommendations before we analyse the recommendations regarding : (i) the distribution of divisible pool, (2) allocation of such divisible pool between the states, and (3) the recommendations in supplementing the resources of the Panchayats and Municipalities in different states.

Some of the Major Recommendations of the 13th Finance Commission are :

1. Initiative to be taken to reduce the number of Centrally sponsored Schemes (CSS) and to restore the predominance of formula-based plan transfers.
2. Both the Centre and the states should conclude a Grand Bargain to implement the Model GST which comprises six elements. To incentivise implementation of the Grand Bargain, the Commission recommends sanction of a grant of Rs. 50,000 crore to meet the compensation claims of state governments if it results revenue losses.
3. The share of states in net proceeds of shareable central taxes shall be 32 per cent in each of the financial year from 2010-11 to 2014-15.

4. The indicative ceiling on over-all transfers to states on the revenue account may be set at 39.5 per cent of gross revenue receipts of the centre.
5. The revenue deficit of the Centre needs to be progressively reduced and eliminated, following the emergence of revenue surplus by 2014-15.
6. A target of 68 per cent of GDP for the combined debt of the Centre and states should be achieved by 2014-15. The fiscal consolidation path embodies steady reduction in the augmented debt stock of the Centre to 45 per cent of GDP by 2014-15 and of the states to less than 25 per cent of GDP by 2014-15.
7. In case of macro-economic shocks, instead of relaxing the states' borrowing limits and letting them borrow more, the Centre should borrow and devolve the resources using the Finance Commission tax devolution formula for *inter-se* distribution between states.
8. Given the exceptional circumstances of 2008-09 and 2009-10, the fiscal consolidation process of the states which was disrupted would try to get back to their fiscal correction path by 2011-12, allowing for a year of adjustment in 2010-11.
9. The National Calamity Contingency Fund is suggested to be merged into the National Disaster Response Fund and the Calamity Relief Fund into State Disaster Response Funds of the respective states. Contribution to the SDRFs is to be shared between Centre and states in the ratio of 75:25 for general category states and 90:10 for special category states.
10. Apart from non-plan revenue grants of Rs. 51,800 crore recommended to 8 states, there are other grants like performance grant, grant for Elementary Education, Environment, Improving outcomes, maintenance of Roads and Bridges and State specific needs. There is also a High Level Monitoring Committee headed by the Chief Secretary to review the utilisation and take corrective measures.

There are two issues in sharing of taxes, one is vertical and the other is horizontal. Since the Eleventh Finance Commission for the first time made provision for sharing of all taxes (as per eightieth amendment), we only make a reference to the recommendations of both Eleventh Finance Commission and 12th Finance Commission but analyse in detail the recommendations of the 13th Finance Commission whose recommendations have been accepted by the Government. The Eleventh Finance Commission considered the aggregate shares of states in the net proceeds of all Union taxes and duties, excluding surcharges and cesses during the last two decades and found that it varied between 26.2 per cent (1988-89) and 31.8 per cent (1993-94), the average varying from a low of 27.3 per cent to a high of 28.8 per cent. The Eleventh Finance Commission stipulated the ratio at 29.5 per cent. The 12th Finance Commission considered the views of both the Union Government and State Governments and decided to use grants to a larger extent as an instrument of transfers and recommended that the shares of the states in net proceeds of shareable central taxes to be raised from 29.5 per cent to 30.5 per cent.

For this purpose additional excise duties in lieu of sales tax on textiles, tobacco and sugar are treated as part of the general pool of central taxes. If, however, the tax rental arrangement is terminated and if states are allowed to levy sales tax (or VAT) on these commodities without any prescribed limit, the share of the states in the net proceeds of shareable central taxes will be 29.5 per cent. The 12th Finance Commission has also treated the service tax as shareable. The position will change after the 88th constitutional amendment is notified. Any legislation that is enacted in respect of service tax must ensure that the revenue accruing to a state under the legislation should not be less than the share that would accrue to it had the entire service tax proceeds been part of the shareable pool.

SHARING OF UNION TAX REVENUE

(a) Vertical Distribution

One of the core tasks of a Finance Commission as

stipulated in Article 280(3)(a) of the Constitution is to make the recommendations regarding the distribution between the Union and the states of the net proceeds of taxes which are to be, or may be, divided between them and the allocation between the states of such proceeds. There are two aspects here, Vertical Devolution and Horizontal Sharing. While considering vertical distribution, the Finance Commission has considered the revenue raising capacity of the Centre and states as well as emerging pressures on their expenditure commitments. It is found that the Centre has the advantage of buoyancy of Central taxes, resorting to levy of cesses and surcharges to meet some of its expenditure commitments, scope for an increase in non-tax revenues, particularly from royalties and telecommunication sector while the states will have to meet certain obligations in respect of CSS, matching contributions in respect of central schemes, pressure for increasing urban population and implementation of the recommendations of Sixth CPC along with some other disabilities. Taking all these factors into account, the 13th F.C. increased the indicative ceiling on all revenue account transfers to 39.5 per cent of the Centre's gross revenue receipts while the Eleventh Finance Commission and Twelfth Finance Commission had fixed it at 37.5 per cent and 38 per cent respectively.

(b) Horizontal Sharing

Different Finance Commissions have followed different criteria in determining the principle of distribution. Recent Finance Commissions have used equity and efficiency as the two guiding principles while recommending *inter-se* shares of states in tax devolution. The principle of equity addresses the problem of differences in revenue raising capacity and cost of disabilities across states. The principle of efficiency is intended to address this issue and to motivate the states to exploit their resource base and manage their fiscal operations in a cost effective manner. On this basis of above principles the criteria used in the past for these purposes can be grouped under : (a) factors reflecting needs such as population and income measured either as distance from the highest income or as reverse, (b) cost disability indicators such as area and infrastructure distance, and (c) fiscal efficiency indicators such as tax effort and fiscal discipline. The importance given to any of the above criteria has varied by different commissions. We mention below the recommendations of only the 13th Finance Commission.

TABLE 6

Criteria	*Weight (percent)*
Population (1971)	25.0
Area	10.0
Fiscal Capacity Distance	47.5
Fiscal Discipline	17.5

The recommendations of the Commission on tax devolution are based on the consideration of the need, fiscal deficiency and adequate incentivisation for better performance.

SEPARATE GRANTS FOR LOCAL BODIES

For the first time the Eleventh Finance Commission was required to augment the consolidated fund of the states to enable them to supplement the resources of the local bodies. The 12th Finance Commission made a detailed study of the financial problem of local bodies and recommended a total grant of Rs. 20,000 crore for the Panchayati Raj Institutions and Rs. 5000 crore for the urban local bodies during the period 2005-10. It also made a number of recommendations in respect of powers and functions of local bodies so as to serve the social and economic needs of the people. The other conditions prescribed are: The PRIs should be encouraged to take over the assets relating to water supply and sanitation and utilise the grants for repair/rejuvenation as also O&M costs. The PRIs should however, recover atleast 50 per cent of the recurring costs in the form of user charges. In respect of urban local bodies the Commission suggested that atleast 50 per cent of grants provided to each state for the urban local bodies should be earmarked for the scheme of solid waste management through public partnership. The municipalities should concentrate on collection, segregation and transportation of solid waste. The cost of these activities, whether carried out in house or outsourced could be met from the grants.

The Thirteenth Finance Commission (THFC) has made some significant departures from the past and made recommendations that could help to strengthen the process of democratic decentralisation in the country if they are fully implemented. First substantial grants have been recommended by THFC as compared to other Finance Commissions as given in Table 7.

Table 7
Grant Allocation of Different Commissions to Local Governments

Commission	*Total Grant (Rs. in crore)*	*% of Divisible Pool*
TFC (1995-2000)	5380.93	1.38
EFC (2000-05)	10,000	0.78
TWFC (2005-10)	25,000	1.24
THFC (2010-15)	87,519	2.28@

@ Defacto only 1.93%, *Source* : THFC Report 151, 174.

TFC : Tenth Finance Commission

EFC : Eleventh Finance Commission

TWFC : Twelfth Finance Commission

THFC : Thirteenth Finance Commission

The increase from TWFC's Rs. 25,000 crore to the THFC's Rs. 87,519 crore is more than 3.5 times.

1. Unlike the report of the predecessors, the THFC upheld the view that local governments should be supported through 'a predictable and buoyant source of revenue' of the Centre and States. Since the scope of increasing buoyancy of central taxes, the Panchayat and Urban local bodies may receive additional grants beside the grant prescribed.
2. Another important recommendation of the THFC is the decision to relate grants to local governments to a share in the divisible pool of the Union tax revenue. In this way, the THFC has made local governments

an integral part of the public finance of the country. They are now recognised as entities that are linked to the union tax revenue pool almost like the state governments.

3. The local grant recommended by the THFC has two components: a basic component and a performance-based component. The basic grant is equivalent to 1.5 per cent of the previous year's divisible tax revenue to be further adjusted when the final accounts are available. All states will have access to this grant for all the five years (2010-15). A small portion of this grant is earmarked to special areas such as those covered by Schedule V and Schedule VI. The performance grant effective from 2011-12 will be 0.5 per cent for 2011-12 and 1 per cent after that upto 2014-15. The performance grant allocated to each state is subject to their fulfilling a nine point conditionality package. This should help promote result-based accountability.
4. Along with the fixation of the size of vertical transfers, there is a need to determine the horizontal share on the basis of relevant criteria. The following criteria have been fixed in respect of distribution of the allotment of funds to the local bodies by THFC.

TABLE 8

Criteria and Weight allotted for Grants to Local Governments

Criteria	*Weight Allotted*	
	PRIs	*ULBs*
Population	50	50
Area	10	10
Distance from highest per capita sectoral income	10	20
Index of devolution	15	15
SC/ST proportion in Population	10	—
FC Local Government Grant Utilisation Index	5	5
Total	100	100

Source : THFC Report 177.

Two comments are worth mentioning. One is Index of devolution dcpends on tax effort. Many local bodies do not make any effort to impose taxes. There is every justification to allot 15 per cent on tax effort. Second is the Index of Utilisation. If a particular local body does not utilise the grant it should be deprived of performance grant. The THFC has made many general comments. We can only mention one which emasculates local governments both financially and operationally. The local self-government is supposed to implement plans for economic development and social justice and prepare a draft district development plan. The Union and state governments are to help this process of decentralised planning and governance with funds, functionaries and technical support. Instead when there is manifold growth of parallel agencies (like Local Area Development Scheme entrusted to MPs and Assembly Members) that trangress the functional domain entrusted to local governments and distort their role in the federal structure of India.

Other Measures of Grants and Assistance to improve economic well-being along *with measure for Improving Outcome, etc.*

Measures which include in this category are: Disaster Relief, Grants-in-aid, Elementary Education, Environment, Improving Outcome, Maintenance of Roads and Bridges, State Specific Grants and Monitoring. All these are a part and parcel to strengthen the federal structure of the country. The total assistance given by some of the recent Finance Commissions are given below in Table 9.

As can be seen from Table 9 in all these cases the share in taxes has been much more than grants given by the Finance Commissions. And in Thirteenth Finance Commission, both share in taxes and grants have been much more than the previous Finance Commissions.

FINANCIAL ASSISTANCE BY PLANNING COMMISSION AND OTHER AGENCIES

Federal transfers to states are mediated through three agencies: Finance Commission, Planning Commission and through Ministries of Central Government. Planning

TABLE 9

Transfers Recommended by Finance Commissions

Finance Commission	*Grants in Aid*		*Share in Taxes*		*Total Amount*
	Amount (Crore)	*% share*	*Amount (Crore)*	*% share*	*Amount in Crore*
(1)	*(2)*	*(3)*	*(4)*	*(5)*	*(6)*
Tenth	20,300	8.96	2,06,343	91.04	2,26,643
Eleventh	58,587	13.47	3,76,318	86.53	4,34,905
Twelfth	1,42,640	18.87	6,13,112	81.13	7,55,752
Thirteenth	3,18,581	18.03	14,48,096	81.07	17,66,677

Source : Thirteenth Finance Commission (Annex 6.1).

Commission generally provides grants for developmental programmes. Though there is a little bit of pull and pressure in Planning Commission grants, by and large, priority is often given to the basic needs of the states on the basis of revised Gadgil formula. Broadly speaking plan assistance is provided for two types of plan schemes viz. (i) plan schemes sponsored by the state government and (ii) plan schemes sponsored by the Union Government. In regard to vertical plan transfers, it is found that the transfers of plan finance have been consistently decreasing. While during the period 1989-95, total plan assistance to the States and Union Territories was 15.54 per cent of the gross revenue receipts of the Centre, it has come down to about 11 per cent during the 10th Plan period. In respect of horizontal transfer, the plan transfers were not helpful to poorer states since the loan component was 70 per cent of the grant. Now that the TWFC has emphasized needs and cost disabilities in transfer of funds along with a number of other recommendations regarding withdrawal of loan component, debt relief, conversion of old debts with lower rate of interest, the poorer states are likely to receive substantial assistance from the THFC for rectifying their economic and social disabilities.

The fiscal transfer norm that has been enunciated by THFC is important because the transfers mediated by FC constitute the principal component of revenue flows from the Centre to the states. While all states depend on central transfers in varying degrees, forming an average about one-third of their revenue (in the case of poorer states the proportion is nearly 50 per cent), over two thirds of the total transfers flow from the dispersion of the FC. Therefore, transfers mediated by the FC and its other recommendations in response to matters additionally referred to, they have a profound impact on the budgets of all states.

The transfer of funds under various centrally sponsored schemes has created some adverse effect on the state finances due to matching grants in some of the schemes. Since many of the poorer states are unable to meet such grants due to their financial difficulty, they cannot avail of such privileges. Though in principle it has been stipulated to hand over such schemes to local institutions through the state governments, the manner of allocation has not yet been finalised. Since there is a pressure from the states and different NDC meetings have unanimously resolved to transfer such schemes to the states, it is hoped the Centre will respond to it in a positive manner. However, since grants under such schemes are not substantial, it will not materially change the plan finance of the states.

CHAPTER

17

Hazards of a Billion Plus Population

INDIA HAS A DEMOGRAPHIC DIVIDEND

Research on the relationship between population change and economic development provides very divergent views. For example, India which is a young nation has a promise of demographic dividend with great potentialities of rapid growth. The dividend is illustrated by the fact that majority of people is under the age of 35 years. The India's National Youth Policy (NYP, 2003) considers all individuals in the age group of 13-35 years as youth population. Their number in India comes to 459 million or 38 per cent of the total population and will reach close to 574 million by 2020. Again by 2020, the average Indian will be 29 compared to 37 in China and the US, 45 in Western Europe and 48 in Japan. It is said that young Indians will show the way with innovation, gumption and determination. Gandhiji said once upon a time that young people are salt of the nation with ability to change the course of history. What will be our tomorrow is what young people decide today.

BUT DIVIDEND WILL HELP OF QUALITY IMPROVES

But what sort of society do the youth want to build? It is not the size of population but the quality of the human resource which is of paramount importance. If the young people are not able to dream with imagination and excel with innovation, increase in population will not be a dividend but a disaster. As pointed out by Isher Judge Ahluwalia, Chairperson, Indian Council for Research on International Economic Relations (ICRIER), the current GDP growth rate cannot be termed sustainable as a large chunk of society is not able to reap the benefit. According to him, this can become both an economic and social problem. Economic because an additional 110 million youngsters are to be added to the workforce by 2010. How can the economy provide so much productive employment? If productive employment cannot be created, poverty which is now colossal may further worsen. How can we provide good jobs to all these young people?

And social because of the diverse composition of this force, for instance 40 per cent of the literate youth are OBCs and 62 per cent in rural areas. In addition, the question of human resource development which depends primarily on the levels of education and status of health are almost dismal. As NKC Chairman Sam Pitroda notes only 11-12 per cent of Indian population of relevant age enter higher education, which is half of Asian average. And what is most distressing is that most of them are unemployable. It is estimated that by 2020, the working age population in India is expected to grow by more than 47 million people. If the new generation of work force is not equipped with skill and knowledge, the nation cannot harness human capital. Similarly our record in health care is shameful. According to UN Development Report, India has in respect of community health services, slipped in world ranking from 128 to 134. Further the third National Family Health Survey of 2005-06 attests that 25 million children in India are wasted and 61 million stunted. The Food and Agriculture Organization estimates that over 250 millions in India are chronically undernourished. In fact, India's mal-nourished children are double the population of sub-Sahara Africa. How can we harness India's Youth Power?

In view of all this, there is every reason to believe that a rapidly growing population in India will retard the process of economic development. Economic development to a great extent depends upon higher level of income, higher level of saving, increased capital formation, improved technology, increased productivity of various resources and improved quality of human life. A rapidly growing population in an over populated country adversely affects all the above factors and increases dependency load. As the first Indian Prime Minister, Pandit Jawaharlal Nehru put it, "to plan when population growth is unchecked is like building a house where the ground is constantly flooded".

The obvious reason why increased pressure of population retards economic growth is that most of the developing countries invest almost 50-60 per cent of their total investment in maintaining the existing level of per capita income, whereas the corresponding figure in many developed countries comes to less than 25 per cent. Therefore, the developing countries have hardly any investible surplus to increase the productivity of land and labour, create additional employment opportunities through increased capital formation, reduce the number of unproductive consumers and improve the level of living of all those who are poor or deprived. Most of the economists are therefore, agreed that one way of accelerating economic development is to reduce the rate of growth of population. Stphe Enke succinctly puts it as "Where labour has a very low marginal product relative to that of capital which is reported to be the case in most backward as compared with most advanced countries, practically all economic democratic models indicate that a gradual lowering of fertility over several decades raises income per head substantially" and thus helps in increasing capital formation and economic development along with human development.

RATE OF GROWTH OF POPULATION

If rapid growth of population is a barrier to economic development, what should be done in India so that we can be able to control the rate of growth of population. But before we answer this question, let us examine the position of population growth and factors contributing to such growth. India's population in the year 1951 was about 361 million. By 1st March, 1991, the number increased to 846.3 million including the projected population of 7.72 million for Jammu and Kashmir where census was not conducted. In 2001, the total population comes to 1027.02 million. The following table shows the rate of growth of population from 1951-2001 along with density and sex ratio. (The detailed report of 1911 census has not yet been published. The preliminary figures show that India's population in 1911 has come to 1.21 billion with a growth rate of 17.64 per cent in comparison to 21.15 per cent in 2001).

TABLE 1

Population Growth (1951-2001)

Census year	*Population (In Million)*	*Decadal Growth (Per cent)*	*Average annual Growth (per cent)*	*Density (per sq. km)*	*Sex Ratio (Females per 1000 males)*
1951	361.09	13.31	1.25	117	946
1961	432.23	21.64	1.96	142	941
1971	548.16	24.80	2.20	177	930
1981	683.33	24.66	2.22	216	934
1991	846.39	23.86	2.14	267	927
2001	1027.02	21.34	1.93	324	933

Source : Economic Survey, 2001-02.

Though population has become one billion plus, the decrease in decadal growth and average annual growth is more or less marginal. The U.N. has estimated that world population grew at annual rate of 1.4 per cent during 1990-2000 and China registered a much lower annual growth rate of population which comes to 1 per cent. India is now the second country in the world after China to cross one billion mark. It is now estimated that by 2050, India will most likely overtake China to become the most populous country on the earth with 17.2 per cent population living here. India now accounts for 2.4 per cent of the world surface area (135.79 m sq.kms) with 16.7 per cent of world population. It may be noted here that from 16.7 per cent to 17.2 per cent is not a small jump under world standards.

The two other factors that are noticed in the table are : (1) density per sq.km is increasing (from 117 in 1951 to 324 in 2001—almost an increase of 28 per cent), and (2) there is no significant change in sex ratio—there is a great deal of fluctuation in number of females to 1000 males. This does not seem to be a sign of healthy development. Further, the census figures also show that the rate of growth of population is not uniform among different states. While Kerala, Tamil Nadu and Andhra Pradesh registered a low growth in population during 1991-2001, States like Bihar, Haryana, Uttar Pradesh, Sikkim, Nagaland, Delhi, Chandigarh and Gujarat have shown an upward swing in population growth rates during the same period. It is surprising that developed states like Haryana, Delhi, Chandigarh and Gujarat have not been able to reduce the rate of growth of population.

The National Population Policy (NPP) has a medium term objective to bring down the Total Fertility Rate (TFR) to the replacement level of 2.1 by 2010. The current TFR (per women on average) is about 2.7 (2007) compared to 6.0 in 1951, 4.5 in 1981 and 3.6 in 1991. The demographic profile across States reveals that 9 States and Union Territories including Kerala, Tamil Nadu and Punjab are reported to have already reached the replacement level of fertility. These States account for about 15 per cent of total population. Another 10 states with about 41 per cent of the country's population are likely to achieve replacement rates by 2010. The remaining 11 states and UTs which account for 44 per cent of the country's population and include the more populous States like Uttar Pradesh, Rajasthan, Bihar, Madhya Pradesh may not achieve replacement rates.

The Registrar General of India has also made projections of population for the year 2021 under different fertility assumptions. If TFR is assumed to be 2.0 during the period 2006-11, the projected population by 2021 would be about 1233 million. But if the TFR reaches 2.0 by 2011-16, the projected population by 2021 would be more than 1972 million. And if the TFR is assumed to reach 2.0 during 2016-21, the projection of population by 2021 would be about 1327 million. One does not exactly know what would be the trend of fertility rate in different periods given above. It all depends on measures taken to control the fertility rate. The projection of population of India by the State of the World Population Report, 1994, for the year 2025 comes to about 1.4 billion. According to the Ministry of Health and Family Welfare India's population is increasing by 1.4 per cent per year during the last 5 years. China's increase in population during the same period is 0.6 per cent per year. During the last 100 years India's population increased five-fold. It is now estimated by the Ministry that India's population will exceed China in 2050. By that year, India's population would be 161.38 crore whereas China's 141.7 crore.

The increase in population under different assumptions of fertility will bring about changes of population, under different age groups. Assuming that the population will increase to the extent of 1272 by the year 2021 (fertility level reaches 2 sometime during 2011-16), there will be tremendous increase in the population in working age group 15-59. This population is likely to increase from 488 million in 1991 to about 849 million of 2021—an increase of 361 million within a short period of 30 years. One constraint of the high increase in the working age group is that large number of workers will come to the labour market for additional jobs.

Even now about 60 to 65 per cent of the working population is dependent on agriculture. Because of heavy dependence on agriculture, we have not been able to achieve the full potential of our agriculture which is at least twice as much as we are currently producing. Our area under food grain crops, as well as our irrigated area, exceeds those of both USA and China. But our productivity per hec. is not even half of those countries. Our total production is less than half of what has been achieved in China and less than two-thirds of that of USA. On per capita basis USA is producing five times more foodgrains than what we are. In spite of the green revolution, our per capita availability of foodgrains is less than two-thirds of the world average. We appear to be self sufficient only because one-third of our population cannot afford to buy enough foodgrains for its adequate nutrition. It follows from this that increased growth of population and consequent heavy dependence on agriculture cannot reduce hunger from India. In fact India now ranks at 66 among 88 in the Global Hunger Index.

IMPACT OF INCREASED GROWTH

Per capita real income is generally taken as an index of economic development, even though in recent years HDI has assumed more importance than per capita real income. However, if we judge economic development only on the basis of per capita income, a high growth rate of population will reduce the level of per capita income. During 1960-61 and 1988-89, net national product at factor cost (at 1980-81 prices) increased by about 184 per cent, but on account of a rise in population by 80 per cent, per capita income increased only by about 54 per cent. The annual average growth rate of national income works out to be 3.8 per cent (compound) whereas per capita income comes of only 1.6 per cent. However, in recent years there has been some improvement in per capita income due to increase in annual growth of national income since Eighth Plan. For example, the annual average of per capita net national product at 1999-2000 prices increased by 4.5, 3.3 and 6.1 per cent respectively during 8th, 9th and 10th plan periods.

But this was not sufficient to improve the economic well being of the poor mainly because there was no increase in the productivity of the working population. Increase in per capita income ultimately depends upon the productivity of workers. When there is increase in population, more labourers are generally used in a unit of productive activity resulting in lower productivity of each worker. That is what is happening today in India in most of the economic activities. And thus a continuing growth of population and labour force is an impediment to raising of personal incomes and the alleviation of poverty.

Rapid population growth also prevents change in occupational distribution. Since most of the developing countries cannot afford to risk large scale unemployment, rapid population growth in these countries postpones the transformation of traditional economy into one dominated by the manufacturing sector. This is because of the fact that relative investment costs of job creation in manufacturing sector are much more than the traditional sector and a developing country cannot afford to have such investments due to paucity of capital. Postponement of such transformation increases the number of unproductive workers. There is evidence that capital is moving away from inefficient low productive sectors to efficient more productive sectors. But what is less noticed is the lack of similar mobility of labour from inefficient to efficient sectors. If a large number of workers remains underemployed or works in inefficient sectors the marginal productivity of such workers becomes less than one apart from the fact there is huge wastage of manpower arising both from underemployment and unemployment.

Increase in the growth of population will not only decrease the number of productive workers, but also increase the number of unproductive consumers. Unproductive consumers constitute persons who are not engaged in any economic activity. Broadly speaking, children, old persons and some of the people in the age group of 15-59 who are unemployed are included among the non productive consumers. Total number of unproductive consumers has increased from 256 million in 1961 to 464 million in 1981 (from 57.0 per cent to 62.4 per cent). In 1991 census, the number of people under 15 years of age constituted 320 million and those aged 60 years and above came to 52.8 million. The estimates of Human Development Report, 2009, show that in 2010, child dependency ratio is 47.9 and old age dependency ratio is 7.7. This means additional health care has to be provided to treat the aged who are susceptible to different kinds of diseases. Children also require more nutritious food and health care for their healthy growth.

However, according to the projections of the Registrar General of India, child population (below the age of 15 years) may decline to 286 million and the aged may increase to 137 million by 2021. The total, therefore, come to 423 million. As mentioned in Economic Survey 2009-10, the rate of growth of labour force increased per annum by 2.62 per cent between 1999-2000 to 2004-05 whereas during the same period the rate of growth of employment was 1.25 per cent per annum. The latest figures of poverty in India are given by both NSS 61st round and Tendulkar Committee for the year 2004-05.

According to NSS 61st round, it is 27.5 per cent (by URP method) and by Tendulkar Committee 37.2 per cent. But there is no doubt that with the increase of population, the number of unproductive workers will increase. It is not possible now how many people will be absorbed in productive activity by 2021. According to NSS 61st round, the CDS estimates of unemployment rate which is the broadest and also highest come to 8.2 for rural areas and 8.3 for urban areas. Therefore, there is no doubt that a large number of workers will go without work and therefore, the number of unproductive consumers will go on increasing along with population explosion.

It may also be mentioned here that of the total labour force of 40.3 per cent only 7 per cent is employed in organized sector and the rest 93 per cent is employed in informal sector. Of the 7 per cent who are employed in organized sector, 66.7 per cent is employed in public sector and 33.3 per cent in private sector. Those who are working in the informal sector, neither their employment nor wage level is certain. The Report of National Commission for Enterprises in the unorganized sector states that 836 million Indians (i.e. 77 per cent of our people) live on Rs. 20 a day or less.

RAPIDLY GROWING POPULATION REDUCES INVESTIBLE SURPLUS AND QUALITY OF LIFE

It follows from this that a rapidly growing population does not provide adequate investible surplus for capital formation. Because a rapid growth of population makes increasing demands on resources for maintaining the existing level of consumption, thus hindering capital accumulation. In the sixties and seventies, the rate of growth of population of India was about 2.2 per cent per year and the capital output ratio on average varied from 4.5 to 5 per cent. This implies that capital accumulation of the order of 11 per cent (2.2×5) is necessary to maintain a constant level of consumption. Dr. Zaidan has estimated that whereas in developed countries the proportion of GNP that is required to keep per capita income at a constant level, is less than 5 per cent, in developing countries, it is more than 10 per cent. This implies that a large proportion of national income will be invested in producing consumer goods at the expense of investment goods, thereby slowing down the rate of economic growth.

Another worry in rapid growth of population is deterioration in the quality of life. As it is, we do not have sufficient food, adequate educational and medical facilities, even drinking water is not available in many parts of India, infant mortality is quite high and as we have already discussed the level of poverty and unemployment is colossal. Malthusian nightmare is still haunting us. The following table shows some selected social indicators.

TABLE 2

Selected Social Indicators

Crude Birth Rate (per 1000 persons)	22.8	(2008)
Crude Death Rate (per 1000 persons)	7.4	(2008)
Maternal Mortality Rate (per 100,000 live births)	254	(2004-05)
Infant Mortality Rate (per 1000 live births)	53	(2008)
Child Mortality Rate (0-4 years per 1000 children)	16	(2007)
Total fertility rate (per woman)	2.7	(2007)
Life Expectancy at Birth (in years)	64.2	(2002-06)
Male	63.5	(2002-06)
Female	64.2	(2002-06)
Adult Literacy Rates (% aged 15 years and above)	66.0	(1999-2007)

Source : Ministry of Health and Family Welfare, *Economic Survey*, 2009-10, Table 11.9, p. 284.

The table shows that from the point of view of Human Development Index (HDI), India's position comes to 0.612 (2007) whereas it is 0.772 in China—during the same year. In many of the developed countries it varies from 0.930 to 0.940.

If we consider the measures taken by the Government to improve the quality of life we find that they are far from satisfactory. The following table shows the commitment to health, access, services and resources.

Even some of the developing countries (not to speak of developed countries) have got better facilities than that of India.

TABLE 3

Commencement to Health, Access, Services and Resources

1.	One year old fully immunized against TB (2002)	81%
2.	One year old fully immunized against measles (2002)	67%
3.	Population with sustainable access to affordable essential drugs (1999)	0.49%
4.	Contraceptive prevalence (1995-2002)	48%
5.	Physicians (per 100,000 people, (1990-2003)	51
6.	Health expenditure per capita (PPPUS $) 2001	80

Source : Human Development Report, 2004, Table 6, p. 158.

Another dimension which is likely to create further hurdles in improving the quality of life is increasing urbanization. Urban population in India has increased from 18 per cent in 1951 to 22.44 per cent in 1991 and 27.8 per cent in 2001. The metropolitan cities have increased from 5 in 1951 to 21 in 1991 and 35 in 2001 with Greater Mumbai the highest at 16.4 m followed by Kolkata, Delhi, Chennai, Bangalore and so on. And in most of the metropolitan cities, slums account for about 35 to 40 per cent of the population. In Greater Mumbai the slum population comes to more than 60 per cent and about 1 per cent of India's population lives in the slums of Maharashtra. Life lived in these cities is not worthy of human dignity. Further, the Registrar General of India estimated in 2006 that 67 per cent of the population growth in the next 25 years is expected to take place in urban areas alone. Human Development Report 2009 indicates urban population in India at 30.1 per cent in 2010. This increase will prove greater worry to improve the economic and social conditions of urban areas.

We may also mention here that HDI as defined by UNDP Report does not adequately measure the basic contents of the quality of life in India with its over population and poverty. Human Development widely used for the purpose of inter country comparison utilizes such indicators as life expectancy, literacy rate and per capita real income for the construction of the HDI. For example, long life expectancy, in the midst of poverty, illness and deprivation of the basic facilities of life, can be more painful than any benefit. Similarly, high literacy rates improve the capabilities of an individual but if he does not get adequate employment, his abilities are not utilized in which case he feels more frustrated than any pleasure from his improved ability. In case of India, a large number of educated people are unemployed and their number is increasing. Even per capita income alone cannot convey the true meaning of quality of life when there is widespread inequality in the distribution of income. As Table 4 indicates there is wide gap in income between the rich and poor.

TABLE 4
Distribution of Income by Per capita Income Quintile—All India

Per capita Quintile	*Share of each Quintile to total income*		
	1993-94	*2004-05*	*2009-10*
Q5—Top Quintile (81%-100%)	36.7	47.9	53.2
Q4—Fourth Quintile (61%-80%)	24.7	20.8	18.9
Q3— Third Quintile (41%-60%)	18.4	14.4	12.6
Q2—Second Quintile (21%-40%)	12.9	10.4	9.2
Q1—Bottom Quintile (0%-20%)	7.3	6.5	6.1
Total	100	100	100

Source : NSHIE 2004-05 data, NCAER-CMCR Analysis.

It is true that we retain per capita income as a proxy for the quality of life of an individual. It is considered as an index of economic growth. A high rate of economic growth manifested by a high GDP may help in improving per capita income but may not be a sufficient condition for improving the quality of life. This is particularly so because economic growth does not automatically transform itself into human development. All depends on the nature and extent to which policies and programmes of an economy are geared to harmonise economic growth with human development. If the policies and programmes are implemented to improve the basic amenities of life such as clean drinking water, sanitation and good housing facilities and access to electricity, information technology and so on for people at large, we can say that economic growth and human development are complementary (Amartya Sen).

In order to measure the human development from a comprehensive point of view, we have to take into account various aspects of human development such as levels of living, employment and wages, nutrition, effectiveness of such public services as public distribution system, education and health care as well as the demographic characteristics. The NCAER studied the rural sector of 16 major states and assessed the overall scenario of human development. The study shows that 14% of the people belonging to lowest strata have access to Rs. 3 per person per day and the next 18% Rs. 5.30, about 50 per cent of those who live below the poverty line spend one-fifth of their per capita income on health care alone. Adult literacy is alarmingly low, about 5 per cent among the SCs and STs especially in Uttar Pradesh, Bihar, Madhya Pradesh and Rajasthan. Programmes of poverty alleviation, too have not had much impact. On the whole, the states in the south are relatively in a much better position as far as the indicators of human development are concerned (Keya Sengupta).

Population explosion is not only a stumbling block for the development of economically backward countries, it also leads to uncontrolled exploitation of the nature. One of the pertinent questions is how many people can the earth accommodate—5.66 billion as in mid-1994, six billion by the turn of the century or 12 billion in the year 2058? Most of the UN organizations concerned with population, development, industrialization, employment, food, health, education and environmental protection point to the limits of growth. The quantities of raw materials, potable water, arable land and marine resources are limited. And the North-South divide in respect of basic necessities, education and health is colossal. Taking the reality of 2001 into account, it is doubtful whether the earth can accommodate for another addition in billions to population. We are now consuming 40 per cent more than what the earth can sustain. As a matter of fact environmental degradation has increased so much that inhabitants of many countries do not get fresh air, pure water, and traffic and industries release so much pollutants that the entire atmosphere becomes unhealthy. For example, indiscriminate industrialization has given rise to toxic gases, depletion of ozone layer, threat of acid rain, pollution of air, water and land surface, etc., in fact nothing is spared resulting in total pollution. And some of the cities in India are worst sufferers of environmental pollution (Misra). In fact climate report rings alarm bells for humanity.

The present scenario of the world is terribly grim. About 1.1 billion people are in dire poverty, earning about $1 per day, and two billions lack atleast one of the basic foods necessary for nourishment. Another 800 million continue to be undernourished, although by global standards there is no shortage of food. Some 192 million children suffer from chronic protein deficiency and about 13 million die every year before the age of five as a result of infection and starvation.

What is most distressing is that the people of the industrialized nations, who constitute 25 per cent of the world's population, consume 88 per cent of all raw materials and produce 400 million tonnes of garbage annually. Traffic and industries in the North are mostly responsible for releasing into the atmosphere the emissions that can cause global warming known as the green house effect. Even agriculture is in a precarious situation. Monocultures, pesticides, excessive use of fertilizers, salinity, shifting cultivation and erosion are blighting the once fertile top soil. According to the FAO, two billion hectares of agricultural land—double the surface of the USA—have become infertile and 295 million hectares are virtually lost forever. Some 35 per cent of pasture land is over used and 30 per cent of land in general suffers from deforestation and fires. About 16 million hectares of forests are cut down by man every year. One fatal consequence is that at least 40 animal and plant species are dying each day (World Conservation Union and Worldwide Fund for Nature). All this shows that the tug of war between comfort and naked survival is gathering momentum.

The above analysis reveals different approaches both for the North and South to prevent uncontrolled exploitation of nature. Though the North has to reduce the high life style of the consumerist society which exploits nature's resources at an unsustainable pace, the south has to emphasize control of population to improve the level of living and quality of life of its inhabitants. The latter should not of course try to imitate the North in increasing its level of consumption. The North is not only endangering the earth by increasing environmental pollution, it is also facing shortage of some basic materials for development. One example will indicate the gravity of the situation. Japan, for instance, got a foretaste of problems to come when 2000 factories and business had to close down recently because of a water shortage.

HOW TO CONTROL THE GROWTH OF POPULATION

Any way, since our theme in this paper is population explosion in relation to development, we may analyze some of the important measures to control population in the developing countries with particular reference to India.

As Jacob Viner has said there are no easy and certain remedies for the over population problem in developing countries. We have to concentrate on several measures like family planning, improvement in education and health programmes and acceleration of economic development. All these are interrelated. We cannot avoid family planning programmes because to wait for education and economic development to bring about a drop in fertility is not a practical solution. Moreover, family planning does not only mean controlling numbers. It relates to health, education and contraceptive services. It has been broadening to include provision of reproductive health services, reduction of infant mortality, improvement in maternal health, education and women empowerment (J.S. Singh—Creating a New Consensus on population). The very increase in population makes economic development slow and more difficult of achievement. The time factor is so pressing, and the population growth so formidable, that we have to get out of the vicious circle through a direct assault upon this as a national commitment. As pointed out by the Planning Commission, "It is almost axiomatic that economic development can in the long-run bring about a fall in the fertility rate". But it simultaneously and rightly mentions, ". . . developing countries with large population cannot afford to wait for development to bring about a change in the attitudes of couples to limit the size of families as the process of development itself is stifled by population growth".

Again an exclusive reliance on family planning, in a country like India, where widespread illiteracy exists even today, may not be very effective. It is difficult to effectively implement family planning programme both due to poverty and low level of consciousness. Various surveys conducted in recent years in different parts of the country have revealed that only 25 to 30 per cent women in the country side and 45 to 50 per cent women in cities are aware of birth control measures. According to the Human Development Report, 2004, the contraceptive prevalence rate in India, was as low as 48 per cent during 1995-2002 as against 84 in China during the same period. This was mostly due to greater awareness by the people of China. Though family planning programme in India has to be voluntary, certain amount of reasonable restrictions seem to be necessary even in a democracy. In this connection the prescription of sterilization in the country and a minimum age for marriage to influence the size of family are important steps in family planning programme.

But the main disincentive in sterilization is high infant mortality. Unless effective health programmes are initiated to reduce infant mortality, sterilization cannot be successful. Similarly, since fertility depends to a great extent on the age at marriage, it is necessary that every possible social, legal and educative measures are undertaken to raise it. There are many difficulties for which parents want their girl child to marry early. One such difficulty is the fear in rural areas about the safety of an unmarried daughter. Then there are lack of awareness about the impact of fertility on early marriage, wide spread illiteracy, inadequate coverage of the vital registration system which can generate evidence of age and so on. Professor Krishna's study of Kerala shows that higher rates of female literacy increases the age of marriage and decreases birth rate. And in China, Malaysia and Sri Lanka, there has been substantial increase in the age of marriage and reduction of fertility both due to improvement in education and expansion of health programme.

The role of education in enhancing women's social power is undisputed. An educated woman finds it easier to understand contraception, negotiate with her husband and extended family and take advantages of available services. These changes lead to better child spacing, improvement in maternal and infant survival and better health of family members.

Another factor which stands in the way of family planning is that peasants prefer to have more children as they are a source of income to the family. As Mamdani has argued, the people in the rural areas think that the benefit from an additional child is greater than the cost of his upbringing. The obvious reason for this is that children contribute at an early age to agrarian production and a traditional source of security in the old age of parents. P.C. Joshi in his 'Population and Poverty' analyses this problem in a succinct manner. As he puts it, ".... Circumstances of economic insecurity, the poorer classes tend to associate economic security not with a reduction but with an increase in the number of children. The poor has no other economic asset than their own labour and the more the number of earners in the family, the more the amount of family earnings. The lower survival rate further reinforces the preference for children". This shows why economic costs of children for poor parents are low and economic and other benefits of children are high and having many children becomes preferable.

It follows from this that economic development along with human development and change in occupational pattern is important components for the success of family planning programmes. Economic development not only increases income but provides scope for social security system. Parents with higher income have greater motivation for small families to reduce the excessive burden of family life and provide more scope for their children's improvement. Human development creates the necessary awareness and provides scope and opportunity to limit the number of children.

In the final analysis, women have to play a major role in controlling the rate of growth of population. Better education, health care and economic opportunity enable women to make their own decisions, for example, in the size and spacing of their families. By increasing women's decision-making capacity, women's status and ability to contribute to social and economic development will also be strengthened. Experience shows that population and development programmes are most effective in conjunction with action to improve the status of women.

According to the State of World Population Report, empowering women extending choices: Choices about if and when to get married, choices about education, employment opportunities, controlling the social and physical environment, choices about if and when to get pregnant and ultimately about family size. Empowerment requires that husbands, partners, family members and communities help to promote a healthy environment free from coercion, violence or abuse, in which women are free to use community services on a basis of equality. If women are given such empowerment, there is every hope to reduce the size of family and the rate of growth of population in a healthy and decent environment.

References

Economic Survey, 2009-10, Government of India.

Human Development Reports, 2004 and 2009, UNDP.

Joshi, P.C., Population and Poverty, The Moral Discord in Ashish Bose *et. al.* (eds.), Population in India's Development (Delhi, 1974).

Mamdani, Mahmood, The Ideology of Population Control, *EPW*, Special Number, 1976, p. 1143.

Sen, Amartya, Development as Freedom, Oxford India Paper Backs, New Delhi, 2000.

Sengupta, Keya, Indian Economy : Economic Growth and Human Development, Man and Development, March, 2002.

Tenth Five Year Plan, Government of India.

CHAPTER

18

Challenges of Aging

Old age is not a disease; it is a part of life. If one has to grow, he or she has to pass through different stages of life. And a time comes when one becomes old, though the time varies from place to place and person to person. Further along with improvement in economic and social structure which increases longevity, old age comes very late in life. In forties and fifties, many people in rural areas of India were becoming old even at the age of forty or fifty-five. Now it has extended to sixty or more than sixty. In many of the developed countries like the USA, Britain or Japan, one has to wait for seventy or seventy-five to consider himself old. Bertrand Russell married for the fourth time at the age of eighty-two and was mentally so alert that he could write satirical articles which had profound impact on the society. Age didn't make Galbraith invalid even at the age of ninety. And thus the aging problems vary from person to person, while some people suffer from aging problems at a very young age, there are others who carry on with their normal work, even at a very advanced age without any hazard of old age.

But since aging hazards are becoming common for most of the people in India due to environmental degradation, we have to think up the problems of aged in India. Their numbers are gradually increasing due to increase in longevity; the life expectancy at birth, which was about 36/37 in 1951, has now come to 63.4 during the period 2007. If we assume old age at 60+, it is seen that the proportion of people of 60+ in the population shows a definite increasing trend from about 5.97 per cent in 1971 to 7.0 per cent or 7.5 per cent in 2006. The analysis of census data of past decades clearly reveals that the rate of increase of the population 60+ is higher than the rate of increase in the general population. This trend is also expected to continue in future implying thereby that the numbers of the aged would increase at a much faster rate than even before. The demographic shift of the aging population needs a detailed study of the challenges of the growing number of aged people in our country. It is pertinent because while the child crosses the dependency stage with alarming speed, the aged in many cases becomes increasingly dependent on others. We therefore propose to study the issues like : (a) The socio-economic aspect of aging, (b) The emotional and psychological problems of the aged, and (c) The health and medical aspects of aging. These three aspects are most relevant in understanding the problems of the aged and their impact on the society.

SOCIO-ECONOMIC ASPECTS OF AGING

When we consider the socio-economic aspects of aging, we find a number of changes in the economy, which have altered social aspects of life. The following may be considered as important :

(i) There is change in occupational pattern due to growth of industrialisation and urbanization. The joint family system was a part and parcel of agricultural economy. When the importance of agriculture was reduced due to industrial development and increase in the growth of service sector, people tended to move from agriculture to these new avenues of employment. The joint family system in the past provided the aged with needed security, status, love and affection and also mental satisfaction. Their knowledge and also the experience in agricultural operations encouraged the family members to look to them for guidance not only in economic matters but also in social sphere. Parents, both aged men and women, served as guides to younger generation and as such they commanded respect from the younger generation. The community life in villages thus ensured such social values like discipline, respect and obligation.

(ii) The forces of modernization, technological change, improvement in educational system, mobility and explosion of latest transmission of knowledge changed the outlook of younger generation. The knowledge and the experience of older generation became less relevant in solving some of the problems arising in the new social and economic environment. One can easily imagine why one of the sons in BAGBAN had to tell his Dad that the knowledge and experience gathered by him in a small establishment were not relevant in multi-national corporations as they are more challenging and abstruse. Naturally therefore the utility of earlier knowledge and experience in solving present day problems become less relevant and therefore, younger generation's dependence on the aged is greatly reduced.

(iii) The change in educational system provides opportunities to younger generation for different types of jobs for which they have to move sometimes from place to place. When they live in new surroundings, they hardly get suitable accommodation to accommodate their aged parents with them. Particularly in some of the mega cities, housing is a big problem and even a small house costs quite a great deal, so much so that they have to spend a major portion of their income on housing. This works as a constraint in providing accommodation to their parents in their own houses.

(iv) Then they have to think of their children, their health, their education and future prospects. It also happens that both the family members have to take up different types of occupation to maintain their livelihood and meet the increasing demand of their children. This compels them to ensure nuclear family.

(v) There is also a fundamental change in life style of the people in the new environment. New wants are emerging. A family requires many modern amenities to maintain a decent life, you require a television, a fridge, a washing machine, a personal computer, a sofa set and so on which have become a part of modern life. And then there are professional expenses, you have to travel to attend different conferences, invite people on social occasions, and attend parties if you want to make your mark in a society. In this competitive age you can't live an isolated life. But when you wish to be a part of the changed society, your aged parents become isolated having lost all their glamour and prestige. These physical and social constraints sometimes compel some people in the younger generation to remain separate from their parents. But they are not indifferent to them.

But there are cases where some people in younger generation become completely indifferent to their parents; sometimes it is because of their perversion or because of family conflict. Both husband and wife may not have the same common feeling for the parents of either one leading to the negligence of parents.

THE EMOTIONAL AND PSYCHOLOGICAL PROBLEMS OF THE AGED

The aged when left alone feel terribly frustrated which eventually leads to depression. The depression arises because of the fact that Indians are living in a period of transition. For a long time the aged were privileged communities. They were getting the love and respect of their children. They were expecting that when their children grow up, take up some jobs and earn some money, they will take care of them. They bring up their children with great care, suffer sleepless nights when they suffer from some ailments, provide them with a decent education and now when they grow up, stand on their own legs, secure good jobs with good money, they forget the needs of their parents. This is a psychological problem. When one faces lonely days in one's twilight years, one finds difficulty in reconciling to changing family and social equations.

A time has come when the aged should remember that their children have their own problems in these days of competitive struggle; they have to work very hard to establish their own position. Job market is not so easy now a days. If one has to make any significant contribution in any field, one has to work for 9 to 10 hours everyday. We see how young men and women are working now; they go to their office or work centre at about 7.30 A.M. and come back sometimes at 10 or 11 P.M. The work program is terribly arduous. Second, they have to respect the sentiments of their spouses. Conflict or differences of opinion are not unusual in present day social life. If your son/daughter has to live a peaceful life, you should not impose yourself on them to make their life miserable. Thirdly, you must understand that they have to think of their children, bring them up properly, give them good education so that their children are able to survive in this competitive world. We do not mean to say that the children should neglect their parents. In most cases they do not. If there are some who deliberately do this they should by all means be blamed. But parents should have their own responsibilities. If they expect too much from their children, they are bound to feel disappointed. Children cannot possibly come, stay with them and take care of them. If the parents want their children to prosper and succeed in their career, they must not trouble them with minor troubles. Children should of course shoulder the responsibility of their parents when they are in acute trouble. Mutual adjustment is what is necessary to avoid bitter bickering.

THE HEALTH AND MEDICAL ASPECT OF AGING

Aging process has its own problems of health hazards.

Age quite often is found to be associated with respiratory and digestive problems, deficiency disease and diseases of reproductive system. While most suffer with financial disorders, some have organic disorders particularly in higher age group. The ailments, which are commonly associated with later years, include many others like falling eye sight and hearing capacity, forgetfulness, slow and faltering sleep and so on. All these are aggravated when the aged lose many things including friends, spouses, job, power, income and influence. Alienation increases loneliness making their living miserable. Particularly, when they compare their life pattern with the young who have a decent life style with a number of improved amenities, they become more frustrated.

All such problems are a part and parcel of socio-economic phenomena. It is not possible to go back to joint family system or prevent the economic advancement. In such a setting what is required is to provide more facilities for the care of the aged. Retiring rooms for the aged will not solve the problem. The aged want to live with the young, play with children, and participate in different social activities so as to feel that they are wanted in the society. They have their own rich experience. Such experience should be used as far as possible to improve the economic and social structure of the country. What is necessary is to develop a healthy and encouraging attitude towards the aged. Their advice should not be bypassed because they are old nor should they be neglected because of their age. The old age needs more care and therefore all the different institutions, government, civic society, voluntary organizations and individuals should make a co-ordinated effort to create a package of services, both physical, medical, intellectual, and social which will involve them, assist them and make them useful to the broad development of the society. We again repeat, old age is not a disease; all it needs is more care, not in the form of sympathy or compassion, but as a part of duty and obligation to the older generation.

CHAPTER

19

Trend and Pattern of Urbanization in India

Urban growth in India is gradually increasing. The urban population in India at the beginning of 20th Century was only 25.8 million constituting 10.8 per cent of total population in 1901. By about 1951 urban population increased to 62.44 million comprising 17.29 per cent of the total population. The census of 2001 shows that the total urban population came to 286.12 million comprising about 28 per cent. The detailed report of 2011 census is not yet published and as such we have no information on urban population in 2011 census. However, it is now estimated that the urban population in India may cross 35 per cent by 2011. Urban India contributes about 60 per cent of GNP of India. All over the World, there is a trend in the growth of urban population. But the pattern of urbanisation is very unequal between the developed and developing countries. Majority of the population in developed countries lives in urban areas compared to the majority living in rural areas in the developing countries.

In developed countries, the process of urbanisation speeded up in the wake of industrial revolution. India could not make any dent on industrialisation during the British period since the colonial government did not attach any importance to industrial development. Almost about 80 per cent of people in India lived in rural areas at the time of independence whose main occupation was agriculture. There was a trend against urbanisation among most of the influential people as they thought that urbanisation pertained to commercial activities. Indian culture had an antipathy for commercial activities. The politicians also thought that cities do not belong to India. Even Gandhiji's message which implied that cities were built on the blood of villages added lusture to rural life and politicians tried to idealise rural culture even though many of them tried to live in emerging towns. It is only Pandit Nehru who gave an impetus to industrialisation during his Prime Ministership creating an atmosphere for a change in attitude of people in favour of urban centres. Nehru himself facilitated for the creation of a number of new urban centres with modern facilities. All the same, it took sometime before urban life could draw peoples' attention. In sixties and seventies, Green Revolution increased productivity of agriculture and powerful political leaders by emphasising rural development marginalised urban development.

However, economic development and the surge of IT/ BPO industries in Bangalore and elsewhere changed the political winds of India in favour of urbanisation. In addition, a number of other factors increased the importance of urban centres. Growth of cities along with increased number of malls, department stores, colleges and universities, hospitals, law courts, hotels and rest houses and particularly cinemas drew people from rural areas in large numbers. Another major shift which brought about a change in attitude is the Delimitation Commission which revised Parliament and state assembly seats and provided adequate urban representation in Parliament and Assemblies. The political leaders who represented urban constituencies naturally added their voice for the growth of urban centres. The emergence of middle class and the NGOs along with a large number of private organisations heightened urban consciousness. Then there was 'migration of escape' from rural areas of many people coming to urban areas both in search of employment and to enjoy the privileges of urban facilities. When the new technology which had increased the productivity of agriculture became fatigued and agriculture could not provide adequate income nor generate sufficient employment, distressed people had to migrate to urban centres in search of new areas of avocation. In other words poverty in rural areas was exported to urban areas. As such political winds in India began to change the direction in favour of urban India. The Planning Commission which considered urbanisation as an 'unhealthy process in the 1970s and 1980s started thinking urban growth as a natural outcome of the growth of the economy'.

Along with surging crowds of different sections of the community and the rise of middle class with social and political ferment tended to generate new ideas and intellectual thoughts across science and economics which may be named as Renaissance, giving rise to new culture, called urban culture as distinct from rural one. Leaders like Ambedkar recognised this and found the Indian city liberating after the 'sink of localism, the den of inequity'. And Andre Beteille telling Nandan Nilekani that the caste system persisted in rural areas decades after decades because land was economic power in villages, and the upper castes wielded much of their power through family ownership. But in urban areas, wealth is flexible and can be earned in many possible ways providing upward mobility for different castes. Improved transport in urban areas also added scope for limiting the vicious nature of caste relations.

It may be mentioned here that though communal riots and partition of India were a great tragedy in India which killed thousands of people and injured millions who were destabilised and lost their homes and property, came to cities for rehabilitation. Many new towns and cities were created to absorb all these people who had no shelter anywhere. As urban centres increased and many enterprising people shifted to urban areas to test their luck in different enterprises, rural life was often neglected. The 'Garibi Hatao' programme by the government gave a new thrust to rural life but did not succeed in improving the quality of rural people. At this stage, there was a change in political scene by an introduction of 73rd and

74th amendments in the constitution, the 73rd providing empowerment for rural people through Panchayati system with some financial powers to improve their economic and social wellbeing and the 74th amendment created urban bodies like Municipalities and Corporations with definite financial and administrative powers to meet the growing needs of urban people. Not that these could function effectively, but these amendments provided some scope to identify the problems of both the areas and prepare plans and programme atleast to try to solve them. These two separate bodies indicated that the rural and urban areas had many problems which were distinct from each other and therefore needed action by separate elected bodies. But this did not however, mean that the growth of urban areas was completely divorced from rural areas. Some of the people who settled in urban areas had their roots in rural areas. They had their families and also some land from which they were getting some income. On the other hand there were others who were working in urban areas also remitted some money from their income for the maintenance of their families who were staying in villages. There was a great deal of interdependence between urban and rural areas. One economist suggests that a two and half dollar increase in spending on consumption in urban India increased rural household income by just under one dollar.

TRENDS IN URBANISATION

Along with increase in the importance of urbanisation there was not only change in the growth of urban people, but also increase in number of cities and towns and greater migration of rural people to urban centres. Census figures show that the number UAs/Towns which were only 2,843 in 1951 increased to 4,378 in 2001. Similarly, there was an increase in urban population during this period. In 1951, the urban population which was 62.44 million increased to 286.12 million in 2001. Percentage was, it was 17.29 in 1951 which increased to 27.86. The above figures show that the number of towns has not grown as fast as the urban population. When we compare the urbanisation of different states and UTs, we find that Goa tops the list among the states with nearly 50 per cent level of urbanisation followed by Mizoram with 49 per cent, Tamil Nadu with 44 per cent and Maharashtra with 42 per cent in 2001. On the other hand the states like Himanchal Pradesh, Assam, Odisha, Bihar (including Jharkhand) and Utter Pradesh (including Uttarnchal) are the least urbanised states with urbanization levels varying from 10 to 21 per cent, i.e. much lower than the national average of 27.7 per cent in 2001. These are some of the poorer states in India. On the other hand, the levels of urbanisation among UTs are very high as some of them like Delhi, Chandigarh, Pondicherry have city dominance and their rural population are very small. Also, except Dadra Nagar Haveli, the other Union territories show higher level of urbanisation than the national average.

We also make a classification of size class of cities and urban growth. The following table shows a six-fold classification of cities and towns on the basis of population which has been given in Table 1.

Table 1 shows nearly 45 per cent of population lived in cities with population 100 thousand and more in 1951 which increased to 69 per cent in 2001. The number of such cities was only 396 out of the total 4378 urban agglomerations and towns in India. It is not only the cities that dominate India's urban population, but the metropolitan cities within them have far greater sway. According to census 2001, there are 35 million plus cities consisting of 107.9 million urban population and constitute nearly 39 per cent urban population in the country. India's top 20 cities account for just 10% of the country's, but earn more than 30% of national income, spend 21% and account for close to 60% of the surplus income.

However, as Doshi points out, an elephant or a human being or even an ant, after maturity does not grow beyond its ultimate size. If it does it automatically gets destroyed succumbing to external pressures like the dinosaurs of Jurassic era. It is the same with mega cities. By improving their infrastructure, we will improve their functioning, but we cannot upgrade the quality of life. By focussing development in one city we are depriving the smaller towns of their small scale crafts and industries, and encouraging migration to mega cities, which will eventually be crushed under their own burden. Expansion means larger distances and more time and energy to

TABLE 1
Percentage of Distribution of Urban Population by Size-Class of Towns

Census Year	*Cities Class-I 1 lakh or more*	*Large towns Class-II 50000-99000*	*Medium Towns Class-III 20,000-49,999*	*Small Towns*			
				Class-IV 10000-19999	*Class-V 5000-9999*	*Class-VI Less than 5000*	*Total*
(1)	*(2)*	*(3)*	*(4)*	*(5)*	*(6)*	*(7)*	*(8)*
1951	44.63	9.96	15.72	13.63	12.97	3.09	29.69
1981	60.42	1163	14.33	9.54	3.58	0.50	13.62
1991	65.20	10.95	13.19	7.77	2.60	0.29	10.66
2001	68.82	9.73	12.29	6.80	2.33	0.23	9.36

commute for living, working or for cultivating the body, mind and spirit.

To avoid the increasing size of mega cities, it will be better if we can have multiple growth poles spread across the length and breadth of the country. The experience of last several years shows that small cities are showing robust economic growth. Some of the small cities are located even in BIMARU regions. It is suggested by some that these small cities can serve as magnets for intra-state migration and reduce pressure in metros. This will have positive trickle down effect and galvanise the rural economy. Size of cities is not so important as the quality of physical and social infrastructure. Mega cities like Delhi, Mumbai, Kolkata or Bangalore are now struggling with their size and depending overly on exhaustible resources such as water, energy, land and human energies that keep becoming expensive while the quality of life keeps dropping. Needless to say, as against 'small is beautiful', we are talking of 'the bigger the better', and only look towards the west, which has traversed this path, for approval and funding.

Another feature which we notice in mega cities is that inequality is quite high in the top 20 cities, 53 per cent of households in the top most income quintiles are to be found there. For the other cities, the figure is 30% and just 12 per cent in rural India. The Gini co-efficient, a measure of inequality is 0.41 for the top 20 cities and 0.43 for other cities and rural areas. This occupation structure coupled with the variability in earnings across the top 20 cities and rural areas is what causes the big difference in income and savings levels. An average graduate earns Rs. 1,80,000 per year in the leading cities, the comparable rural figure is just Rs. 91,000. The difference in fact is higher for illiterates as well average Rs. 70,000 in the elite towns versus just Rs. 22,500 in the villages (Rajesh Shukla).

If we analyse the growth story of urban centres we find that small cities and towns appear to be doing more to power India's growth story than big metros. Income tax statistics indicates that Tier II and Tier III cities (cities like Patna, Lucknow, Meerut and Kanpur) have far outstripped big metros (like Delhi, Mumbai, Chennai and Kolkata) in terms of personal and corporate tax collections. In fact, Patna has seen as much as 95% growth in personal income tax figures over the 2009-10 period compared to merely 4 per cent for Delhi and 6 per cent for Mumbai. Such a shift towards growth driven by regional centres can help mitigate the problems ensuing from unequal development and, therefore, needs to be encouraged.

TREND AND PATTERN OF URBAN GROWTH

Urbanisation is crucially linked to both natural increase and migration. Natural increase from 1971 to 2000 shows that both during 1971-80 and 1981-1990, the rate of increase per one thousand was 19.3. But during 1991-2000, it came down to 15.8. The obvious reason for this was both birth rate and death rate per 1000 came down in urban areas during these periods. While birth rate during 1991-2000 was 22.3, the death rate came down to 6.5 during the same period. In future, urban growth is further likely to slow down because there is much scope for the urban birth rate of about 22 per 1000 observed during the decade 1990-2000 to further decline whereas urban death rate observed on average during the same period may not decline any more.

Urbanisation is also crucially linked to migration. Whether migration is a strong or a weak force in urbanisation, much depends upon the nature and pattern of migration. In India, migration occurs not only due to economic reasons but a host of social, cultural and other factors as well. As per 2001 census, the total number of internal migrants were 309 million based on place of last residence (which was considered as the basis of calculation). The percentage of total internal migrants to total population was nearly 31 per cent in 2001. The growth rates of intra-district as well as inter-state were much higher than the national population growth rate of 21.4 during this decade as shown in Table 2. One remarkable features of all types of internal migration is that it is dominated by females. This is because women move to their husband's place of residence after marriage.

Three distinct features are noticed in this Table. All the three Intra-district, inter-district and Inter-State migration have been quite significant except during the period 1981-91. Second, international migration has been negative in all these

Table 2
Migrants Classified based on Place of Last Residence in 2001 and their Growth Rates during 1999-2001 (All duration)

Migrants	*2001 (in million)*	*P.C. Distribution 2001*	*Sex Ratio (Males per 1000 females) 2001*	*Growth Rates %*		
				1971-81	*1981-91*	*1991-2001*
(1)	*(2)*	*(3)*	*(4)*	*(5)*	*(6)*	*(7)*
Intra-District	193.5	61.6	323	24.9	8.3	37.0
Inter-District	74.6	23.7	481	44.3	13.7	26.3
Inter-State	41.1	13.1	865	28.1	11.7	53.6
International Migrants	5.1	1.6	1085	-9.1	-6.1	-13.4
All Migrants	314.3	100.0	422	27.0	9.8	34.7
Total Population	1028.6	—	1072	24.7	23.7	21.4

periods. And total number of migrants have been more than the growth of population in the first and third period.

Along with natural increase in urban population which we have already analysed, migration has also contributed to the growth of urban population. Most of the studies show that both push and pull factors have dominated much of the migration. Push factors like low income, low literacy, dependence on agriculture and high poverty are cited as some examples associated with place of origin. On the other hand high income, high literacy, dominance of industries and services and affluence are the pull factors associated with place of destination. While push factors are responsible for out migration, the pull factors attract in migration (Bhagat & Mohanty). There are also many examples to show that it is not only the poor who move out from the rural areas, but those with some education and capital also move out in anticipation of better prospects.

OVERVIEW OF URBANISATION IN INDIA

About 30 per cent of Indian lives in cities generating two-thirds of the GDP and 90 per cent of the Government revenue. It is estimated that about 140 million people will move to Indian cities by 2020 and 700 million by 2050. Five of the world's 20 most densely populated cities are in India. In 1981, there were 12 cities with a population greater than one million in India. According to some projections, there may be 68 such cities by 2020. Already in numerical terms, India's urban population is the second largest in the world after China and is higher than the total urban population of all countries put together barring China, USA and Russia. That is why United Nations tell us that we are living in the urban century, where for the first time more people are living in cities and towns rather than villages. During the last 50 years though the population of India has grown two and half times, urban India has grown by nearly five times.

Comparing Indian cities in the Global Cities Index 2010, it is said that New Delhi and Mumbai are ranked 45 and 46 respectively, Bangalore is 58 and Kolkata 63. Bamzai therefore, says that our cities are like countries. Four urban cities in India alone have a population of 35 million people (nearly 78 million, including wider metropolitan regions and Delhi's National Capital Region) and an economy valued at nearly $ 360 billion within their agglomerations. Employment in urban India during 1981-91 was 38 per cent against 16% in rural areas and 26.1 per cent in the country as a whole. All this shows, at their best, they can mould the destiny of the country. In fact, cities have been the driving force in economic and social development. Urban areas are the engines of economic growth in the country. This is manifested in the contribution of urban sector to national income.

TABLE 3
Urban Contribution to National Income

Year	*% of urban to total population*	*Estimated Contribution to National Income*
1951	17.3	29%
1981	23.3	47%
1991	25.7	55%
2001	30.5 (It came to 28%)	60%

Source : Ministry of Urban Affairs.

Some of the main forces which are driving urbanisation are shifting of people from rural areas to urban areas and the concentration of economic and social opportunities in the urban areas associated with higher incomes, improved health, higher literacy, improved quality of life and many other benefits. But along with benefits, there are many environment and social ills like shortage of housing, lack of water supply and sanitation facility, poor physical infrastructure, lack of proper waste disposal facility, traffic congestion, dilapidated roads and so on—all of which lead to spread of communicable diseases and damage environment. It is not possible to discuss all these maladies in one short paper. We will just emphasise two problems which create great damage to urban life. These two major problems are, urban transportation and urban waste. The other problems like water supply, housing, slum improvement, etc. can be managed by JNNURM which has been started to tackle these problems.

URBAN TRANSPORTATION

Transportation system in urban centres and particularly in cities and large towns contributes to the decay of urban environment and reduces the quality of life due to atmospheric emissions and noise pollution. Urban centres are groaning under the weight of thousands of vehicles of different types. Bangalore which was once a garden city is converted now as a city of vehicles and broken roads. Nobody knows how to control the number of vehicles that jam the roads. The same thing is noticed almost in each city, whether it is Bombay or Delhi. It is tough on the police who end up monitoring and guiding millions of vehicles that ply in metropolis. The Chairperson of Infosys Foundation in one article, called "Geek Tragedy' writes that more than 500 people are killed annually in Bangalore city roads. Same thing happens in many cities though the number of accidents cannot be categorically stated. Poor maintenance of vehicles, degraded condition of roads, and use of unpure fuels primarily precipitate the problems of air and noise pollution arising from operation of motorized vehicles.

Writing on city roads Nandan Nilekani writes that the consequence of two many rules has obviously been that everyone has agreed to ignore them. Across cities, roads and pavements are dug up and left open for days on end, inconveniencing pedestrians and traffic. Even so often, children fall into these open ditches and get badly hurt—and recovering them out of these storm drains, holes and open wells becomes human interest stories covered by newspapers and TV. Jeffrey Sachs once commenting on the state of Indian cities said that it is impossible to take a jog or even walk from place to place in an Indian city. The broken pavements, the chaos of the roads endanger the casual pedestrian. We think this is the experience of all those who are living in Indian cities. Infrastructure is not just tarring roads and leaving them for years without any repair, erecting flyovers which remain incomplete for a decade or so and building big malls without any space for parking cars. This is not urban planning. All that we can hope that Municipalities and Corporations will rise to the occasion and improve the quality of life of urban citizens by improving public transport and repairing dilapidated roads.

THE PROBLEM OF URBAN WASTE MANAGEMENT

Our cities are choking with garbage thanks to our consumption mania. A nation's life style is nothing but the integrated life styles of its people, which in turn, is nothing but the living pattern of individuals. And when the living pattern goes on increasing, you find pile of garbage that collects in the kitchen and is thrown out at the end of the day. When you start walking in the morning or evening, you see over-flowing bins in the streets and some of these might be yours. Gopal Krishna Gandhi in one article points out that of the 377 million tonnes of solid waste urban India generates only 295 million tonnes are collected. The rest 37 or 38 m tonnes are left somewhere on our dear land's vacant lots, which are allowed to shrink each passing day. The balance 295 m tonnes which are being moved to the edges of cities and towns are dumped in water bodies, marshes or fields and so on. Those are also the places where or near where our aquifers are being tapped for the drinking water we buy. With water underneath sinking and garbage above rising, without proportionate recycling, it will not be very long before people would start choking.

It is estimated that urban India will grow from the present size 400 million to nearly 600 million by 2030 along with increase in per capita income to the extent of 4 times. If the same process of garbage deposit continues and increases along with increased consumption, how long the earth can tolerate? When the land is misused, unmercifully pounded, poisoned with chemicals and mindlessly exploited, the only protest it can make is to die. Land is not immotal, it can also die. It is important to remember that this is not all. If the ocean becomes toxic due to over flow of garbage and then dry what will happen to mankind? Therefore, a time has come when we have to reduce our consumption pattern and at the same time recycle the accumulated garbage instead of depositing them on the face of earth. Gandhiji has rightly said that nature has enough for man's need, but not for man's greed. It is said by a social scientist that R's of waste management should imply three Rs.—one R means Refuse to buy items that you do not really need. The less you buy, the lesser the waste management. Second R is Reuse the amount of waste produced. Before throwing away any item, try to see whether it can be reused in any way. Something useless can be used for any other purpose. And the third R is Recycle. This method is increasingly becoming popular as it does not cause air, water or soil pollution or harm to the environment. And this may also be noted that waste management is not any one's sole responsibility, but a joint venture to a clean and happy environment.

WHAT SHOULD BE THE URBAN AGENDA?

Time is ripe now to prepare a comprehensive agenda to tackle some of its problems. We cannot now neglect urban areas since 17% of the world population lives in urban India. The present number of our 35 million plus population cities will go up to 68, 13 of these will have population of more than four million each and six will be mega cities with population crossing 10 million. Mumbai and Delhi from this category will be among the five largest cities of the world by the year 2030. As ADB publications identify India does not provide sufficient attention to improve urban life. We have now a flagship programme, Jawaharlal Nehru National Urban Renewal Mission (JNNURM) which was launched in 2005 with focus on 65 mission cities with a view to drastically improving basic infrastructure services of the above cities. This mission is of 7 years duration and mid-term appraisal shows the progress of improvement is far from satisfactory. All that JNNURM has done so far is that it has renewed focus on the urban sector across the country. There is a conscious need to attack the major maladies of urban centres.

A few suggestions are offered to effectively implement some of the reform programmes. First, there must be a target to attain 100 per cent level of success in basic infrastructure of facilities in some major cities within a fixed period, let us say five years and provide necessary funds for the same. With regard to other cities and towns, the period may be extended so as to make a phased programme in order to avoid constraint on resources. Second, those who will be entrusted with the responsibility in implementing these programmes must be accountable for proper use of funds. One of the major difficulties in our development programmes is that there are heavy leakages in our development resources. Such development work should be properly monitored to see that the resources have been properly used and wherever possible the assistance of residents of the locality must be taken to see that there is no pilferage. Third, Planning Commission should set apart the required funds for the purpose of urban development and the Municipalities and Corporations may also raise some development funds to improve basic infrastructure of urban centres. The World Bank also stands committed to $ 1 billion assistance to the urban sector which could go up to $ 5 billion. The India Infrastructure Development Fund will probably take shape soon and this could be another source of funding. In fact if a time-bound programme in respect of water supply, solid waste management, sewerage, walkable roads, and drainage which are essential requisites of an urban centre is done to the satisfaction of the community, resources will not be a problem to attain these basic facilities.

Though it is difficult to predict the future level of urbanisation of a country like India because urbanisation level not only depends upon demographic trends, but economic, social and political factors as well. Since economic growth is increasing and urban facilities are providing better opportunities for education, health and cultural activities, contribution to migration may be an important factor in increasing urban population. It has been observed that the growth of migration has significantly accelerated during 1990s after a considerable deceleration in the previous decade. The same process may continue in future. It is also important to remember that because of changing demand of labour market as persons with skills and education would be more able to meet this demand, many skilled persons will move to urban areas. Our political debates are tinged with the recognition of an urban India. The recent remarks of many political authorities including the Planning Commission clearly imply that urban growth is a natural outcome of the growth of the economy. Nilekani therefore, points out that there lies a real, tangible shift in the city's place within the Indian landscape. As he remarks "The day is turning and the sun is rising on the city—the place where as many of us are beginning to recognise, our biggest success will take shape".

References

Bhagat, B. Ram and Mohanty Soumya, 2008. Trends and Patterns of India's Urbanisation : A Demographic Assessment—Paper presented in the Annual Meeting of Population Association of America, New Orleans, USA, 16-19th April.

Gandhi, Gopal Krishna, Dying a slow death, 2010, *Hindustan Times*, Kolkata, May 22.

India Today, September, 20, 2010, A Number of Articles by different writers on different aspects of Urbanisation which have enabled me to appreciate many of the problems of urban areas.

Nilekani, Nandan, Imagining India, Ideas for the New Century, 2009, Revised and Updated, Penguin Group.

Ramachandran, M., Times Right Set the Urban Agenda, 2010, *Economic Times*, 30.11.

Shukla, Rajesh, Inclusive Urbanisation needed, 2010, *Economic Times*, 4.10, Director, NCAER.

Index